# ESTATE PUBLICATIONS

# SUR~~VEY~~

C000185436

## Street maps with index
## Administrative Districts
## Population Gazetteer
## Road Map with index
## Postcodes

### COUNTY RED BOOKS

This atlas is intended for those requiring street maps of the historical and commercial centres of towns within the county. Each locality is normally presented on one or two pages and although, with many small towns, this space is sufficient to portray the whole urban area, the maps of large towns and cities are for centres only and are not intended to be comprehensive. Such coverage in Super and Local Red Books (see page 2).

Every effort has been made to verify the accuracy of information in this book but the publishers cannot accept responsibility for expense or loss caused by any error or omission. Information that will be of assistance to the user of these maps will be welcomed.

The representation of a road, track or footpath on the maps in this atlas is no evidence of the existence of a right of way.

Street plans prepared and published by ESTATE PUBLICATIONS, Bridewell House, TENTERDEN, KENT, and based upon the ORDNANCE SURVEY mapping with the permission of the Controller of H. M. Stationery Office.

The Publishers acknowledge the co-operation of the local authorities of towns represented in this atlas.

© Estate Publications 088 L          ISBN  1 84192 063 0          © Crown Copyright 398713

# CONTENTS

## TOWN CENTRE STREET MAPS:

## LEGEND TO STREET MAPS

| | | | |
|---|---|---|---|
| One-Way Street | → | Post Office | ● |
| Pedestrianized | ▨ | Public Convenience | ⊡ |
| Car Park | ℗ | Place of Worship | + |

Scale of street plans: 4 Inches to 1 mile (unless otherwise stated on the map).

County boundary
District boundary

BROMLEY
LEWISHAM
LAMBETH
WANDSWORTH
HOUNSLOW
RICHMOND upon-Thames
KINGSTON-upon-Thames
CROYDON
Tandridge
East Grinstead
Forest Row
SUTTON
MERTON
WIMBLEDON
EPSOM & EWELL
REIGATE & BANSTEAD
Mole Valley
DORKING
LEATHERHEAD
ELMBRIDGE
WALTON-on-Thames
SPELTHORNE
STAINES
SUNBURY
EGHAM
RUNNYMEDE
CHERTSEY
WEYBRIDGE
WOKING
GUILDFORD
WAVERLEY
GODALMING
HASLEMERE
HINDHEAD
FARNHAM
ALDERSHOT
FARNBOROUGH
FRIMLEY
CAMBERLEY
Surrey Heath
WINDSOR
BRACKNELL
HORSHAM
CRAWLEY
HORLEY
CATERHAM
COULSDON
PURLEY
WALLINGTON
CARSHALTON
MORDEN
ASHFORD

©Estate Publications

# GAZETTEER INDEX TO ROAD MAP
## with Populations  County of Surrey population 1,018,003

**SURREY Districts:**

| | |
|---|---|
| Elmbridge | 114,479 |
| Epsom and Ewell | 67,007 |
| Guildford | 122,378 |
| Mole Valley | 79,220 |
| Reigate & Banstead | 117,777 |
| Runnymede | 71,789 |
| Spelthorne | 89,987 |
| Surrey Heath | 79,073 |
| Tandridge | 76,316 |
| Waverley | 113,212 |
| Woking | 86,765 |

| | | |
|---|---|---|
| Abinger Common | | 7 E5 |
| Abinger Hammer **1,780** | | 6 D4 |
| Addlestone | | 6 C2 |
| Albury **1,188** | | 6 D4 |
| Alfold **1,086** | | 6 D6 |
| Artington **370** | | * |
| Ash, **15,519** | | 6 B4 |
| Ashford, **25,739** | | 6 D1 |
| Ashstead, **13,363** | | 7 E3 |
| Bagshot (& Windlesham) **16,147** | | 6 B2 |
| Banstead, **43,404** | | 7 F3 |
| Beare Green | | 7 E5 |
| Betchworth **937** | | 7 F4 |
| Bisley **3,542** | | 6 C3 |
| Blackheath | | 6 C4 |
| Blackwater | | 6 A3 |
| Bletchingley **2,858** | | 7 G4 |
| Blindley Heath | | 7 G4 |
| Bowlhead Green | | 6 B5 |
| Bramley **3,163** | | |
| Brockham **2,669** | | 7 E4 |
| Brook | | 6 B5 |
| Brookwood | | 6 B3 |
| Buckland **584** | | 7 F4 |
| Bucks Horn Oak | | 6 A5 |
| Burgh Heath with Kingswood, **6,340** | | 7 F3 |
| Burnham | | 6 C4 |
| Burrowhill | | 6 C2 |
| Burstow. **4,591** | | 7 G5 |
| Busbridge **892** | | 6 C5 |
| Byfleet **7,120** | | 6 D3 |
| Camberley (& Frimley) **51,894** | | 6 B3 |
| Camelsdale | | 6 B6 |
| Capel **3,481** | | 7 E5 |
| Caterham (& Warlingham), **32,752** | | 7 G3 |
| Charlwood **1,969** | | 7 F5 |
| Chelsham & Farleigh **576** | | 7 G3 |
| Chertsey **43,067** | | 6 D2 |
| Chiddingfold **2,852** | | 6 C6 |
| Chipstead, (with Woodmansterne and Hooley) **6,319** | | 7 F3 |
| Chobham **4,144** | | 6 C2 |
| Church (with Hindhead) | | 6 A5 |
| Claygate **6,495** | | 7 E2 |
| Cobham **10,252** | | 6 D3 |
| Coldharbour | | 7 E5 |
| Compton **964** | | 6 C4 |
| Copthorne | | 7 G5 |
| Cranleigh **11,479** | | 6 D5 |
| Crowhurst **2,907** | | 7 H4 |
| Croydon (Gtr. Ln.) | | 7 G2 |
| Deepcut | | 6 B3 |
| Dockenfield **405** | | * |
| Donkey Town | | 6 B3 |
| Dorking **24003** | | 7 E4 |
| Dormans land | | 7 H5 |
| Dunsfold **1,066** | | 6 C6 |
| East Clandon **283** | | 6 D4 |
| East Horsley **4,081** | | 6 D4 |
| East Molesey **5,613** | | 7 E2 |
| Effingham **2,499** | | 6 D3 |
| Egham **28,722** | | 6 C1 |
| Ellen's Green | | 6 D6 |
| Elstead **2,436** | | 6 B5 |

| | |
|---|---|
| Englefield Green **7,118** | 6 C1 |
| Epsom (with Ewell) **67,007** | 7 E3 |
| Esher **62,559** | 7 E2 |
| Ewell (with Epsom) **67,007** | 7 F2 |
| Ewhurst **2,369** | 6 D5 |
| Farleigh & Chelsham **576** | 7 G3 |
| Farley Green | 6 D5 |
| Farncombe | 6 C5 |
| Farnham **36,284** | 6 A4 |
| Felbridge **1,916** | 7 G5 |
| Felcourt | 7 H5 |
| Fetcham **8,317** | 7 E3 |
| Flexford | 6 B4 |
| Forest Green | 6 D5 |
| Frensham **2,740** | 6 A5 |
| Frimley (with Camberley) **51,894** | 6 B3 |
| Godalming **20,086** | 6 C5 |
| Godstone **5,515** | 7 G4 |
| Gomshall | 6 D4 |
| Grayshott | 6 B6 |
| Grayswood | 6 B6 |
| Great Bookham (with Little Bookham) **10,421** | 7 E3 |
| Guildford **59,976** | 6 C4 |
| Hambledon **664** | 6 C5 |
| Hascombe **292** | 6 C5 |
| Haslemere **15,235** | 6 B6 |
| Headley **709** | 7 E3 |
| Hersham **11,853** | 6 D2 |
| Hindhead (with Churt) | 6 B6 |
| Holmbury St Mary | 6 D5 |
| Holmwood **892** | * |
| Hookwood | 7 F5 |
| Horley **19,267** | 7 F5 |
| Horne **895** | 7 G5 |
| Hydestile | 6 C5 |
| Kingston upon Thames (Gtr.Ln.) | 7 E1 |
| Kingswood with Burgh Heath **6,340** | 7 F3 |
| Knaphill | 6 B3 |
| Laleham **7,330** | 6 D2 |
| Leatherhead **41,819** | 7 E3 |
| Leigh **844** | 7 F4 |
| Lightwater | 6 B2 |
| Limpsfield **3,456** | 7 H4 |
| Lingfield **8,161** | 7 H5 |
| Littleton | 6 D2 |
| Long Ditton **3,996** | 7 E2 |
| Loxhill | 6 C6 |
| Lyne | 6 C2 |
| Mayford | 6 C3 |
| Merstham | 7 G4 |
| Mickleham **484** | 7 E3 |
| Milford | 6 B5 |
| Millbridge | 6 A5 |
| Mytchett | 6 B3 |
| Newchapel | 7 G5 |
| Newdigate **1,499** | 7 E5 |
| Newlands Corner | 6 D4 |
| Normandy **2,499** | 6 B4 |
| North Holmwood **5,427** | 7 E4 |
| Norwood Hill | 7 F5 |
| Nutfield **2,682** | 7 G4 |
| Oakwoodhill | 6 D6 |
| Ockham **407** | 6 D3 |
| Ockley **864** | 7 E5 |
| Ottershaw | 6 C2 |
| Outwood | 7 G5 |
| Oxshott (with Stoke) **5,708** | 7 E2 |
| Oxted **10,063** | 7 H4 |
| Parkgate | 7 E5 |
| Peaslake | 6 D5 |
| Peper Harow **164** | 6 B5 |
| Pirbright **3,862** | 6 B3 |
| Pitch Place | 6 C4 |

| | |
|---|---|
| Poyle | 6 C1 |
| Puttenham **532** | 6 B4 |
| Pyrford | 6 C3 |
| Reigate (with Redhill) **52,007** | 7 G4 |
| Richmond (Gtr. Ln.) | 7 E1 |
| Ripley **1,697** | 6 D3 |
| Rowledge | 6 A5 |
| Rowly | 6 D5 |
| Runfold | 6 B4 |
| Rushmoor | 6 A5 |
| St Martha **674** | * |
| Salfords and Sidlow **3,099** | 6 C3 |
| Seal & Sands **851** | * |
| Send **3,975** | 6 C3 |
| Shackleford **650** | 6 B5 |
| Shalford **3,781** | 6 C4 |
| Shamley Green | 6 D5 |
| Shepperton **11,589** | 6 D2 |
| Shere **3,373** | 6 D4 |
| Shottermill | 6 B6 |
| Smallfield | 7 G5 |
| South Holmwood | 7 E5 |
| South Nutfield | 7 F4 |
| Staines **54,254** | 6 D1 |
| Stanwell **9,317** | 6 D1 |
| Stanwell Moor | 6 D1 |
| Stoke D'Abernon (with Oxshott) **5,708** | 6 D3 |
| Stoughton | 6 C4 |
| Sunbury **50308** | 6 D1 |
| Sunningdale | 6 C2 |
| Sutton | 6 D4 |
| Sutton (Gtr. Ln.) | 7 F2 |
| Tadworth and Walton on the Hill **6,370** | 7 F3 |
| Tandridge **678** | 7 H4 |
| Tatsfield **1,816** | 7 H3 |
| Thames Ditton **5,000** | 7 E2 |
| Thorncombe Street | 6 C5 |
| Thorpe **5,182** | 6 C1 |
| Thursley **635** | 6 B5 |
| Tilford **742** | 6 B5 |
| Titsey **94** | * |
| Tongham (with Seale) **2,073** | 6 B4 |
| Virginia Water **4,120** | 6 C2 |
| Walliswood | 6 E5 |
| Walton-on-Thames and Weybridge **51,920** | 6 D2 |
| Walton on the Hill and Tadworth **6,370** | 7 F3 |
| Wanborough **301** | * |
| Warlingham (with Caterham) **32,725** | 7 G3 |
| West Clandon **1,309** | 6 D4 |
| West End **3,346** | 6 C2 |
| West Horsley **2,728** | 6 D3 |
| West Humble | 7 E4 |
| West Molesey | 6 D2 |
| Westcott **2,118** | 7 E4 |
| Weybridge and Walton-on-Thames **51,920** | 6 D2 |
| Wheelerstreet | 6 B5 |
| Whiteley Village | 6 D2 |
| Whiteley Village | 6 D2 |
| Whyteleafe **3,166** | 7 G3 |
| Windlesham (with Bagshott) **16,147** | 6 B2 |
| Wisley **171** | * |
| Witley **7,290** | 6 B5 |
| Woking **86,765** | 6 C3 |
| Woldingham **1,993** | 7 H3 |
| Wonersh **3,332** | 6 C5 |
| Woodham | 6 C2 |
| Woodmansterne, with Chipstead and Hooley **6,319** | 7 F3 |
| Wood Street | 6 C4 |
| Worcester Park | 7 F2 |
| Worplesdon **8,175** | 6 C3 |
| Wotton **578** | 7 E4 |

Population figures are based upon the 1991 census and relate to the local authority or parish as constituted at that date. Places with no population figure form part of a larger local authority area or parish. Boundaries of local authority areas are shown on page 4.

Population figures in bold type.                    *Places not included on map due to limitation of space.

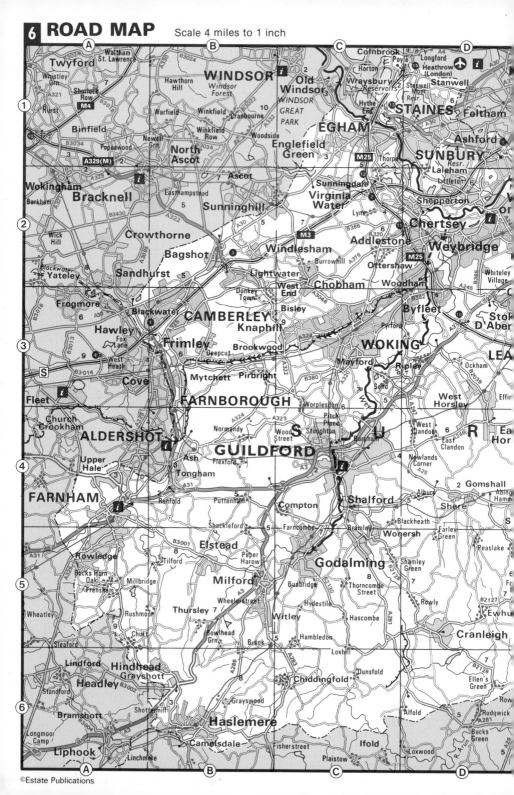

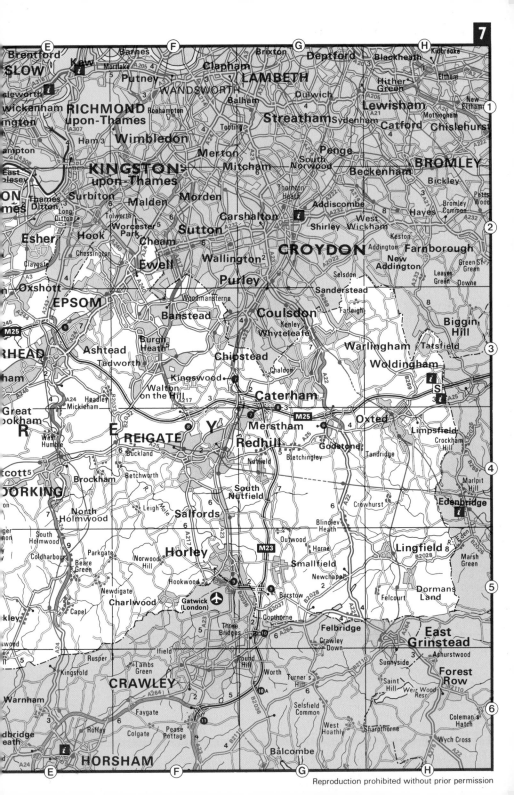

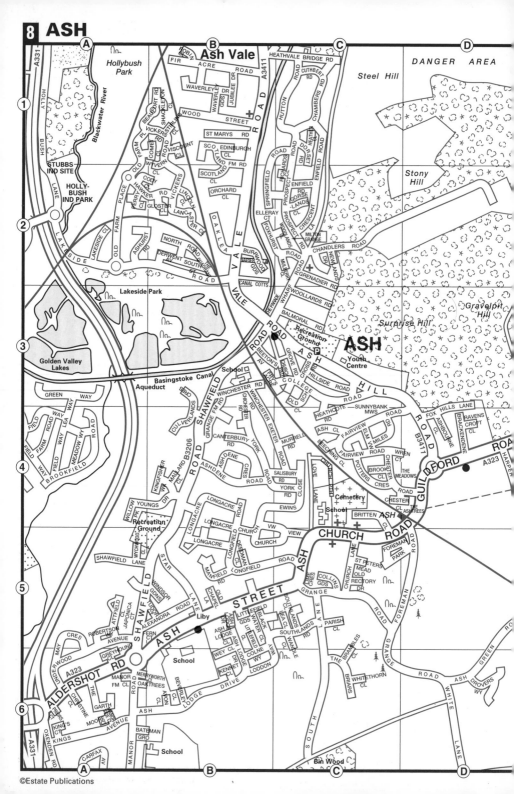

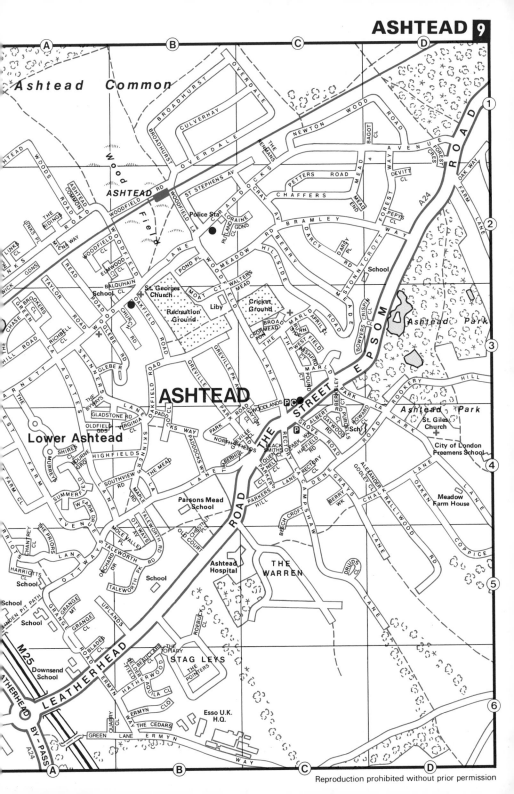

ASHTEAD 9

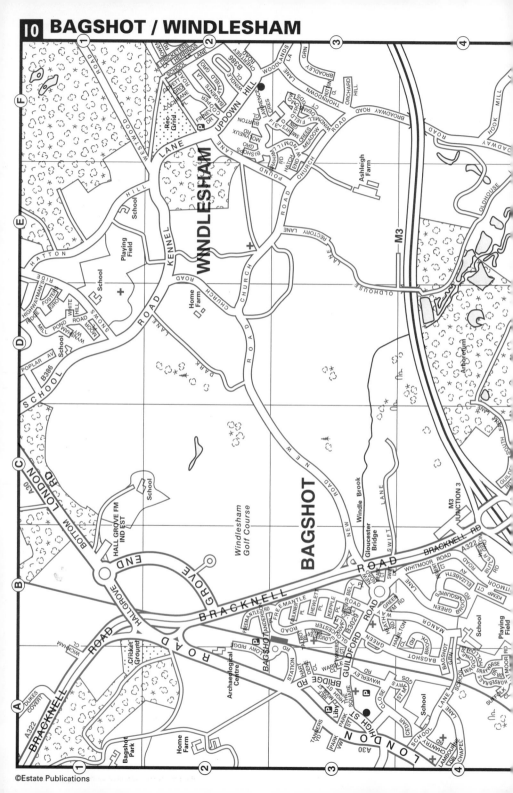

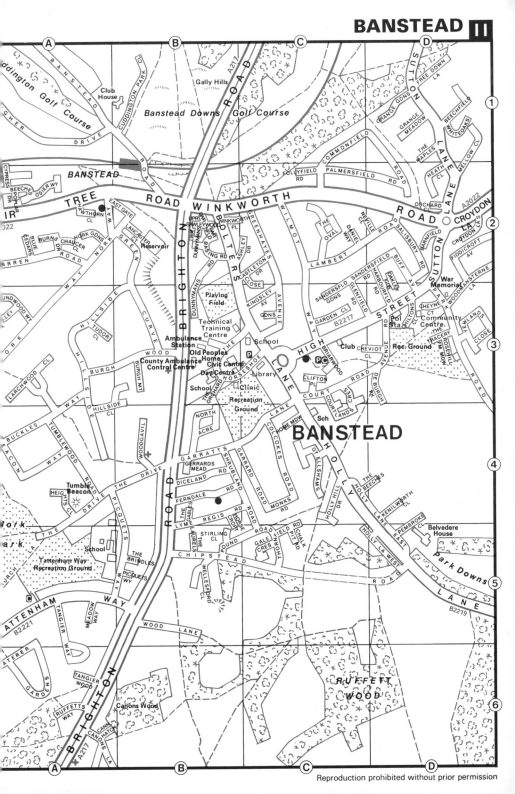

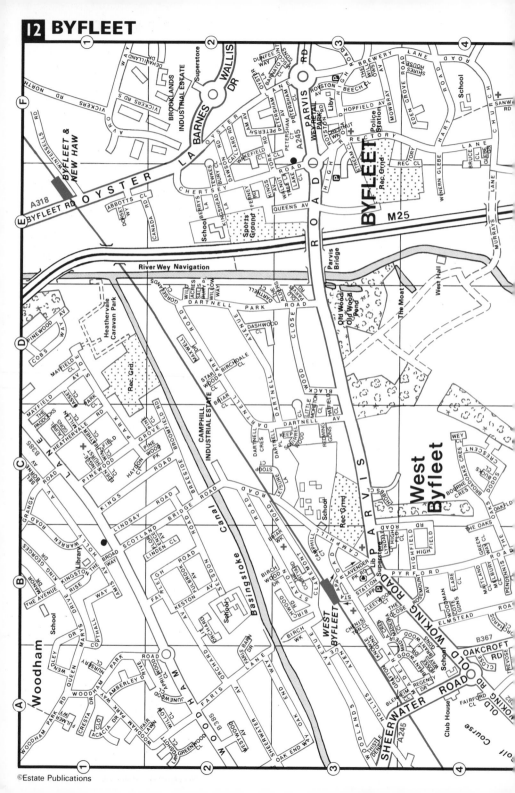

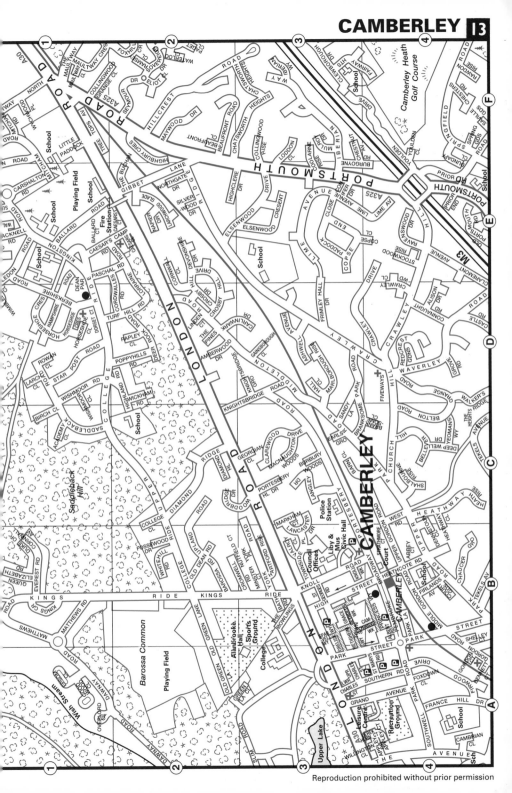

# CAMBERLEY 13

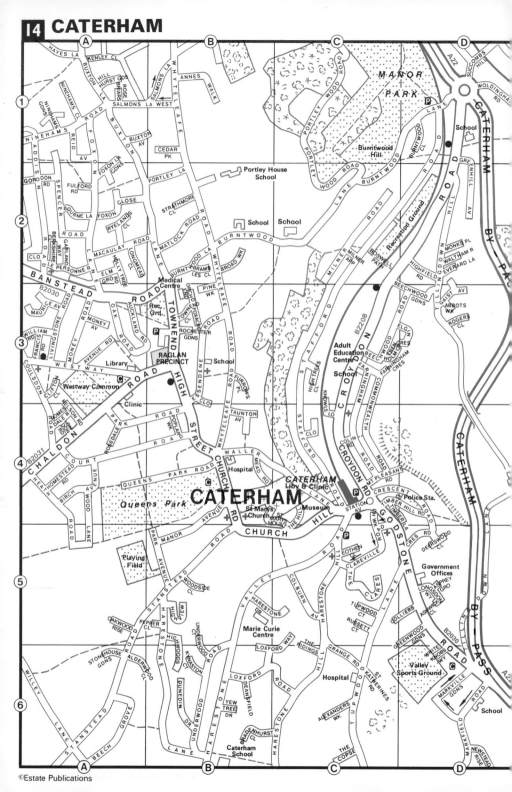

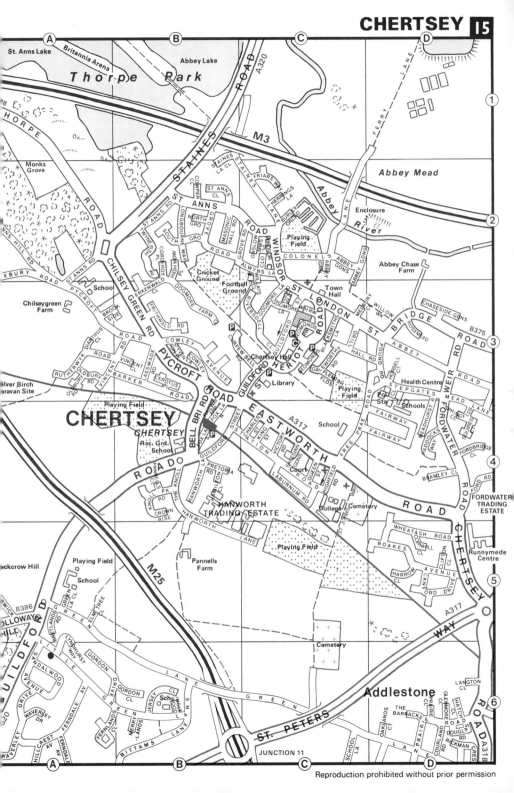

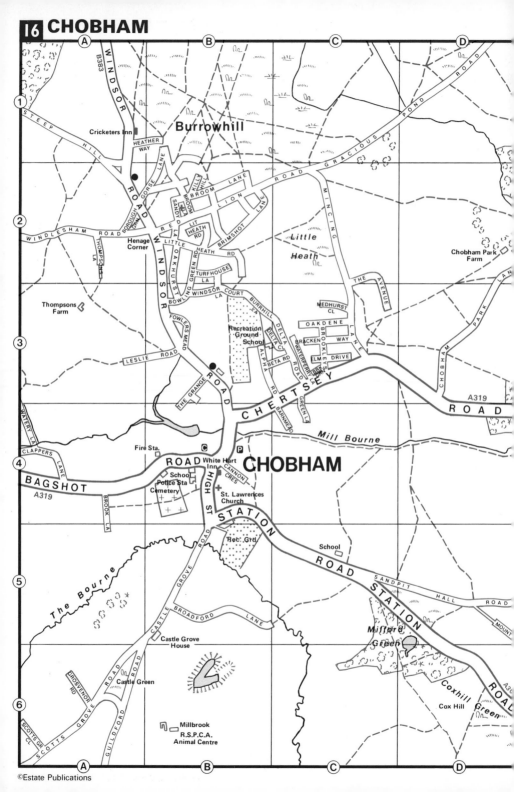

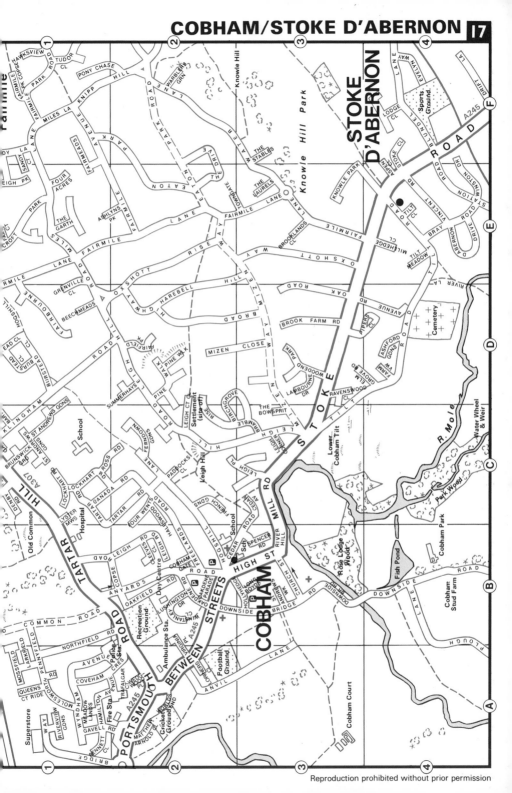

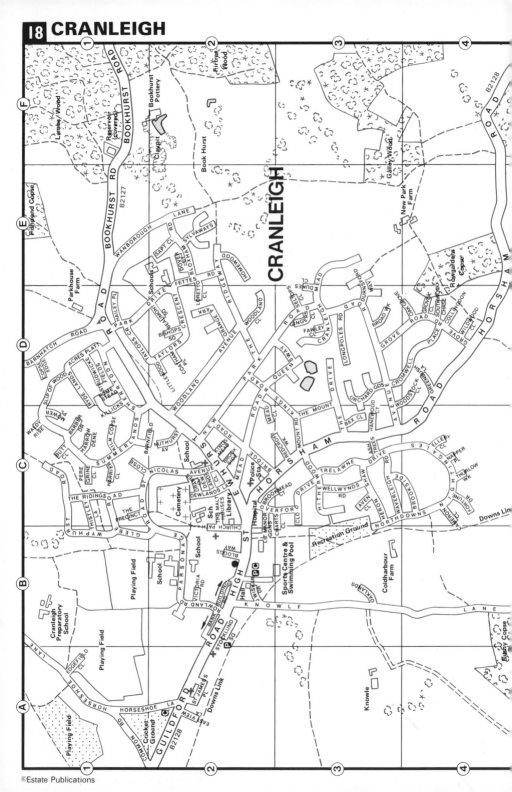

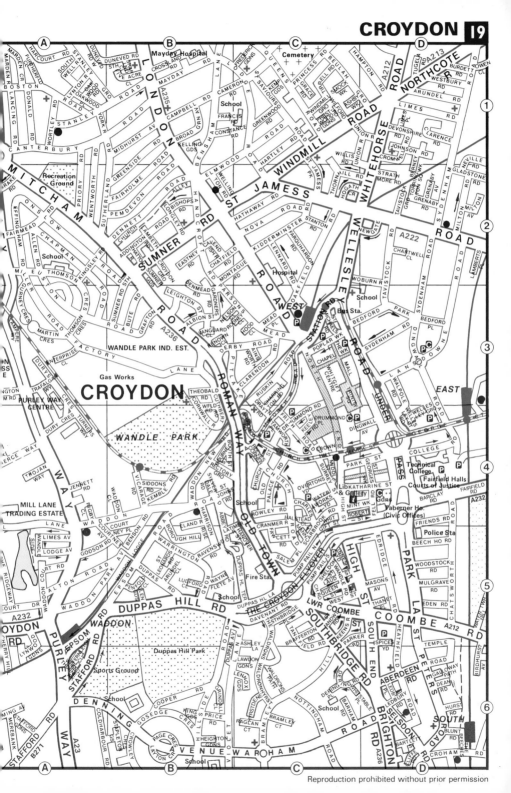

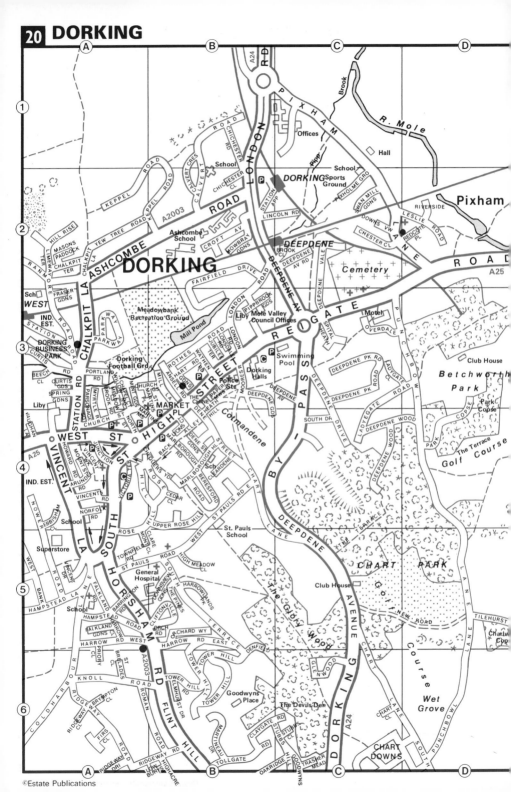

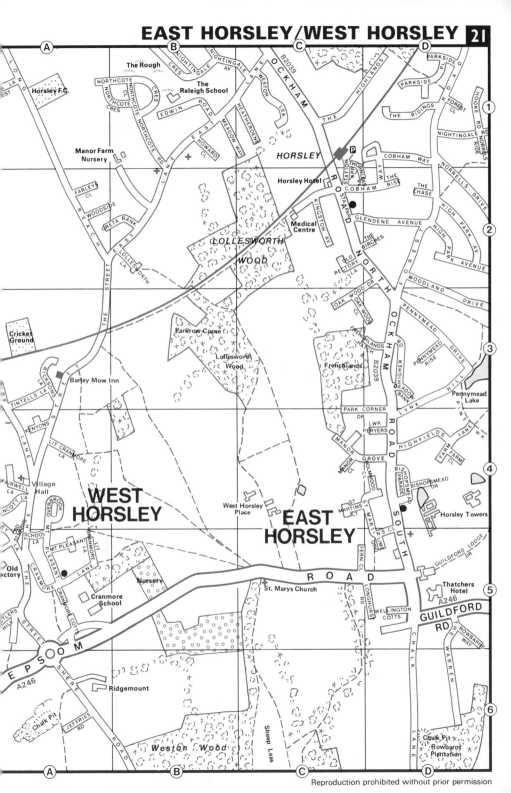

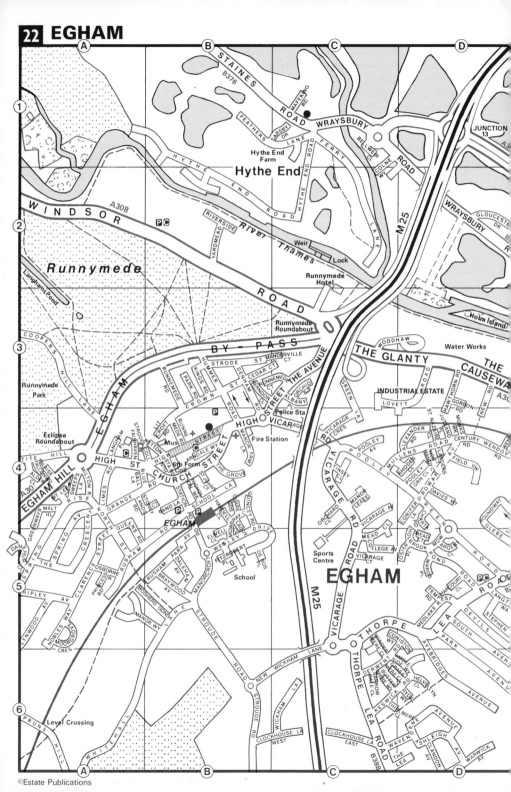

©Estate Publications

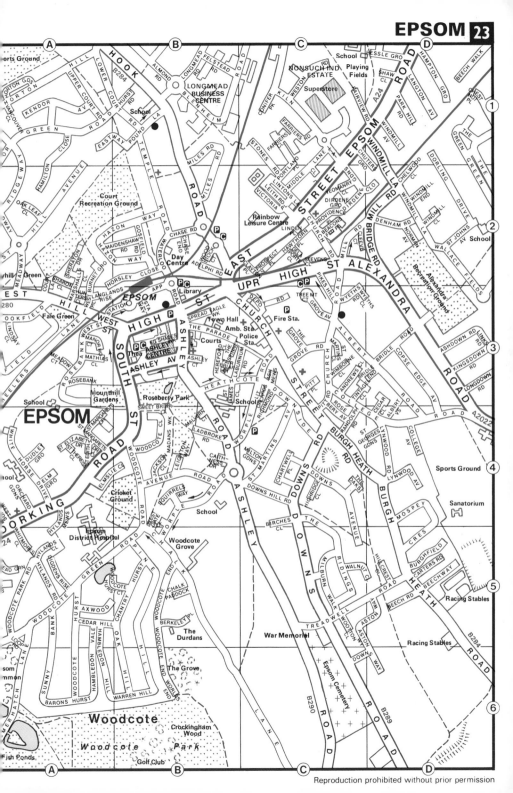

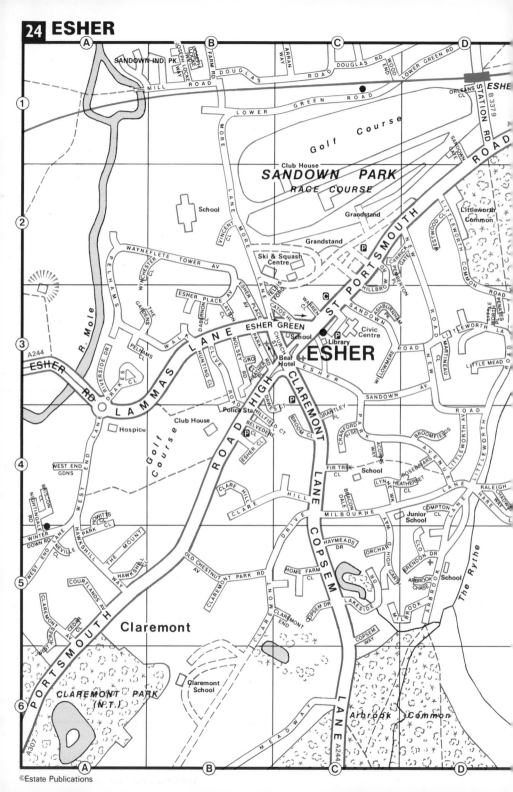

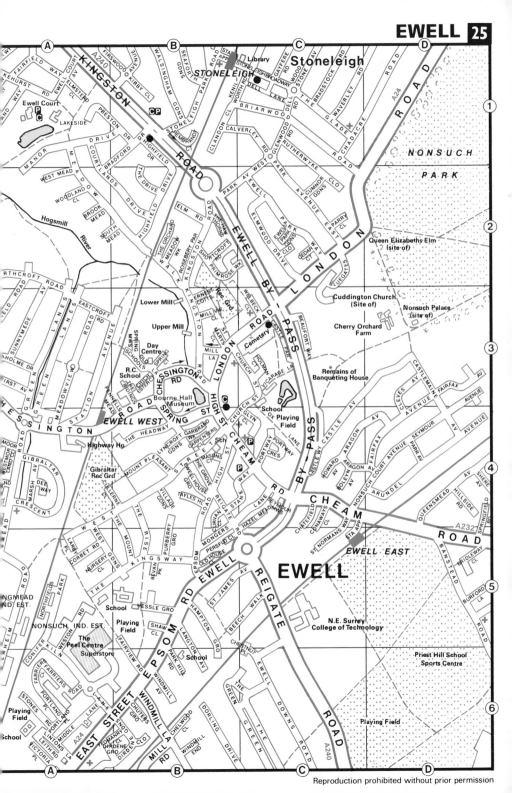

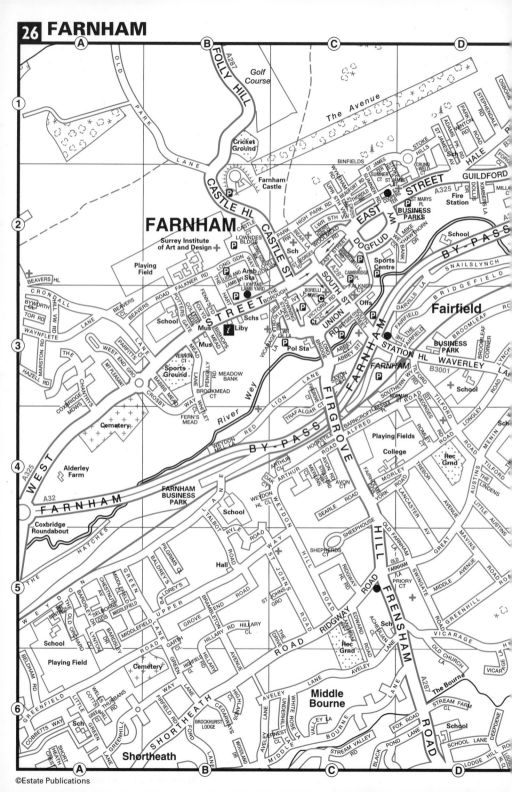

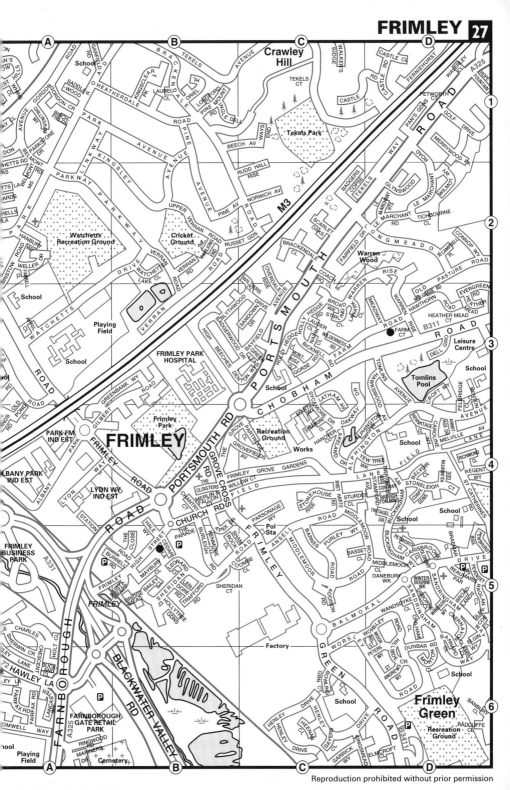

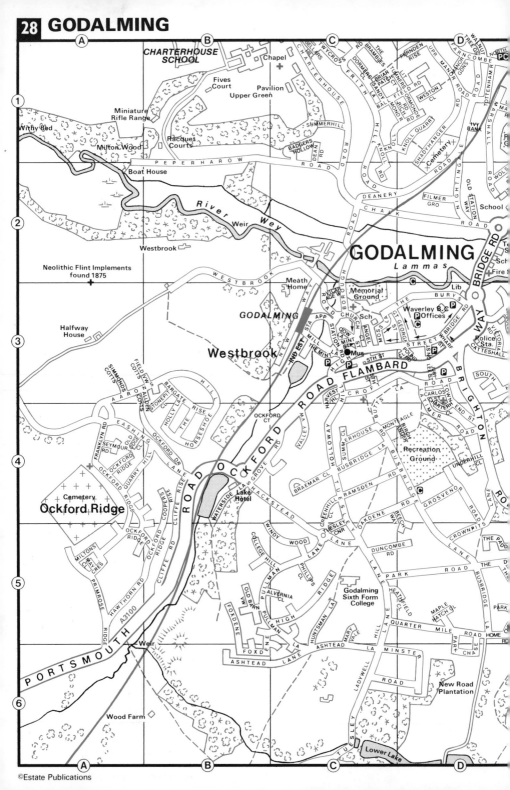

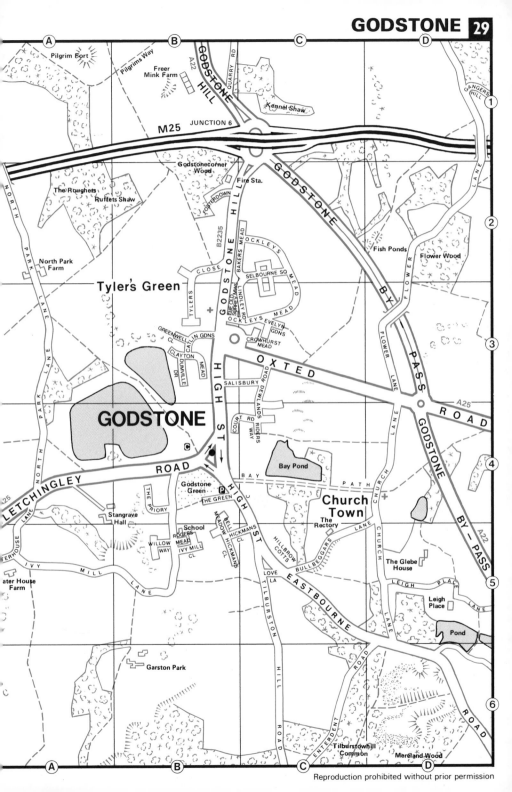

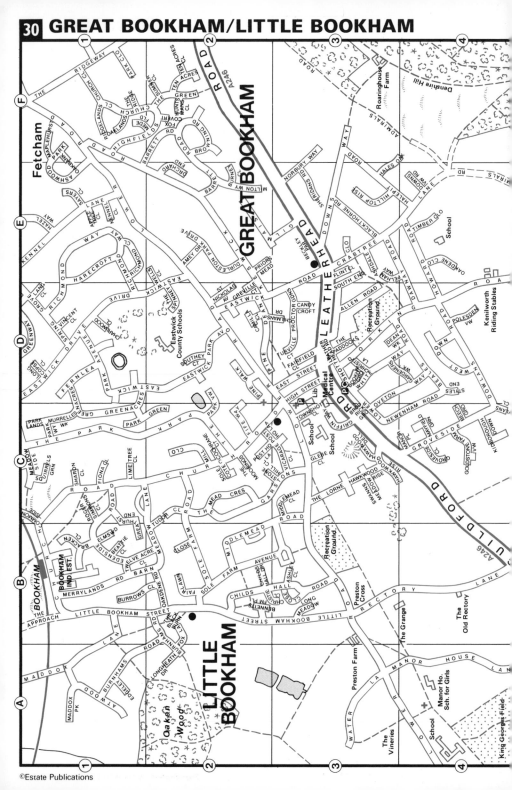

GREAT BOOKHAM

LITTLE BOOKHAM

LEATHERHEAD

Fetcham

GUILDFORD ROAD A246

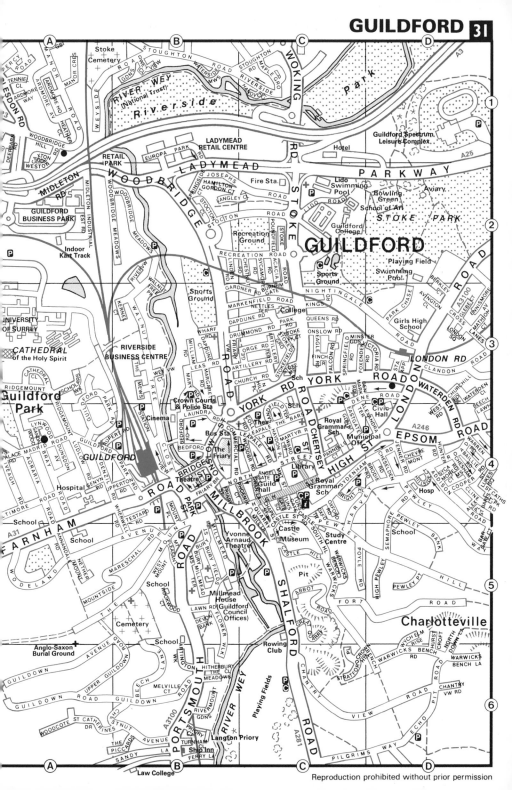

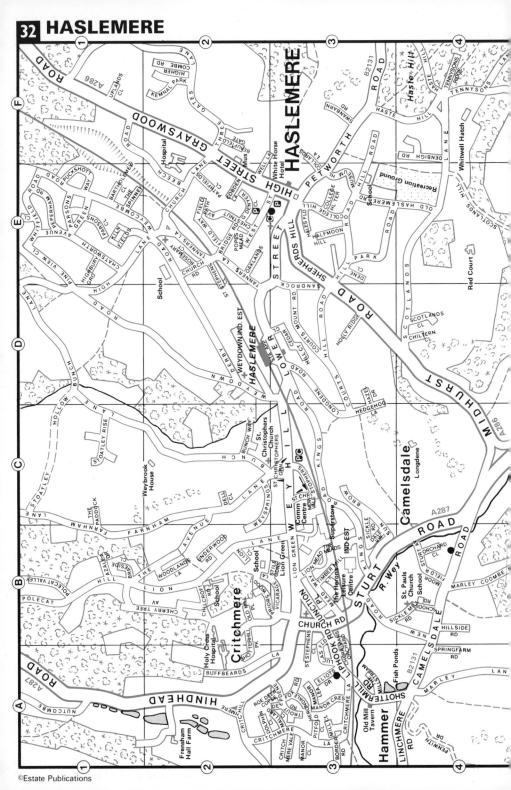

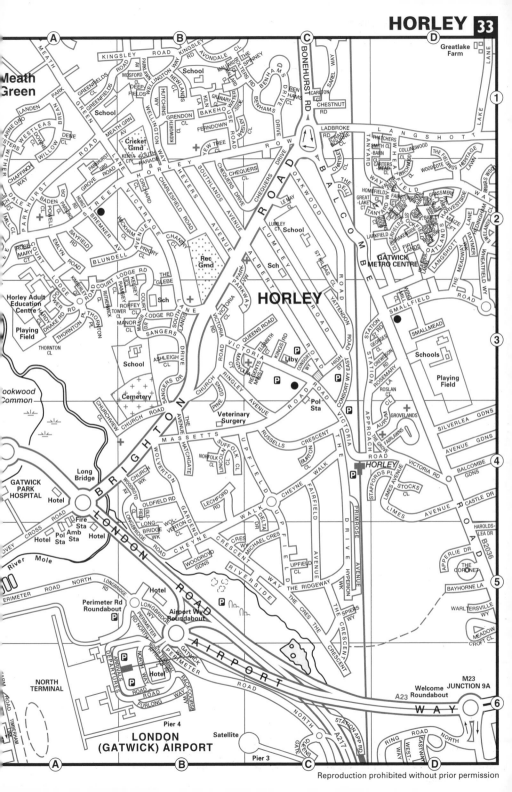

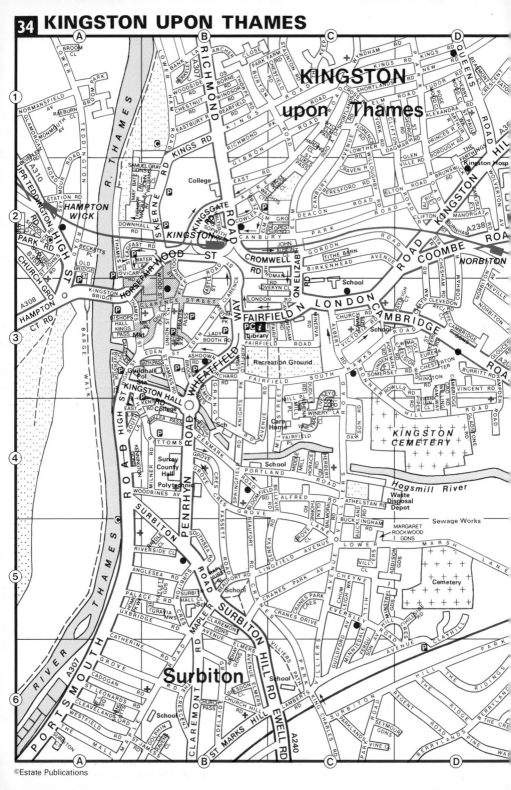

KINGSTON
upon Thames

Kingston Hosp

NORBITON

College

HAMPTON
WICK

KINGSTON

FAIRFIELD

LONDON

CAMBRIDGE

School

School

School

Library

Recreation Ground

KINGSTON
CEMETERY

Guildhall
Pol
Sta

KINGSTON HALL

College

Care
Home

School

Surrey
County
Hall

Polytechnic

Hogsmill River

Waste
Disposal
Depot

Sewage Works

MARGARET
ROCKWOOD
GDNS

Cemetery

Surbiton

School

School

School

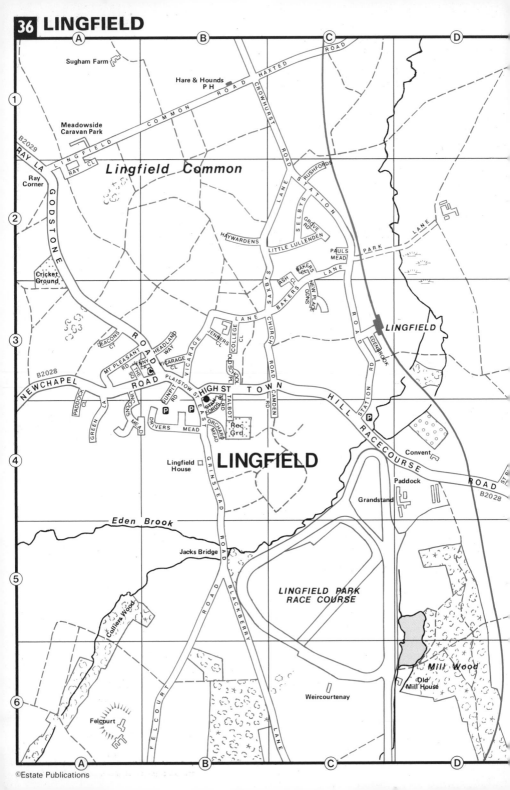

A   B   C   D

1

Sugham Farm

Hare & Hounds
P H

Meadowside
Caravan Park

B2029

Lingfield Common

Ray
Corner

2

Cricket
Ground

HAYWARDENS

LITTLE LULLENDEN

PAULS
MEAD

PARK

LINGFIELD

3

DEACONS
CT

B2028

MT PLEASANT
RD

HEADLAND
WAY

GARAGE
CL

JENNERS
CL

COLLEGE
CL

EDENBROOK

NEWCHAPEL

PADDOCK
CL

GREEN LA

LINCOLNS MEAD

DRIVERS MEAD

PLAISTOW ST

VICARAGE

HIGH ST   TOWN

TALBOT
RD

CAMDEN
RD

RACECOURSE

HILL

STATION
RD

Convent

4

Lingfield
House

GRINSTEAD ROAD

ORCHARD MEAD

Rec
Grd

**LINGFIELD**

Paddock

Grandstand

ROAD
B2028

Eden Brook

Jacks Bridge

5

Colliers Wood

BLACKBERRY

FELCOURT ROAD

**LINGFIELD PARK
RACE COURSE**

Mill Wood

Old
Mill House

6

Felcourt

Weircourtenay

LANE

A   B   C   D

©Estate Publications

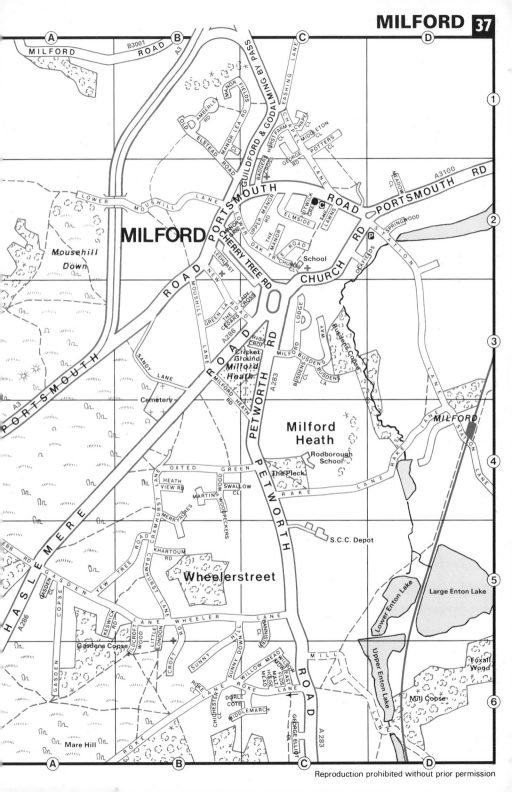

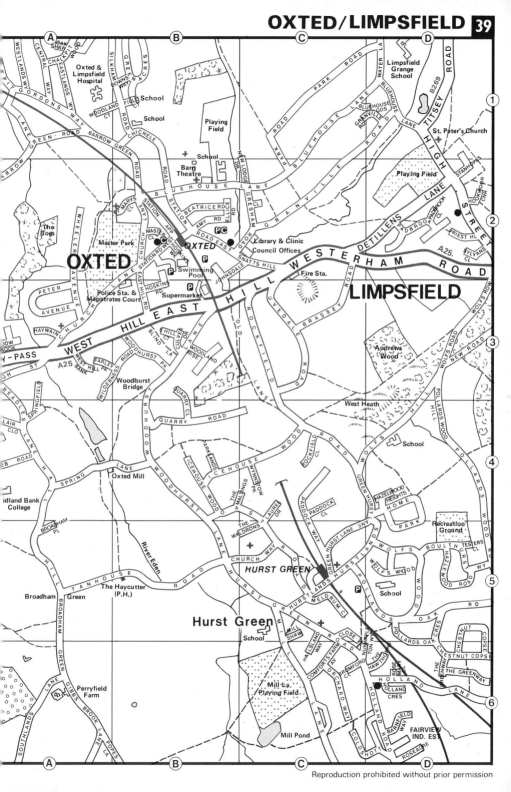

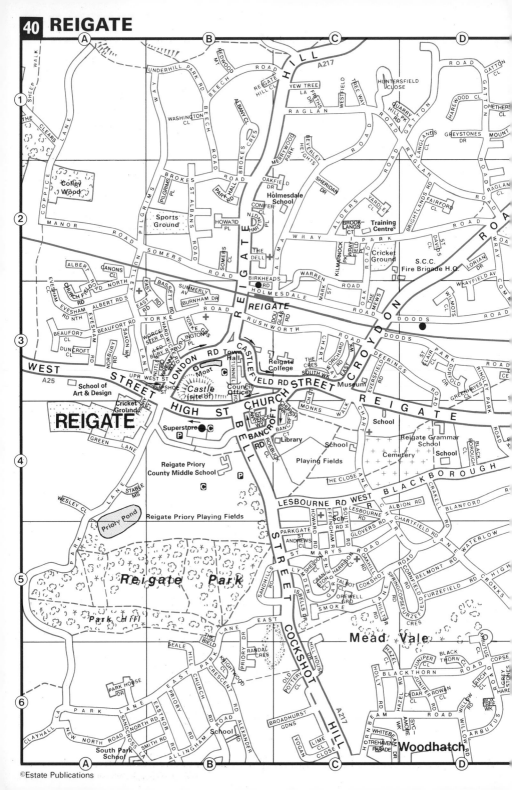

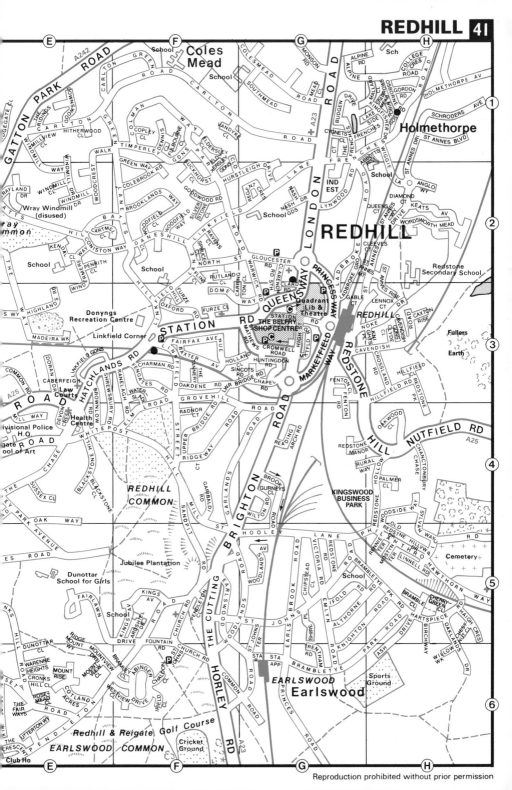

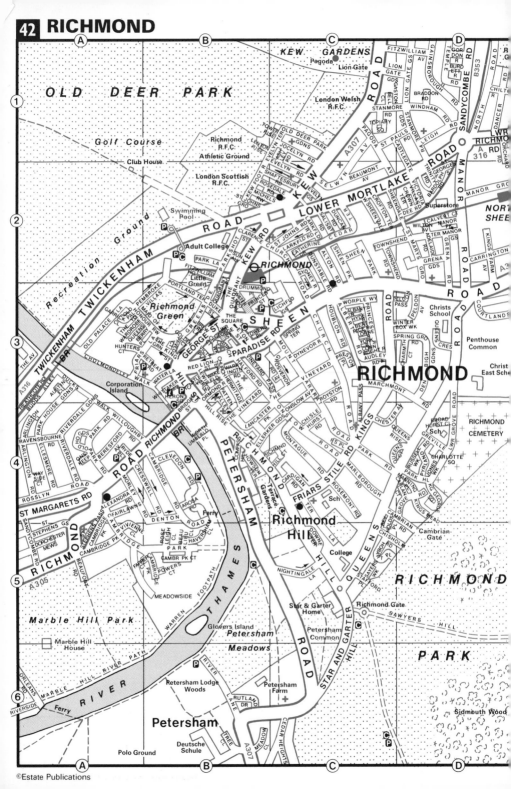

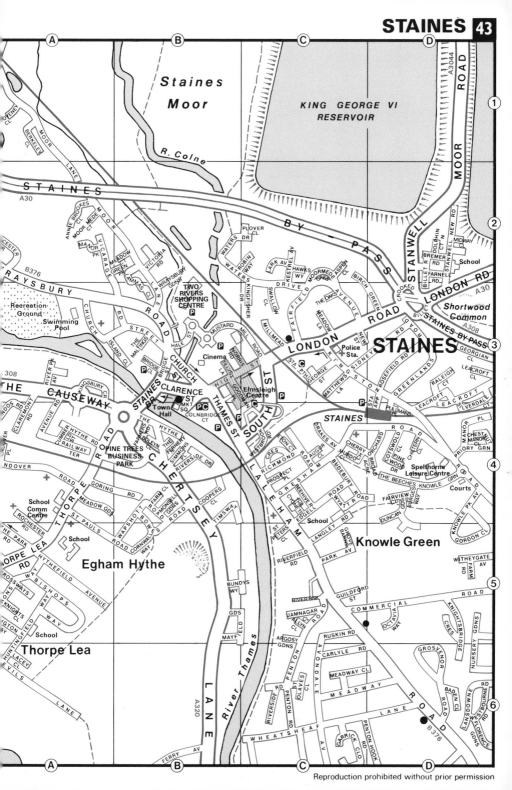

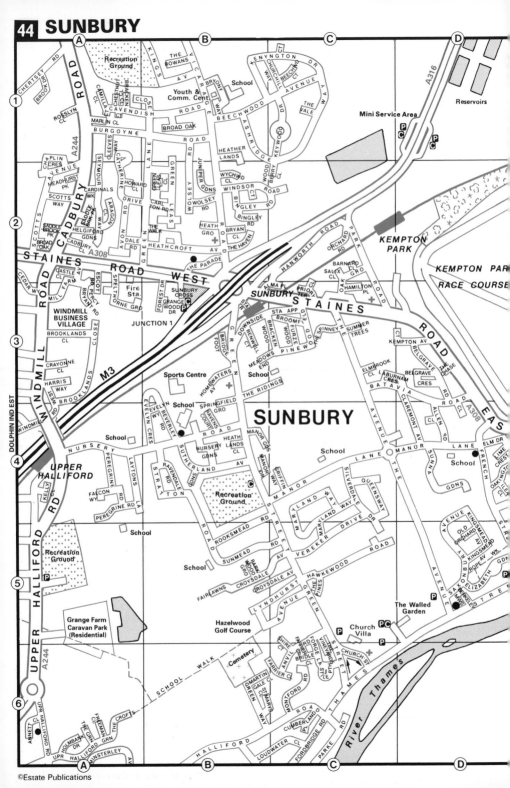

# 44 SUNBURY

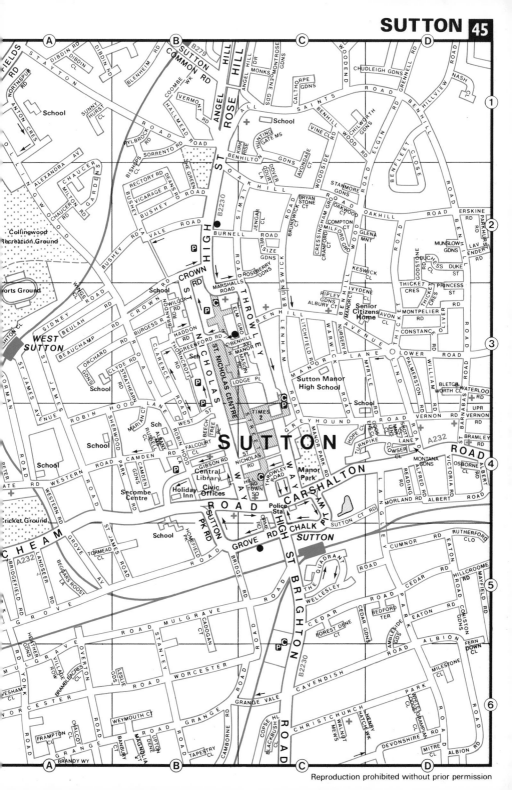

SUTTON 45

Reproduction prohibited without prior permission

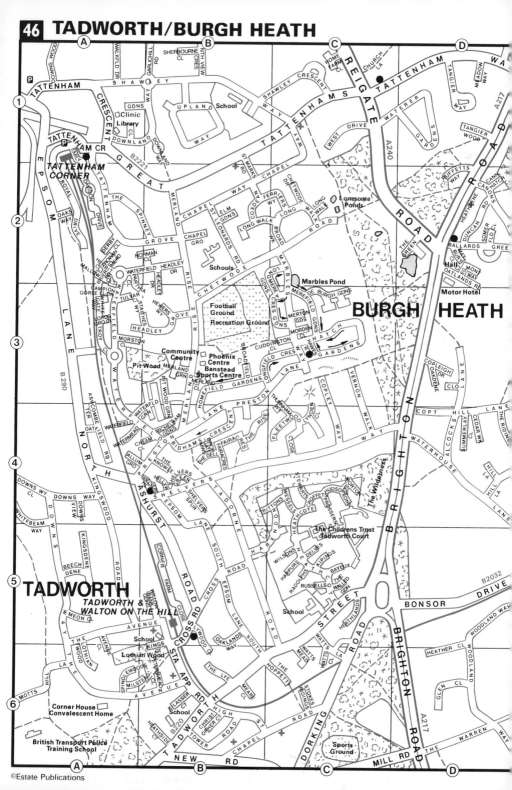

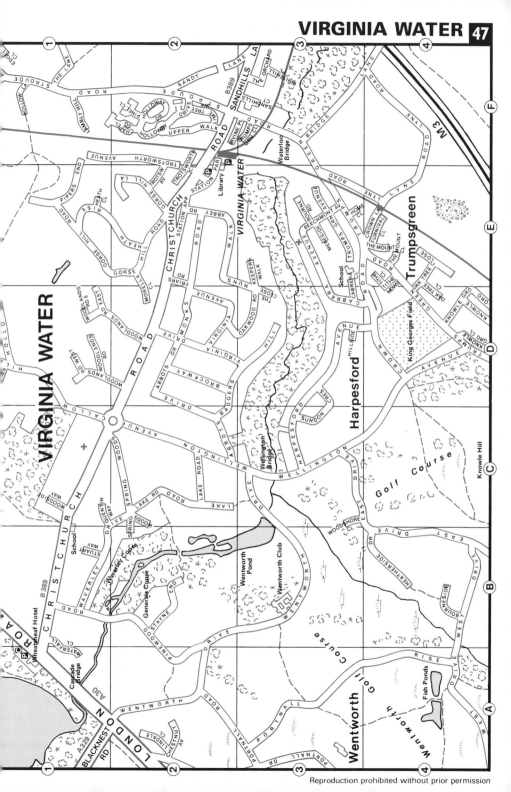

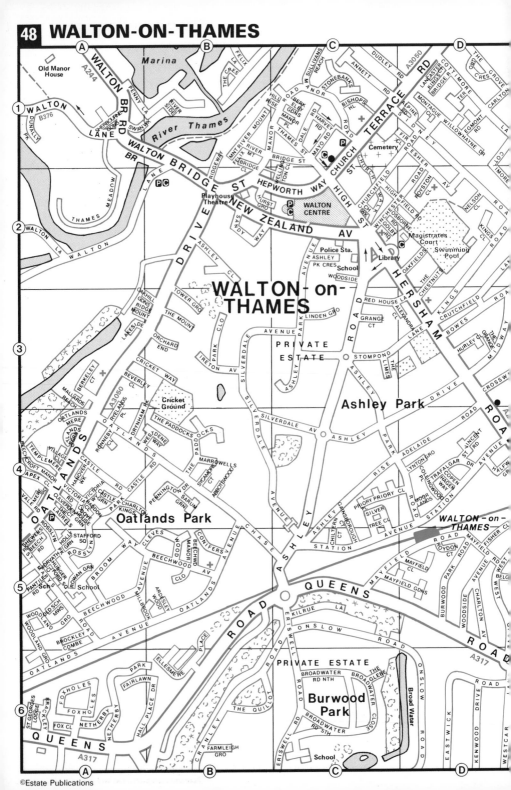

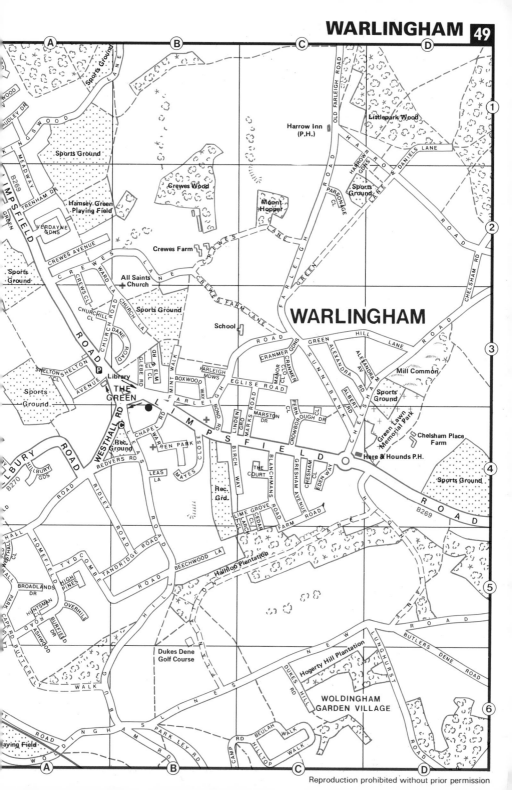

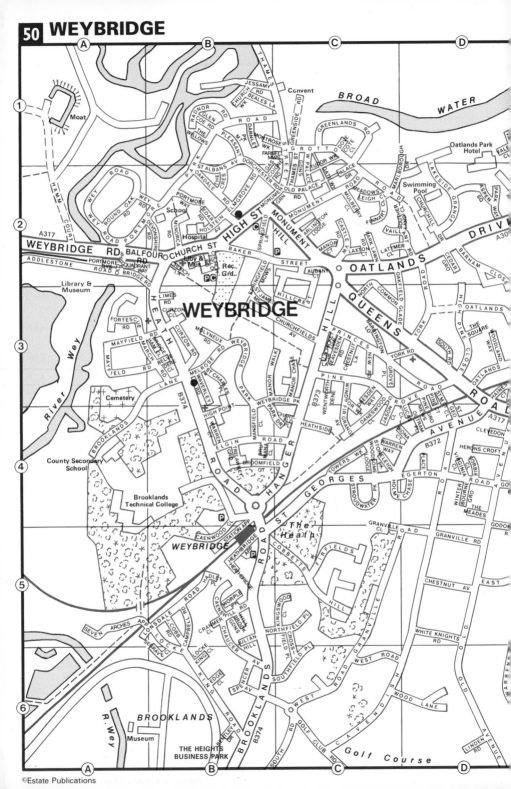

WEYBRIDGE

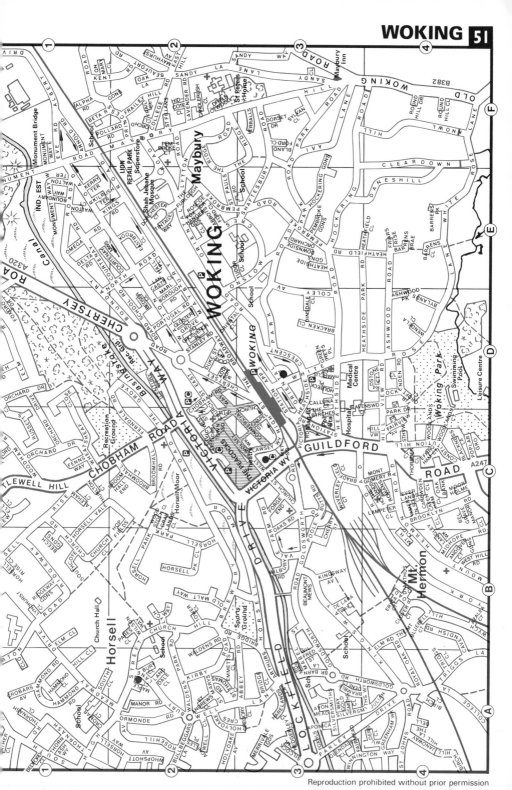

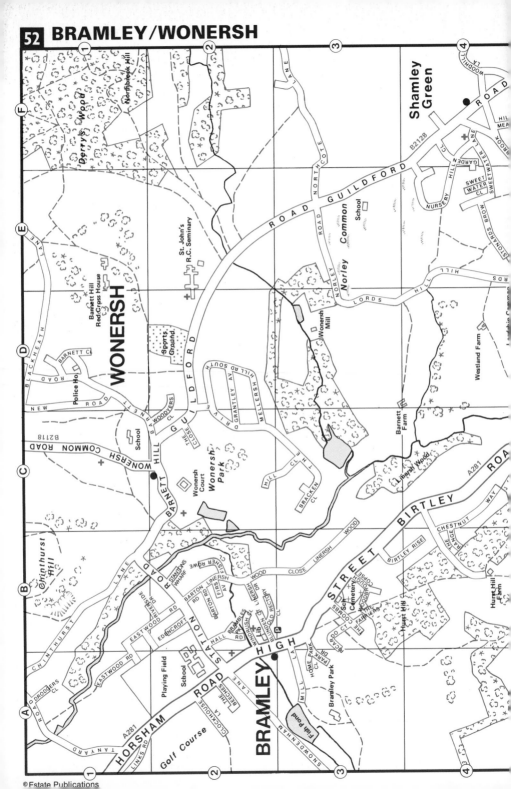

WONERSH

BRAMLEY

Shamley
Green

he Index includes some names
or which there is insufficient
pace on the maps. These
ames are preceded by an *
nd are followed by the nearest
djoining thoroughfare.

## ASH

- Hart Dene Clo. GU19 10 A3
- Hatch End. GU20 10 E3
- Hatton Hill. GU20 10 E1
- Heath Rd. GU19 10 B3
- Herrings La. GU20 10 F2
- Hewlett Pl. GU19 10 B3
- High St. GU19 10 A3
- Highwaymans Ridge. GU20 10 D1
- Hook Mill La. GU18 10 F4
- Horsebrass Dri. GU19 10 A4
- Hutton Clo. GU20 10 F3
- **INDUSTRIAL & RETAIL:**
- Hall Grove Farm Ind Est. GU19 10 B1
- Kemp Ct. GU19 10 B4
- Kennel La. GU20 10 E2
- Kepple Pl. GU19 10 B3
- Lambourne Dri. GU19 10 A4
- Lawrence Cres. GU20 10 F2
- London Rd. GU19 10 A4
- Lory Ridge. GU19 10 A2
- Manor Way. GU19 10 B4
- Mill Pond Rd. GU20 10 D1
- Molyneux Rd. GU20 10 F2
- Moor Pl. GU20 10 D1
- New Rd. GU20 10 C3
- Old House La. GU20 10 D3
- Orchard Hill. GU20 10 F3
- Owen Rd. GU20 10 F2
- Park St. GU19 10 A3
- Park View. GU19 10 A3
- Parkers Ct. GU19 10 A3
- Poplar Av. GU20 10 D1
- Pound La. GU20 10 E3
- Rectory La. GU20 10 E3
- Regent Ct. GU19 10 B4
- St Marys Gdns. GU19 10 A4
- School La, Bagshot. GU19 10 A4
- School La, Windlesham. GU20 10 F2
- School Rd. GU20 10 C1
- Shire Clo. GU19 10 A4
- Meade Ct. GU19 10 B3
- Smithys Grn. GU20 10 F3
- Snows Ride. GU20 10 D1
- South Farm La. GU18 10 C4
- Station Rd. GU19 10 A3
- Suffolk Clo. GU19 10 A4
- Swift La. GU19 10 B3
- Talbot Pl. GU19 10 B3
- Tanners Yd. GU19 10 A3
- The Square. GU19 10 A3
- Thorndown La. GU20 10 F3
- Updown Hill. GU20 10 F2
- Waggoners Hollow. GU19 10 A4
- Wardle Clo. GU19 10 A3
- Waverley Rd. GU19 10 A3
- Weston Gro. GU19 10 B4
- Westwood Rd. GU20 10 F1
- White Hill. GU20 10 D1
- Whitmoor Rd. GU19 10 A4
- Wickham Clo. GU19 10 A1
- Windle Clo. GU20 10 F2
- Windmill Field. GU20 10 F3
- Woodlands La. GU20 10 F2
- Wynsham Way. GU20 10 D1


## BANSTEAD


- Ashley Dri. SM7 11 C2
- Avenue Rd. SM7 11 D3
- Banstead Rd. SM7 11 A1
- Barnfield. SM7 11 D2
- Basing Rd. SM7 11 B2
- Beacon Way. SM7 11 A4
- Beechfield. SM7 11 D1
- Blue Cedars. SM7 11 A2
- Bolters La. SM7 11 B2
- Briarwood. SM7 11 C3
- Brighton Rd. SM7 11 A6
- Buckles Way. SM7 11 A4
- Buff Av. SM7 11 D2
- Burgh Mt. SM7 11 B3
- Burgh Wood. SM7 11 A3
- Burns Dri. SM7 11 A2
- Cann Hatch. SM7 11 A6
- Canons La. SM7 11 A6
- Castleton Clo. SM7 11 C2
- Castleton Dri. SM7 11 C2
- Chalk Pit Rd. SM7 11 C5
- Chaucer Clo. SM7 11 A2
- Cheviot Clo. SM7 11 D3
- Cheyne Ct. SM7 11 D3
- Chiltons Clo. SM7 11 D3
- Chipstead Rd. SM7 11 B5
- Clifton Pl. SM7 11 C3
- Colcokes Rd. SM7 11 C4
- Commonfield Rd. SM7 11 C1
- Court Rd. SM7 11 C3
- Courtlands Cres. SM7 11 C3
- Croydon La. SM7 11 D2
- Croydon Lane Sth. SM7 11 D2
- Cuddington Park Clo. SM7 11 B1
- Cypress Way. SM7 11 A2
- Daniel Way. SM7 11 C2
- De Burgh Pk. SM7 11 D3
- Diceland Rd. SM7 11 B4
- Dunnymans Rd. SM7 11 B3
- East Gate. SM7 11 A2
- Ferndale Rd. SM7 11 B4
- Fiddicroft Av. SM7 11 D2
- Fir Tree Rd. SM7 11 A1
- Follyfield Rd. SM7 11 C2
- Free Down La. SM7 11 D1
- Gale Cres. SM7 11 C5
- Garden Clo. SM7 11 C3
- Garrard Rd. SM7 11 C4
- Garratts La. SM7 11 B4
- Gerrards Mead. SM7 11 B4
- Glenfield Rd. SM7 11 C3
- Grange Gdns. SM7 11 D1
- Grange Meadow. SM7 11 D1
- Great Ellshams. SM7 11 C4
- Green Curve. SM7 11 B2
- Greenhayes Av. SM7 11 C2
- Greenhayes Gdns. SM7 11 C3
- Harbourfield Rd. SM7 11 D2
- Hawthorn Clo. SM7 11 A2
- Heath Clo. SM7 11 D2
- Heights Clo. SM7 11 A4
- High Beeches. SM7 11 A2
- High St. SM7 11 C3
- Higher Dri. SM7 11 A1
- Hillside. SM7 11 A3
- Hillside Clo. SM7 11 A4
- Holly Hill Dri. SM7 11 C4
- Holly La. SM7 11 C4
- Holly La East. SM7 11 C4
- Holly La West. SM7 11 D5
- Home Meadow. SM7 11 C4
- Horse Croft. SM7 11 B4
- Kenilworth Clo. SM7 11 D4
- Kingsley Av. SM7 11 C3
- Lambert Rd. SM7 11 C2
- Lancaster Ct. SM7 11 B2
- Larchwood Clo. SM7 11 A3
- Lower Dunnymans. SM7 11 B2
- Lower Northfield Rd. SM7 11 B2
- Lower Sawley Wood. SM7 11 B2
- Lyme Regis Rd. SM7 11 B4
- Meadow Way. SM7 11 A5
- Mellow Clo. SM7 11 D1
- Monks Rd. SM7 11 C4
- Neville Clo. SM7 11 D2
- Nork Gdns. SM7 11 A2
- Nork Way. SM7 11 A3
- North Acre. SM7 11 B4
- Oakley Gdns. SM7 11 D2
- Orchard Clo. SM7 11 D2
- Osier Way. SM7 11 A2
- Palmersfield Rd. SM7 11 C2
- Park Rd. SM7 11 D3
- Pembroke Clo. SM7 11 D5
- Picquets Way. SM7 11 B5
- Poplar Dri. SM7 11 A2
- Pound Rd. SM7 11 B5
- Rosehill Farm Meadow. SM7 11 D3
- Roundwood Way. SM7 11 A3
- Ruffetts Way. SM7 11 A6
- Salisbury Rd. SM7 11 D2
- Sandersfield Gdns. SM7 11 C3
- Sandersfield Rd. SM7 11 C2
- Shelley Clo. SM7 11 A3
- Shrubland Rd. SM7 11 B4
- Stirling Clo. SM7 11 B5
- Sutton La. SM7 11 D2
- Sycamore Rise. SM7 11 A2
- Tangier Way. SM7 11 A5
- Tangier Wood. SM7 11 A6
- Tattenham Way. SM7 11 A5
- The Beeches. SM7 11 C4
- The Brindles. SM7 11 B5
- The Drive. SM7 11 A4
- The Gables. SM7 11 B4
- The Horseshoe. SM7 11 B3
- The Laurels. SM7 11 B5
- The Maples. SM7 11 D1
- The Orchard. SM7 11 B3
- The Oval. SM7 11 C2
- The Tracery. SM7 11 D3
- Thornfield Rd. SM7 11 C5
- Tudor Clo. SM7 11 A3
- Tumblewood Rd. SM7 11 A4
- *Upper Dunnymans. Basing Rd. SM7 11 B2
- Upper Sawley Wood. SM7 11 B2
- Warren Rd. SM7 11 A2
- Waterer Gdns. SM7 11 A6
- Wellesford Clo. SM7 11 B5
- Whiteoaks. SM7 11 D1
- Wilmot Way. SM7 11 C2
- Winkworth Pl. SM7 11 B2
- Winkworth Rd. SM7 11 C2
- Wood La. SM7 11 B5
- Woodgavil. SM7 11 B4
- Woodmansterne La. SM7 11 D3
- Yewlands Clo. SM7 11 D3


## BYFLEET


- Abbot Clo. KT14 12 E1
- Acacia Clo. KT15 12 A1
- Acacia Dri. KT15 12 A1
- Amberley Dri. KT15 12 A1
- Amis Av. KT15 12 B1
- Aprilwood Clo. KT15 12 A2
- Avro Way. KT13 12 F1
- Barnato Clo. KT14 12 F3
- Barnes Wallis Dri. KT13 12 F2
- Basset Clo. KT15 12 D1
- Beech Clo. KT14 12 F3
- Berrys La. KT14 12 E2
- Birch Walk. KT14 12 B3
- Birchdale Clo. KT14 12 D2
- Birchwood Dri. KT14 12 B3
- Birchwood Rd. KT14 12 B3
- Blackwood Clo. KT14 12 D3
- Blenheim Clo. KT14 12 A4
- Bourne Cres. KT14 12 C4
- Braeside. KT15 12 C2
- Brantwood Dri. KT14 12 A4
- Brantwood Gdns. KT14 12 B4
- Brewery La. KT14 12 F3
- Briar Clo. KT14 12 D2
- Briar Walk. KT14 12 B3
- Broadoaks Cres. KT14 12 C4
- Broomfield Rd. KT15 12 C2
- Bruce Clo. KT14 12 F4
- Bucks Clo. KT14 12 C4
- Byfleet Rd. KT14 12 E1
- Caillard Rd. KT14 12 F2
- Camphill Ct. KT14 12 B3
- Camphill Rd. KT14 12 B3
- Canada Rd. KT14 12 E2
- Cheniston Clo. KT14 12 B3
- Chestnut Walk. KT14 12 F3
- Chertsey Rd. KT14 12 E2
- Church Rd. KT14 12 E4
- Clare Clo. KT14 12 B4
- Claremont Rd. KT14 12 B3
- Cobs Way. KT15 12 D1
- Copthall Way. KT15 12 B1
- Cresta Dri. KT15 12 A1
- Dartnell Av. KT14 12 C3
- Dartnell Clo. KT14 12 C3
- Dartnell Ct. KT14 12 D2
- Dartnell Cres. KT14 12 C2
- Dartnell Park Rd. KT14 12 C2
- Dartnell Pl. KT14 12 C3
- Dashwood Clo. KT14 12 D2
- Dawson Rd. KT14 12 E2
- De Havilland Dri. KT13 12 F1
- Dodds Cres. KT14 12 C4
- Dorset Way. KT14 12 E1
- Dunfee Way. KT14 12 F2
- Eden Clo. KT15 12 C1
- Eden Grove Rd. KT14 12 F4
- Elmstead Rd. KT14 12 B4
- Fairford Clo. KT14 12 A4
- Fairlawns. KT15 12 A2
- Faris Barn Dri. KT15 12 A2
- Faris La. KT15 12 A2
- Farleigh Rd. KT15 12 B2
- Ferney Rd. KT14 12 E2
- Fleetwood Ct. KT14 12 B3
- Florence Av. KT15 12 B2
- Fosse Way. KT14 12 A4
- Fulbrook Av. KT15 12 B2
- Fullmer Way. KT15 12 A1
- Glebe Gdns. KT14 12 F4
- Gorselands Clo. KT14 12 D2
- Grafton Clo. KT14 12 A3
- Grange Rd. KT15 12 C1
- Greenway Clo. KT14 12 B4
- Greenwood Clo. KT15 12 A2
- Hart Rd. KT14 12 F4
- Hatfield Clo. KT14 12 C3
- Haydon Ct. KT15 12 C1
- Heather Clo. KT15 12 C1
- Heathervale Rd. KT15 12 C1
- High Rd. KT14 12 F3
- Highfield Clo. KT14 12 B3
- Highfield Rd. KT14 12 B4
- Hobbs Clo. KT14 12 C3
- Hollies Av. KT14 12 A3
- Holly Av. KT15 12 B1
- Hopfield Av. KT14 12 F3
- **INDUSTRIAL & RETAIL:**
- Brooklands Ind. Est. KT13 12 F2
- Camphill Ind Est. KT14 12 C2
- Wey Retail Pk. KT14 12 F3
- Inglehurst. KT15 12 C1
- Junewood Clo. KT15 12 A2
- Keston Av. KT15 12 B2
- King Georges Dri. KT15 12 B1
- Kings Av. KT14 12 E2
- Kings Rd. KT15 12 C1
- Kingshead La. KT14 12 E2
- Kingston Rise. KT15 12 B1
- Knowle Gdns. KT14 12 A3
- Lake Clo. KT14 12 E3
- Langshott Clo. KT15 12 A2
- Laurel Gdns. KT15 12 C1
- Lavender Park Rd. KT14 12 B3
- Leisure La. KT14 12 C3
- Linden Clo. KT15 12 B2
- Lindsay Rd. KT15 12 C1
- Little Moreton Clo. KT14 12 C3
- Little Orchard. KT15 12 B2
- Lyndale Ct. KT14 12 B3
- Madeira Clo. KT14 12 B3
- Madeira Cres. KT14 12 B4
- Madeira Rd. KT14 12 A4
- Maitland Clo. KT14 12 B4
- Manor Dri. KT15 12 B1
- Maxwell Dri. KT14 12 D2
- Mayfield Av. KT15 12 D1
- Mayfield Clo. KT15 12 D1
- Melbury Clo. KT14 12 B4
- Millan Clo. KT15 12 C1
- Mowbray Av. KT14 12 F3
- Murrays La. KT14 12 E4
- Nursery Clo. KT15 12 A1
- Oak End Way. KT15 12 A3
- Oakcroft Clo. KT14 12 A4
- Oakcroft Rd. KT14 12 A4
- Oakfields. KT14 12 C4
- Old Parvis Rd. KT14 12 D3
- Old Woking Rd. KT14 12 A4
- Orchard Av. KT15 12 A2
- Orchards Clo. KT14 12 B4
- Oyster La. KT14 12 F2
- Park Clo. KT15 12 D1
- Park Side. KT15 12 C1
- Parvis Bridge. KT14 12 E3
- Parvis Rd. KT14 12 C3
- Pendennis Clo. KT14 12 B4
- Petersham Av. KT14 12 F2
- Petersham Clo. KT14 12 F3
- Petersham Ct. KT14 12 F3
- Pine Clo. KT15 12 C2
- Pinewood Av. KT15 12 D1
- Pinewood Gro. KT15 12 C1
- Pinewood Pk. KT15 12 C2
- Pyrford Rd. KT14 12 B4
- Queen Marys Dri. KT15 12 A1
- Queens Av. KT14 12 E3
- Rectory Clo. KT14 12 F4
- Rectory La. KT14 12 F3
- Redwing Gdns. KT14 12 C3
- Regency Dri. KT14 12 A4
- Rosemount Av. KT14 12 B4
- Royston Av. KT14 12 F3
- Royston Rd. KT14 12 F3
- Salisbury Pl. KT14 12 D2
- Sanway Rd. KT14 12 F4
- Scotland Bridge Rd. KT15 12 B1
- Selbourne Av. KT15 12 C
- Selsdon Rd. KT15 12 B
- Sheerwater Av. KT15 12 A
- Sheerwater Rd. KT14 12 A
- Shires House. KT14 12 F
- Squirrel Keep. KT14 12 C
- Squirrel Wood. KT14 12 C
- Starwood Clo. KT14 12 D
- Station App. KT14 12 B
- Station Rd. KT14 12 B
- Stoop Ct. KT14 12 C
- Stream Clo. KT14 12 F
- Tewkesbury Clo. KT14 12 E
- The Alders. KT14 12 D
- The Avenue. KT15 12 B
- The Broadway. KT15 12 B
- The Courtyard. KT14 12 B
- The Close. KT14 12 B
- The Oaks. KT14 12 C
- The Paddocks. KT15 12 C
- The Willows. KT14 12 F
- Thistle Dene. KT14 12 A
- Trevose Av. KT14 12 A
- Vickers Rd Nth. KT13 12 F
- Vickers Rd Sth. KT13 12 F
- Viscount Gdns. KT14 12 F
- Wakefield Clo. KT14 12 F
- Walnut Tree La. KT14 12 E
- Warren Rd. KT15 12 B
- Wendley Dri. KT15 12 A
- Westwood Av. KT15 12 A
- Wey Clo. KT14 12 C
- Wild Acres. KT14 12 D
- Willow Clo. KT15 12 A
- Willow Way. KT14 12 D
- Winern Glebe. KT14 12 E
- Wingfield Clo. KT15 12 C
- Wintersells Rd. KT14 12 F
- Woodham La. KT15 12 A
- Woodham Park Rd. KT15 12 A
- Woodham Park Way. KT15 12 A
- Woodlands Av. KT14 12 A
- Woodmancote Gdns. KT14 12 B
- York Clo. KT14 12 F
- York Rd. KT14 12 F


## CAMBERLEY


- Abbey Ct. GU15 13 B
- Academy Clo. GU15 13 C
- Albert Rd. GU15 13 B
- Alison Dri. GU15 13 D
- Amberwood Dri. GU15 13 D
- Appley Ct. GU15 13 A
- Appley Dri. GU15 13 A
- Ashwell Av. GU15 13 D
- Ballard Ct. GU15 13 E
- Ballard Rd. GU15 13 E
- Barn Clo. GU15 13 C
- Barossa Rd. GU15 13 E
- Bath Rd. GU15 13 E
- Beaufront Clo. GU15 13 F
- Beaufront Rd. GU15 13 F
- Bellever Hill. GU15 13 C
- Belton Rd. GU15 13 C
- Bennett Ct. GU15 13 A
- Berkshire Rd. GU15 13 D
- Bietigheim Way. GU15 13 E
- Birch Clo. GU15 13 C
- Bracknell Clo. GU15 13 E
- Bracknell Rd. GU15 13 E
- Branksome Clo. GU15 13 C
- Branksome Park Rd. GU15 13 C
- Burbury Woods. GU15 13 C
- Burgoyne Rd. GU15 13 E
- Caesars Camp Rd. GU15 13 E
- Caesars Clo. GU15 13 E
- Caesars Ct. GU15 13 E
- Cambrian Clo. GU15 13 A
- Cambridge Walk. GU15 13 E
- Carlinwark Dri. GU15 13 D
- Carshalton Rd. GU15 13 E
- Castle Rd. GU15 13 D
- Chatsworth Heights. GU15 13 F
- Chaucer Gro. GU15 13 E
- Chesters Rd. GU15 13 F
- Chestnut Av. GU15 13 F
- Church Hill. GU15 13 C

# CATERHAM

# CHERTSEY

**Column 1**

Oaklands Ct. KT15 15 D6
Oldbury Rd. KT16 15 A3
Onslow Mews. KT16 15 C2
Paddocks Way. KT16 15 D4
Pannells Clo. KT16 15 B4
Pound Rd. KT16 15 D3
Prairie Clo. KT16 15 D6
Prairie Rd. KT15 15 D6
Pretoria Rd. KT16 15 B4
Pyrcroft Rd. KT16 15 B3
Queen St. KT16 15 C4
Railway App. KT16 15 B3
Rickman Cres. KT15 15 D6
Riversdell Clo. KT16 15 C3
Roakes Av. KT16 15 D5
Rosemead. KT16 15 C4
Rutherwyk Rd. KT16 15 A3
Ruxbury Rd. KT16 15 A2
St Anns Clo. KT16 15 B2
St Anns Hill Rd. KT16 15 A2
St Anns Rd. KT16 15 A2
St Johns Way. KT16 15 C5
St Peters Way. KT16 15 C6
Salesian Gdns. KT16 15 C4
Sandalwood Av. KT16 15 A6
School La. KT15 15 C6
South Gro. KT16 15 B2
Springfields Clo. KT16 15 D4
Squires Ct. KT16 15 D4
Staines La. KT16 15 C2
Staines Lane Clo. KT16 15 B1
Staines Rd. KT16 15 B1
Station Rd. KT16 15 C4
Stepgates. KT16 15 D3
Stepgates Clo. KT16 15 D3
Styventon Pl. KT16 15 B3
The Barracks. KT15 15 D6
The Knoll. KT16 15 B4
Thorpe Rd. KT16 15 A1
Twynersh Av. KT16 15 B2
Victory Rd. KT16 15 C4
Vincent Clo. KT16 15 B3
Vincent Rd. KT16 15 A3
Waverley Dri. KT16 15 A6
Weir Rd. KT16 15 D3
Wheatash Rd. KT16 15 D5
White Hart Row. KT16 15 C3
Willats Clo. KT16 15 C2
Willow Walk. KT16 15 D2
Windsor Pl. KT16 15 D2
Windsor St. KT16 15 C2

## CHOBHAM

Alpha Rd. GU24 16 B3
Bagshot Rd. GU24 16 A4
Barnmead. GU24 16 C4
Beta Rd. GU24 16 C3
Borough Grn. GU24 16 A2
Bowling Grn Rd. GU24 16 B3
Bracken Way. GU24 16 C3
Brimshot La. GU24 16 B2
Broadford La. GU24 16 B5
Brook Grn. GU24 16 C3
Brook La. GU24 16 A4
Brookleys. GU24 16 B2
Broom La. GU24 16 B2
Burrhill La. GU24 16 B3
Cannon Cres. GU24 16 B4
Castle Gro Rd. GU24 16 B5
Chertsey Rd. GU24 16 C3
Chobham Park La. GU24 16 C1
Clappers La. GU24 16 A4
Delta Clo. GU24 16 C3
Delta Rd. GU24 16 C3
Elm Dri. GU24 16 C3
Fowlers Mead. GU24 16 B3
Gorse La. GU24 16 B2
Gracious Pond Rd. GU24 16 C1
Green La. GU24 16 C3
Grosvenor Rd. GU24 16 A6
Guildford Rd. GU24 16 A6
Heather Way. GU24 16 A1
High St. GU24 16 B4
Killy Hill. GU24 16 B2
Leslie Rd. GU24 16 A3
Little Heath Rd. GU24 16 B2
Medhurst Clo. GU24 16 C3
Mincing La. GU24 16 C2
Mount Rd. GU24 16 D5
Oakdene. GU24 16 B2
Oakhurst. GU24 16 B2

**Column 2**

Red Lion Rd. GU24 16 B2
Sandpit Hall Rd. GU24 16 D5
Sandy La. GU24 16 B2
Scotts Gro Clo. GU24 16 A6
Scotts Gro Rd. GU24 16 A6
Station Rd. GU24 16 C5
Steep Hill. GU24 16 A1
The Avenue. GU24 16 C2
The Grange. GU24 16 B3
Thompsons La. GU24 16 A2
Turfhouse La. GU24 16 B2
Vicarage Rd. GU24 16 B4
Waterperry La. GU24 16 C3
Watery La. GU24 16 A4
Windlesham Rd. GU24 16 A2
Windsor Ct Rd. GU24 16 B3
Windsor Rd. GU24 16 A1

## COBHAM/STOKE D'ABERNON

Anvil La. KT11 17 A2
Anyards Rd. KT11 17 A2
Ashcroft Park. KT11 17 E1
Ashford Gdns. KT11 17 D4
Ashlyns Pk. KT11 17 E1
Aspen Clo. KT11 17 E4
Avenue Rd. KT11 17 D4
Beechmeads. KT11 17 D1
Bennett Clo. KT11 17 A1
Between Streets. KT11 17 A2
Birchgrove. KT11 17 C2
Blundel La. KT11 17 F4
Bramble Rise. KT11 17 C3
Bray Rd. KT11 17 E4
Bridge Way. KT11 17 A1
Broad Highway. KT11 17 D3
Brook Farm Rd. KT11 17 D3
Brooklands Clo. KT11 17 E3
Brunswick Gro. KT11 17 C1
Burleigh Park. KT11 17 E1
Burstead Clo. KT11 17 D1
Canada Rd. KT11 17 C1
Cedar Av. KT11 17 C3
Cedar Rd. KT11 17 B2
Church St. KT11 17 B3
Cleves Clo. KT11 17 B2
Cobham Gate. KT11 17 B2
Copse Rd. KT11 17 A1
Coveham Cres. KT11 17 A1
D'Abernon Dri. KT11 17 E4
Denby Rd. KT11 17 C1
Downside Bridge Rd. KT11 17 B3
Downside Rd. KT11 17 B4
Drift La. KT11 17 F4
Eaton Pk. KT11 17 E2
Eaton Park Rd. KT11 17 E2
Elm Grove Rd. KT11 17 D3
Evelyn Way. KT11 17 F4
Fairbourne. KT11 17 D1
Fairfield Rd. KT11 17 D3
Fairmeads. KT11 17 F1
Fairmile Av. KT11 17 E2
Fairmile Ct. KT11 17 E1
Fairmile La. KT11 17 E1
Fairmile Park Copse. KT11 17 F1
Fairmile Park Rd. KT11 17 F1
Farm Vw. KT11 17 D4
Ferndown Clo. KT11 17 C2
Four Acres. KT11 17 E1
Four Wents. KT11 17 C2
Freelands Rd. KT11 17 B2
French Gdns. KT11 17 C2
Gavell Rd. KT11 17 A1
Grenville Clo. KT11 17 D1
Haleswood. KT11 17 C2
Hamilton Av. KT11 17 A1
Harebell Hill. KT11 17 D2
Hawksview. KT11 17 F1
High St. KT11 17 B3
Hogshill La. KT11 17 B2
Hollymedge Rd. KT11 17 B3
Icklingham Gate. KT11 17 C1
Icklingham Rd. KT11 17 C1
Knipp Hill. KT11 17 F1
Knowle Pk. KT11 17 E3
Lambourne Dri. KT11 17 D3
Larkfield. KT11 17 D1
Leigh Corner. KT11 17 C3
Leigh Court Clo. KT11 17 C2
Leigh Hill Rd. KT11 17 C2
Leigh Pl. KT11 17 C3

**Column 3**

Leigh Rd. KT11 17 B2
Lockhart Rd. KT11 17 C1
Lodge Clo. KT11 17 F4
Longboyds. KT11 17 B3
Loriners Clo. KT11 17 A2
Lushington Dri. KT11 17 B2
Lyster Mews. KT11 17 C1
Lytton Pk. KT11 17 F1
Matthew Arnold Clo. KT11 17 A2
Meadowlands. KT11 17 A1
Miles La. KT11 17 E1
Mill Rd. KT11 17 C3
Millhedge Clo. KT11 17 E4
Mizen Clo. KT11 17 D2
Mizen Way. KT11 17 D3
Molesworth Rd. KT11 17 A1
Mossfield. KT11 17 A1
Northfield Rd. KT11 17 B1
Oak Rd. KT11 17 D3
Oakdene Par. KT11 17 B2
Oakdene Rd. KT11 17 B2
Oakfield Rd. KT11 17 B2
Old Common Rd. KT11 17 B1
Oxshott Rise. KT11 17 E3
Oxshott Way. KT11 17 E3
Paddocks Clo. KT11 17 C2
Pennyfield. KT11 17 A1
Pine Walk. KT11 17 D2
Pipers Clo. KT11 17 D3
Plough La. KT11 17 B4
Pony Chase. KT11 17 F1
Portsmouth Rd. KT11 17 A2
Queens Court Ride. KT11 17 A1
Ravenswood Clo. KT11 17 B3
River Hill. KT11 17 B3
River La. KT11 17 E4
Riverview Gdns. KT11 17 A1
Ross Rd. KT11 17 C1
St Andrews Gdns. KT11 17 C1
St Andrews Walk. KT11 17 B3
Sandy Ct. KT11 17 F1
Sandy La. KT11 17 F1
Spencer Rd. KT11 17 B3
Station Rd. KT11 17 E4
Stoke Clo. KT11 17 F4
Stoke Rd. KT11 17 C3
Summerhays. KT11 17 D2
Tartar Hill. KT11 17 B1
Tartar Rd. KT11 17 C1
The Barton. KT11 17 C1
The Bowsprit. KT11 17 C3
The Drive. KT11 17 E2
The Garth. KT11 17 E1
The Laurels. KT11 17 E3
The Stables. KT11 17 F3
Tilt Clo. KT11 17 E4
Tilt Meadow. KT11 17 E4
Tilt Rd. KT11 17 C3
Towngate. KT11 17 E3
Trafalgar Ct. KT11 17 A1
Tudor Clo. KT11 17 F1
Vincent Rd. KT11 17 E4
Virginia Pl. KT11 17 A2
Warblers Grn. KT11 17 F2
Water La. KT11 17 F2
Wedgwood Pl. KT11 17 A2
Winstanley Clo. KT11 17 B2
Winston Dri. KT11 17 E4
Woodend Pk. KT11 17 D3
Worlds End. KT11 17 A2
Wyndham Av. KT11 17 A1

## CRANLEIGH

Acres Platt. GU6 18 D1
Ash Trees. GU6 18 C3
Aven Clo. GU6 18 C3
Avenue Rd. GU6 18 D3
Bank Buildings Rd. GU6 18 B2
Barber Dri. GU6 18 C1
Barhatch Rd. GU6 18 D1
Barnfield. GU6 18 C2
Bax Clo. GU6 18 C3
Beaumont Sq. GU6 18 D2
Bishops Sq. GU6 18 D2
Bloggs Way. GU6 18 B2
Bloxham Rd. GU6 18 E2
Bookhurst Rd. GU6 18 E1
Bridge Rd. GU6 18 C2
Broad Walk. GU6 18 D3
Brookmead Ct. GU6 18 D3
Brookside. GU6 18 C4

**Column 4**

Butt Clo. GU6 18 C1
Cameron Clo. GU6 18 C4
Charts Clo. GU6 18 C3
Church Path. GU6 18 B2
Coatham Pl. GU6 18 D2
Collingdon. GU6 18 D4
Common Rd. GU6 18 A1
Copse Edge. GU6 18 D1
Cranleigh Mead. GU6 18 D3
Cromwell Pl. GU6 18 D4
Dewlands Clo. GU6 18 C2
Dewlands La. GU6 18 C2
Dover Ct. GU6 18 E2
Drakes Clo. GU6 18 B2
Dukes Clo. GU6 18 D3
Durnsford Way. GU6 18 D3
East View La. GU6 18 A2
Edgefield Clo. GU6 18 A1
Ellery Clo. GU6 18 C4
Ewhurst Rd. GU6 18 C2
Fawley Clo. GU6 18 D3
Fettes Rd. GU6 18 E2
Fortune Dri. GU6 18 C4
Gingers Clo. GU6 18 D3
Glebe Rd. GU6 18 B1
Grange Pk. GU6 18 D2
Greenbush La. GU6 18 D4
Grove Clo. GU6 18 D4
Grove Rd. GU6 18 D4
Guildford Rd. GU6 18 A2
Hailey Pl. GU6 18 D1
Hanewood Ct. GU6 18 C3
Harrier Clo. GU6 18 C1
Harrowdene. GU6 18 C1
Heron Shaw. GU6 18 C3
High St. GU6 18 B2
Hitherwood. GU6 18 C3
Homestead. GU6 18 D1
Homewood. GU6 18 E2
Horseshoe La. GU6 18 A1
Horsham Rd. GU6 18 C3
John Wiskar Dri. GU6 18 B2
Killicks. GU6 18 C1
Kiln Copse. GU6 18 C1
Kingsmead. GU6 18 C2
Kings Rd. GU6 18 C3
Knowle La. GU6 18 B3
Little Manor Gdns. GU6 18 B2
Littlewood. GU6 18 D2
Longpoles Rd. GU6 18 D3
Loretto Clo. GU6 18 D2
Mead Clo. GU6 18 C2
Mead Rd. GU6 18 C2
Mount Rd. GU6 18 C3
Mower Pl. GU6 18 C1
Napper Pl. GU6 18 C4
New Park Rd. GU6 18 C2
Nightingales. GU6 18 C4
Northdowns. GU6 18 C3
Nuthurst Av. GU6 18 C2
Oak Gro. GU6 18 D4
Oaklands. GU6 18 B3
Orchard Gdns. GU6 18 D3
Overford Clo. GU6 18 C3
Overford Dri. GU6 18 C3
Park Dri. GU6 18 D1
Parsonage Rd. GU6 18 B2
Peregrine Clo. GU6 18 C1
Queensway. GU6 18 D3
Redcroft Walk. GU6 18 C1
Rowland Rd. GU6 18 B2
Ryde Lands. GU6 18 D1
St James Pl. GU6 18 A2
St Nicolas Av. GU6 18 C2
St Nicolas Clo. GU6 18 C1
Sapte Clo. GU6 18 E2
Seltops Clo. GU6 18 D3
Sherrydon. GU6 18 D1
Slip of Wood. GU6 18 D1
Southwood Chase. GU6 18 D4
Stocklund Sq. GU6 18 D3
Strudwicks Fields. GU6 18 D1
Summerlands. GU6 18 C1
Sylvaways Clo. GU6 18 E2
Taylors Cres. GU6 18 D1
The Drive. GU6 18 C3
The Malt Houses. GU6 18 C1
The Mount. GU6 18 C3
The Precinct. GU6 18 C1
The Ridgeway. GU6 18 C1
The Ridings. GU6 18 C1
Thistley La. GU6 18 C4
Thurlow Walk. GU6 18 C4
Trelawne Dri. GU6 18 D3
Victoria Rd. GU6 18 B2
Waldy Rise. GU6 18 C1

**Column 5 (Cranleigh continuation)**

Wanborough La. GU6 18 E
Waverleigh Rd. GU6 18 C
Wellwynds Rd. GU6 18 E
Wildwood Clo. GU6 18 D
Woodland Av. GU6 18 C
Woodlands Clo. GU6 18 D
Woodstock Clo. GU6 18 D
Wyphurst Rd. GU6 18 B

## CROYDON

Abbey Rd. CR0 19 B
Aberdeen Rd. CR0 19 D
Addington Rd. CR0 19 E
Ainsworth Rd. CR0 19 C
Albion St. CR0 19 E
Allen Rd. CR0 19 A
Alton Rd. CR0 19 A
Ampere Way. CR0 19 A
Arundel Clo. CR0 19 D
Arundel Rd. CR0 19 D
Ashby Walk. CR0 19 C
Ashley La. CR0 19 C
*Baines Clo
  Cliffe Rd. CR2 19 D
Barclay Rd. CR0 19 D
Barham Rd. CR2 19 C
Bartlett St. CR2 19 C
Beddington Fm Rd. CR0 19 A
Bedford Pk. CR0 19 C
Bedford Pl. CR0 19 C
Beech House Rd. CR0 19 C
Bensham La. CR0 19 B
Benson Rd. CR0 19 B
Berney Rd. CR0 19 C
Beulah Gro. CR0 19 C
Birdhurst Av. CR2 19 D
Bishops Rd. CR0 19 B
Blunt Rd. CR2 19 C
Booth St. CR0 19 B
Borough Hill. CR0 19 B
Boston Rd. CR0 19 A
Bourne St. CR0 19 B
Brafferton Rd. CR0 19 C
Bramley Clo. CR2 19 C
Bramley Hill. CR2 19 C
Brighton Rd. CR2 19 C
*Brightwell Clo,
  Sumner Rd. CR0 19 B
Broad Grn Av. CR0 19 B
Broadfield Clo. CR0 19 A
Burdett Rd. CR0 19 C
Bute Rd. CR0 19 C
Cairo New Rd. CR0 19 C
Cameron Rd. CR0 19 B
Campbell Rd. CR0 19 A
Canterbury Rd. CR0 19 A
Cavendish Rd. CR0 19 B
Chapel Walk. CR0 19 C
Chapman Rd. CR0 19 A
Charles St. CR0 19 C
Charrington Rd. CR0 19 C
Chartwell Clo. CR0 19 C
Chatfield Rd. CR0 19 B
Chatsworth Rd. CR0 19 A
Cherry Hill Gdns. CR0 19 A
Church Alley. CR0 19 C
Church Rd. CR0 19 C
Church St. CR0 19 C
Clarence Rd. CR0 19 B
Clarendon Rd. CR0 19 A
Cliffe Rd. CR2 19 D
*Cobblestone Pl,
  Oakfield Rd. CR0 19 A
Coldharbour Rd. CR0 19 A
College Rd. CR0 19 C
Commerce Way. CR0 19 A
Constance Rd. CR0 19 B
Coombe Rd. CR0 19 B
Cooper Rd. CR0 19 B
Cornwall Rd. CR0 19 B
Cosedge Cres. CR0 19 B
Court Dri. CR0 19 A
Courtney Pl. CR0 19 B
Courtney Rd. CR0 19 A
Cranmer Rd. CR0 19 B
Crawley Cres. CR0 19 B
Croham Rd. CR2 19 D
Cromwell Rd. CR0 19 C
Crossland Rd. CR7 19 C
Crown Hill. CR0 19 C
Croydon Gro. CR0 19 B
Croydon Rd. CR0 19 A

Cuthbert Rd. CR0 19 B4
Davenant Rd. CR0 19 C5
Dean Rd. CR0 19 D6
Denmead Rd. CR0 19 B3
Dennett Rd. CR0 19 B2
Denning Av. CR0 19 A6
Derby Rd. CR0 19 C6
Dering Pl. CR0 19 C6
Dering Rd. CR0 19 C6
Devonshire Rd. CR0 19 D1
Dingwall Av. CR0 19 D4
Dingwall Rd. CR0 19 D3
Donald Rd. CR0 19 A1
Drake Rd. CR0 19 A2
Drayton Rd. CR0 19 C4
Drummond Pl. CR0 19 C4
Drummond Rd. CR0 19 C4
Drury Cres. CR0 19 A3
Dunheved Rd Sth. CR7 19 B1
Dunheved Rd West.
  CR7 19 A1
Duppas Av. CR0 19 B6
Duppas Hill La. CR0 19 C5
Duppas Hill Rd. CR0 19 B5
Duppas Hill Ter. CR0 19 C5
Dysart Av. CR0 19 B5
Eastney Rd. CR0 19 B2
Eden Rd. CR0 19 D5
Edridge Rd. CR0 19 D5
Effingham Rd. CR0 19 A2
Eland Rd. CR0 19 B4
Elmwood Rd. CR0 19 B2
*Englefield Clo,
  Queens Rd. CR0 19 C1
Enterprise Clo. CR0 19 A3
Epsom Rd. CR0 19 A5
Euston Rd. CR0 19 A3
Factory La. CR0 19 A3
Fairfield Rd. CR0 19 D4
Fairholme Rd. CR0 19 B2
Fairmead Rd. CR0 19 A2
Faraday Way. CR0 19 A2
Farquharson Rd. CR0 19 C2
Fawcett Rd. CR0 19 C5
Fell Rd. CR0 19 D4
Fernleigh Clo. CR0 19 A6
Five Acre Clo. CR7 19 B1
Francis Rd. CR0 19 B1
Frederick Gdns. CR0 19 C1
Friends Rd. CR0 19 D4
Frith Rd. CR0 19 C4
Furtherfield Clo. CR0 19 A1
Galloway Path. CR0 19 D6
Galvani Way. CR0 19 A3
Gardeners Rd. CR0 19 B3
George St. CR0 19 D4
Gladstone Rd. CR0 19 D2
Glen Gdns. CR0 19 B5
Godalming Av. SM6 19 A6
Godson Rd. CR0 19 A5
Grace Rd. CR0 19 C1
Grafton Rd. CR0 19 B3
Greenside Rd. CR0 19 B2
Greenwood Rd. CR0 19 C1
Grenaby Av. CR0 19 D2
Grenaby Rd. CR0 19 D2
Grindall Clo. CR0 19 B6
Gurney Cres. CR0 19 A3
Halstead Clo. CR0 19 C4
Hampton Rd. CR0 19 D1
Handcroft Rd. CR0 19 B2
Hanover St. CR0 19 C5
Harcourt Rd. CR7 19 A1
Harrisons Rise. CR0 19 B4
Hartley Rd. CR0 19 C1
Hathaway Rd. CR0 19 C1
Hatton Rd. CR0 19 B2
Headley Av. SM6 19 A6
Heathfield Rd. CR0 19 D5
Heighton Gdns. CR0 19 B6
High St. CR0 19 C4
Hillside Rd. CR0 19 B6
Hogarth Cres. CR0 19 C2
Hood Clo. CR0 19 C3
Howley Rd. CR0 19 C4
Hughes Walk,
  St Saviours Rd. CR0 19 C1
Hurst Rd. CR0 19 D6
Hyrstdene. CR2 19 C6
INDUSTRIAL & RETAIL:
Croydon Business
  Centre. CR0 19 A3
Mill La Trading Est.
  CR0 19 A4
Purley Way Centre.
  CR0 19 A3

Wandle Park
  Ind Est. CR0 19 B3
Innes Yd. CR0 19 C5
Jennett Rd. CR0 19 A4
Johnson Rd. CR0 19 D1
Katharine St. CR0 19 D4
Keeley Rd. CR0 19 C4
Keens Rd. CR0 19 C5
Kelling Gdns. CR0 19 B1
Kemble Rd. CR0 19 B4
Kemp Gdns. CR0 19 C1
Kidderminster Rd. CR0 19 C2
King Gdns. CR0 19 B6
Kingsley Rd. CR0 19 A2
Lamberts Pl. CR0 19 D2
Lambeth Rd. CR0 19 B2
Lancing Rd. CR0 19 A1
Lansdowne Rd. CR0 19 D3
Latimer Rd. CR0 19 B5
Laud St. CR0 19 C5
Lawdon Gdns. CR0 19 C6
Layton Cres. CR0 19 B6
Ledbury Pl. CR0 19 D6
Ledbury Rd. CR0 19 D6
Leighton St. CR0 19 B3
Lennard Rd. CR0 19 C2
Lennox Gdns. CR0 19 C6
Limes Av. CR0 19 A5
Limes Pl. CR0 19 D1
Limes Rd. CR0 19 D1
Lodge Av. CR0 19 B4
Lodge Rd. CR0 19 C1
London Rd. CR0 19 B1
Longley Rd. CR0 19 B2
Lower Coombe St. CR0 19 C5
Ludford Clo. CR0 19 B5
Lynton Rd. CR0 19 A1
Lynwood Gdns. CR0 19 A6
Mann Clo. CR0 19 C5
Marden Cres. CR0 19 A1
Marden Rd. CR0 19 A1
Martin Cres. CR0 19 A3
Masons Av. CR0 19 D5
Mayday Rd. CR7 19 B1
Mead Pl. CR0 19 C3
Merebank La. CR0 19 A6
Middle St. CR0 19 C4
Midhurst Av. CR0 19 B1
Mill La. CR0 19 A4
Miller Rd. CR0 19 A4
Milton Av. CR0 19 D2
Milton Rd. CR0 19 D2
Mint Walk. CR0 19 C4
Mitcham Rd. CR0 19 A2
Montague Rd. CR0 19 B2
Mulgrave Rd. CR0 19 D5
Nelson Clo. CR0 19 B3
Neville Rd. CR0 19 D1
Newgate. CR0 19 D2
North End. CR0 19 C3
Northcote Rd. CR0 19 D1
Nottingham Rd. CR2 19 C6
Nova Rd. CR0 19 C2
Oakfield Rd. CR0 19 C2
Oakwood Pl. CR0 19 A1
Oakwood Rd. CR0 19 A1
Old Palace Rd. CR0 19 C4
Old Town. CR0 19 C4
Onslow Rd. CR0 19 A2
*Otterbourne Rd,
  Ruskin Rd. CR0 19 C3
Overtons Yd. CR0 19 C4
Owen Clo. CR0 19 D1
Page Cres. CR0 19 B6
Park La. CR0 19 D5
Park St. CR0 19 D4
Parker Rd. CR0 19 C5
Parsons Mead. CR0 19 C3
Pemdevon Rd. CR0 19 B2
Penfold Clo. CR0 19 B5
Pitlake. CR0 19 C3
Poplar Walk. CR0 19 C3
Prestwood Gdns. CR0 19 C1
Price Rd. CR0 19 B6
Princess Rd. CR0 19 B1
Priory Rd. CR0 19 A2
Progress Way. CR0 19 A4
Pump Pail Nth. CR0 19 C5
Pump Pail Sth. CR0 19 C5
Purley Way. CR0 19 A4
Queen St. CR0 19 C5
Queens Rd. CR0 19 C5
Raglan Ct. CR2 19 C6
Ravensmead Rd. CR0 19 B4
Rectory Gro. CR0 19 B4
Reeves Cnr. CR0 19 C4

Renown Clo. CR0 19 B3
Rigby Clo. CR0 19 A4
Robert St. CR0 19 C4
Rodney Clo. CR0 19 B3
Roman Way. CR0 19 B3
Ruskin Rd. CR0 19 C3
St Andrews Rd. CR0 19 C5
St Georges Walk. CR0 19 D4
St James's Pk. CR0 19 C2
St James's Rd. CR0 19 C2
St Johns Rd. CR0 19 B4
St Leonards Rd. CR0 19 B5
St Michaels Rd. CR0 19 C3
St Peters Rd. CR0 19 D6
St Saviours Rd. CR0 19 C1
Salem Pl. CR0 19 C5
Scarbrook Rd. CR0 19 C5
Selsdon Rd. CR2 19 D6
Sharland Clo. CR7 19 D1
Sheldon St. CR0 19 C5
Siddons Rd. CR0 19 B4
*Singleton Clo,
  St Saviours Rd. CR0 19 C1
Smock Walk. CR0 19 C1
South End. CR0 19 D5
Southbridge Pl. CR0 19 C5
Southbridge Rd. CR0 19 C5
Southwell Rd. CR0 19 A1
Spices Yd. CR0 19 D5
Stafford Gdns. CR0 19 A6
Stafford Rd. CR0 19 A6
Stanley Gro. CR0 19 A1
Stanley Rd. CR0 19 A1
Stanton Rd. CR0 19 C2
Stapleton Gdns. CR0 19 B6
Station Rd. CR0 19 C3
Strathmore Rd. CR0 19 D2
Sumner Rd. CR0 19 B2
Sumner Rd. CR0 19 B2
Sumner Rd Sth. CR0 19 B3
Surrey St. CR0 19 C4
Sutherland Rd. CR0 19 A2
Sydenham Rd. CR0 19 D3
Sylverdale Rd. CR0 19 B4
Tamworth Pl. CR0 19 C4
Tamworth Rd. CR0 19 C4
Tanfield Rd. CR0 19 C5
Tavistock Gro. CR0 19 D2
Tavistock Rd. CR0 19 D2
Temple Rd. CR0 19 D6
Thanet Pl. CR0 19 D5
The Beeches. CR2 19 D6
The Croydon Flyover.
  CR0 19 C5
The Mall. CR0 19 C3
The Ridgeway. CR0 19 A5
The Waldrons. CR0 19 C5
Theobald Rd. CR0 19 B3
Thomson Cres. CR0 19 A2
Thornhill Rd. CR0 19 C2
Thornton Rd. CR0 19 A1
Tirrell Rd. CR0 19 C1
Torrington Sq. CR0 19 D2
Trafalgar Way. CR0 19 A3
Trinity Sq. CR0 19 C3
Trojan Way. CR0 19 A4
Tugela Rd. CR0 19 D1
Turners Way. CR0 19 A4
Under Pass. CR0 19 D3
Union Rd. CR0 19 D1
Vanguard Clo. CR0 19 B3
Vicarage Rd. CR0 19 B4
Violet La. CR0 19 B6
Waddon Clo. CR0 19 B5
Waddon Court Rd. CR0 19 A5
Waddon Lodge. CR0 19 B5
Waddon New Rd. CR0 19 B4
Waddon Park Av. CR0 19 A5
Waddon Rd. CR0 19 A4
Waldronhyrst. CR2 19 C6
Waldrons Path. CR2 19 C6
Walpole Rd. CR0 19 D3
Wandle Rd. CR0 19 C5
Wandleside. CR0 19 A5
Warham Rd. CR2 19 C6
Warrington Rd. CR0 19 B5
Water Tower Hill. CR0 19 D5
Waterworks Yd. CR0 19 C5
Wayneflete Av. CR0 19 B5
Wellesley Ct Rd. CR0 19 D4
Wellesley Gro. CR0 19 D4
Wellesley Rd. CR0 19 C5
Wellington Rd. CR0 19 B2
Wentworth Rd. CR0 19 A2
West St. CR0 19 C5
Westbury Rd. CR0 19 D1

Westfield Rd. CR0 19 B4
Whitehorse Rd. CR0 19 D1
Whitgift Centre. CR0 19 C3
Whitgift St. CR0 19 C4
Whitstable Pl. CR0 19 C6
Willis Rd. CR0 19 C1
*Wilson Clo,
  RH4
  Bartlett St. CR2 19 D6
Windmill Gro. CR0 19 C1
Windmill Rd. CR0 19 C1
Woburn Rd. CR0 19 D2
Woodstock Rd. CR0 19 D5
Wortley Rd. CR0 19 A1
Wranglethorne Walk.
  CR0 19 A6
York Rd. CR0 19 A1

# DORKING

Ansell Rd. RH4 20 B3
*Archway Mws,
  Meadowbrook Rd.
  RH4 20 A3
Arundel Rd. RH4 20 A4
Ashcombe Rd. RH4 20 A2
Back Alley. RH4 20 B4
*Barrington Ct,
  Barrington Rd. RH4 20 A5
Barrington Rd. RH4 20 A5
Beech Clo. RH4 20 A3
Beresford Rd. RH4 20 B4
Brook Clo. RH4 20 C2
Brympton Clo. RH4 20 A6
Calvert Cres. RH4 20 B2
Calvert Rd. RH4 20 B2
Cedar Clo. RH4 20 B4
Chalkpit La. RH4 20 A3
Chalkpit Ter. RH4 20 A3
Chapel Ct. RH4 20 A3
*Chapel Croft,
  Meadowbrook Rd.
  RH4 20 A3
Chart Clo. RH5 20 C6
Chart Downs. RH5 20 C6
Chart La. RH4 20 B4
Chart Lane Sth. RH5 20 C6
Chequers Yd. RH4 20 B4
Chester Clo. RH4 20 C2
Chichester Clo. RH4 20 B3
Chichester Rd. RH4 20 B1
Church Gdns. RH4 20 A3
Church St. RH4 20 A4
Claremont Clo. RH4 20 A5
Claygate Rd. RH4 20 B6
Cleardene. RH4 20 B4
Cliftonville. RH4 20 B5
Coldharbour La. RH4 20 A6
Croft Av. RH4 20 B2
Curtis Gdns. RH4 20 A3
Curtis Rd. RH4 20 A3
Deepdene Av. RH4 20 C4
Deepdene Av Rd. RH4 20 C3
Deepdene Dri. RH5 20 C3
Deepdene Gdns. RH4 20 B3
Deepdene Park Rd. RH5 20 C4
Deepdene Vale. RH4 20 C3
Deepdene Wood. RH5 20 C4
Dene St. RH4 20 B4
Dene St Gdns. RH4 20 B4
Denfield. RH4 20 B5
Dorking By-Pass. RH4 20 C2
Downs View. RH4 20 C2
Downsview Gdns. RH4 20 A5
Ebbisham Clo. RH4 20 A4
Elmhurst Dri. RH4 20 B6
Fairfield Dri. RH4 20 B2
Falkland Gdns. RH4 20 A5
Falkland Rd. RH4 20 A5
Firs Clo. RH4 20 A6
Flint Hill. RH4 20 B6
Fraser Gdns. RH4 20 A3
Glenwood. RH4 20 C6
Goodwyns Rd. RH4 20 C6
Hampstead La. RH4 20 A5
Hampstead Rd. RH4 20 A5
Harrow Clo. RH4 20 A5
Harrow Rd E. RH4 20 B5
Harrow Rd W. RH4 20 B5
Harrowlands Pk. RH4 20 B5
Hart Gdns. RH4 20 B3
Hart Rd. RH4 20 B3
Heath Hill. RH4 20 B4
High Meadow Clo. RH4 20 B5
High St. RH4 20 B4

Highacre. RH4 20 B6
Hill Rise. RH4 20 A2
Horsham Rd. RH4 20 A5
Howard Rd. RH4 20 A4
INDUSTRIAL & RETAIL:
Haverbury Ind Est.
  RH4 20 A3
Jubilee Ter. RH4 20 B3
Junction Rd. RH4 20 A4
Keppel Rd. RH4 20 A2
Knoll Rd. RH4 20 A5
Ladyegate Clo. RH5 20 C3
Ladyegate Rd. RH5 20 C4
Leslie Rd. RH4 20 D2
Limeway Ter. RH4 20 A2
Lincoln Rd. RH4 20 B2
London Rd. RH4 20 B3
Lonsdale Rd. RH4 20 B3
Market Pl. RH4 20 B3
Marlborough Hill. RH4 20 B4
Marlborough Rd. RH4 20 B4
Martineau Dri. RH4 20 B6
Masons Paddock. RH4 20 A2
Meadowbrook Rd. RH4 20 A3
Mill La. RH4 20 B3
Mint Gdns. RH4 20 A3
Moores Rd. RH4 20 B3
Mount St. RH4 20 A4
Mowbray Gdns. RH4 20 B2
Myrtle Rd. RH4 20 A3
New Rd. RH5 20 D5
Norfolk Rd. RH4 20 A4
North St. RH4 20 A4
Nower Rd. RH4 20 A4
Oak Ridge. RH4 20 B6
Orchard Rd. RH4 20 B5
Orchard Way. RH4 20 B5
Overdale. RH5 20 C3
Paper Mews. RH4 20 B3
Park Copse. RH5 20 D4
Parkway. RH4 20 A3
Parsonage Sq. RH4 20 A3
Pippbrook Gdns. RH4 20 B3
Pixham La. RH4 20 C1
Pixholme Gro. RH4 20 C2
Portland Rd. RH4 20 A3
Priory Clo. RH4 20 A5
Punchbowl La. RH5 20 D3
Ranmore Rd. RH4 20 A4
Redcote Pl. RH4 20 A3
Reigate Rd. RH4 20 C3
Ridgeway Clo. RH4 20 A6
Ridgeway Rd. RH4 20 A6
Riverside. RH4 20 D2
Rose Hill. RH4 20 A4
*Rose Hill Arch Mews.
  RH4 20 A4
Rothes Rd. RH4 20 B3
St Brelades Clo. RH4 20 A6
St Martins Pl. RH4 20 B3
St Pauls Rd East. RH4 20 B4
St Pauls Rd West. RH4 20 A5
South Dri. RH5 20 C4
South St. RH4 20 B4
South Ter. RH4 20 B5
Spital Heath. RH4 20 C3
Spring Gdns. RH4 20 A3
Station App. RH4 20 B2
Station Rd. RH4 20 B2
Stubs Clo. RH4 20 C6
Stubs Hill. RH4 20 C6
Swan Mill Gdns. RH4 20 C2
The Chine. RH4 20 B3
The Pines. RH4 20 B5
The Terrace. RH5 20 C5
Tilehurst La. RH5 20 D5
Tollgate Rd. RH4 20 B6
Tower Hill. RH4 20 A4
Tower Hill Rd. RH4 20 A4
Townfield Rd. RH4 20 A5
Trasher Mead. RH4 20 C6
Upper Rose Hill. RH4 20 B4
Vaughan Way. RH4 20 A4
Victoria Ter. RH4 20 B4
Vincent Dri. RH4 20 A5
Vincent La. RH4 20 A4
Vincent Rd. RH4 20 A4
Vincent Walk. RH4 20 A4
Wathen Rd. RH4 20 A4
West Bank. RH4 20 A5
West St. RH4 20 A4
Willow Mead F.P. RH4 20 A3
*Willow Mead,
  Portland Rd. RH4 20 A3
Yew Tree Rd. RH4 20 A2

# EAST HORSLEY/ WEST HORSLEY

Bishopsmead Dri. KT24 21 D4
Bishopsmead Par. KT24 21 D4
Butlers Hill. KT24 21 A5
Chalk La. KT24 21 D6
Cobham Way. KT24 21 D1
Cranmore Cotts. KT24 21 A5
Cranmore La. KT24 21 A5
East La. KT24 21 B2
*Edwin Clo,
    Edwin Rd. KT25 21 B1
Edwin Rd. KT24 21 B1
Epsom Rd. KT24 21 A6
Fairwell La. KT24 21 A4
Farleys Clo. KT24 21 A2
Farm Clo. KT24 21 D4
Farm La. KT24 21 D4
Fern Clo. KT24 21 C5
Forest Clo. KT24 21 D1
Forest Rd. KT24 21 D2
Frenchlands Hatch.
    KT24 21 D3
Glendene Av. KT24 21 D2
Green Lane West. KT24 21 A1
Greta Bank. KT24 21 B2
Guildford Lodge Dri.
    KT24 21 D5
Guildford Rd. KT24 21 D5
Heatherdene. KT24 21 C1
High Park Av. KT24 21 D2
Higher Dri. KT24 21 D3
Highfields. KT24 21 D4
Hooke Rd. KT24 21 D1
Holmwood Clo. KT24 21 D1
Howard Clo. KT24 21 A6
Jeffries Rd. KT24 21 A6
Kenyons. KT24 21 A4
Kingston Av. KT24 21 C2
Lime Gro. KT24 21 D5
Little Cranmore La.
    KT24 21 A4
Lollesworth La. KT24 21 B2
Long Reach. KT24 21 A1
Longhurst Rd. KT24 21 D5
Lower Peryers. KT24 21 D4
Lynx Hill. KT24 21 D3
Manor Clo. KT24 21 D4
Meadow Bank. KT24 21 D3
Meadow Way. KT24 21 B1
Mount Pleasant. KT24 21 B1
Nightingale Av. KT24 21 B1
Nightingale Cres. KT24 21 B1
Nightingale Rd. KT24 21 D1
Norrells Dri. KT24 21 D2
Norrells Ride. KT24 21 D1
Northcote Clo. KT24 21 B1
Northcote Cres. KT24 21 B1
Northcote Rd. KT24 21 B1
Oak Wood Clo. KT24 21 C3
Oak Wood Rd. KT24 21 C3
Ockham Rd Nth. KT24 21 C1
Ockham Rd Sth. KT24 21 D3
Old Rectory La. KT24 21 C2
Old St Marys. KT24 21 A5
Overbrook. KT24 21 A4
Park Corner Dri. KT24 21 C4
Parkside Clo. KT24 21 D1
Parkside Pl. KT24 21 D1
Pennymead Dri. KT24 21 D3
Pennymead Rise. KT24 21 D3
Pincott La. KT24 21 A4
Pine Walk. KT24 21 D4
Ricksons La. KT24 21 A3
Ripley La. KT24 21 A4
Rowbarns Way. KT24 21 D5
St Martins Clo. KT24 21 C4
St Martins Ct. KT24 21 C4
School La. KT24 21 A6
Shere Rd. KT24 21 A6
Silkmore La. KT24 21 A3
Station App. KT24 21 C2
Station Par. KT24 21 C2
The Birches. KT24 21 D2
The Chase. KT24 21 D2
The Highlands. KT24 21 C1
The Ridings. KT24 21 D1
The Rise. KT24 21 D2
The Street. KT24 21 A4
The Warren. KT24 21 D5
Thornleas Pl. KT24 21 C4
Tintells La. KT24 21 A3
Wellington Cotts. KT24 21 D5
Weston Lea. KT24 21 C1
Woodland Dri. KT24 21 D2
Woodside. KT24 21 A2

# EGHAM

Albany Pl. TW20 22 C3
Alder Clo. TW20 22 A4
Alexander Rd. TW20 22 D4
Ambleside Way. TW20 22 D6
Arndale Way. TW20 22 B4
Argent Clo. TW20 22 D5
Ashleigh Av. TW20 22 D6
Ayebridges Av. TW20 22 D6
Band La. TW20 22 B4
Bellweir Clo. TW19 22 C1
Blue Ball La. TW20 22 A4
Borrowdale Clo. TW20 22 C6
Boshers Gdns. TW20 22 A5
Braywood Av. TW20 22 B5
Buttermere Way. TW20 22 C6
Caddy Clo. TW20 22 B4
Cedar Ct. TW20 22 B3
Century Rd. TW20 22 D4
Charta Rd. TW20 22 D4
Church St. TW20 22 B4
Clandon Av. TW20 22 D6
Clare Gdns. TW20 22 B4
Clarence St. TW20 22 A5
Clockhouse La East.
    TW20 22 C6
Clockhouse La West.
    TW20 22 C6
College Av. TW20 22 C5
Colne Way. TW19 22 C1
Conifer La. TW20 22 D4
Coniston Way. TW20 22 D5
Coopers Hill La. TW20 22 A3
Crown St. TW20 22 B3
Daleham Av. TW20 22 B5
Danehurst Clo. TW20 22 A5
Davies Way. TW20 22 D4
De Ros Pl. TW20 22 B5
Denham Rd. TW20 22 B3
Derwent Rd. TW20 22 C6
Devils La. TW20 22 D5
Egham By-Pass. TW20 22 A4
Egham Hill. TW20 22 A4
Elwell Clo. TW20 22 B5
Fairhaven. TW20 22 A4
Falaise. TW20 22 A4
Falconwood. TW20 22 A4
Feathers La. TW19 22 B1
Ferry La. TW19 22 C1
Field Vw. TW20 22 D4
Fitzrobert Pl. TW20 22 B5
Flanders Ct. TW20 22 D4
*Furzedown Clo,
    Danehurst Clo. TW20 22 A5
Glebe Rd. TW20 22 D5
Gloucester Dri. TW18 22 D2
Gordon Rd. TW20 22 D3
Grange Rd. TW20 22 A4
Grasmere Clo. TW20 22 C6
Green La. TW20 22 C3
Greenways. TW20 22 A4
Harcourt Clo. TW20 22 D5
Hardell Clo. TW20 22 B4
Hawthorn Rd. TW20 22 D3
Helvellyn Clo. TW20 22 D6
Herndon Clo. TW20 22 B3
High St. TW20 22 A4
Holbrook Mdw. TW20 22 D5
Hummer Rd. TW20 22 B3
Hythe End Rd. TW19 22 B1
Jutland Pl. TW20 22 D4
Keswick Rd. TW20 22 C6
Kings Rd. TW20 22 D5
Langham Pl. TW20 22 A4
Langton Way. TW20 22 D5
Limes Rd. TW20 22 A4
Little Croft Rd. TW20 22 B4
Lovett Rd. TW20 22 C3
Lynwood Av. TW20 22 A5
Mafeking Rd. TW19 22 C1
Malt Hill. TW20 22 A4
Mandeville Ct. TW20 22 C3
Manor Farm La. TW20 22 B4
Manor Way. TW20 22 A5
Manorcrofts Rd. TW20 22 B5
Manorleaze. TW20 22 C4
Mead Clo. TW20 22 B4
Mead Ct. TW20 22 D5
Medlake Rd. TW20 22 D5
Milton Rd. TW20 22 A4
Mons Walk. TW20 22 D4
Moorgrove Cres. TW20 22 A5
Mount Lee. TW20 22 A4
Mowbray Cres. TW20 22 B4
Mullens Rd. TW20 22 D4
New Rd. TW20 22 D3
New Wickham La.
    TW20 22 B6
Nicholson Walk. TW20 22 B4
Nobles Way. TW20 22 A5
Normandy Wk. TW20 22 D4
North St. TW20 22 A4
Oak Av. TW20 22 D6
Orchard Clo. TW20 22 C4
Orchid Ct. TW20 22 C3
Osborne Rd. TW20 22 A5
Osier Pl. TW20 22 D5
Park Av. TW20 22 B3
Park Rd. TW20 22 B3
Pond Rd. TW20 22 D5
Pooley Av. TW20 22 C4
Pooley Grn Clo. TW20 22 D4
Pooley Grn Rd. TW20 22 C4
Princess Rd. TW20 22 A5
Prune Hill. TW20 22 A6
Queens Rd. TW20 22 A4
Quincy Rd. TW20 22 B4
Ripley Av. TW20 22 A5
Riverside. TW20 22 B2
Roundway. TW20 22 D4
Rowan Av. TW20 22 D4
Runnemede Rd. TW20 22 B3
Runnymede Ct. TW20 22 C3
Rusham Pk Av. TW20 22 B5
Rusham Rd. TW20 22 A5
Rydal Way. TW20 22 D6
St Johns Ct. TW20 22 B4
St Nazaire Clo. TW20 22 D4
Sarsby Dri. TW19 22 C1
School La. TW20 22 B4
South Av. TW20 22 D5
Spring Av. TW20 22 A5
Spring Rise. TW20 22 A5
Staines Rd. TW19 22 B1
Station Rd. TW20 22 B4
Station Rd Nth. TW20 22 B4
Stephen Clo. TW20 22 D5
Stoneylands Ct. TW20 22 A4
Stoneylands Rd. TW20 22 A4
Strode St. TW20 22 B3
Strodes College La.
    TW20 22 B4
Stroude Rd. TW20 22 B5
Sweeps La. TW20 22 A4
Tempest Rd. TW20 22 D5
The Avenue. TW20 22 C3
The Causeway. TW20 22 D3
The Crescent. TW20 22 A5
The Glanty. TW20 22 C3
The Grove. TW20 22 B4
The Lea. TW20 22 D6
Thirlmere Clo. TW20 22 D6
Thorpe Lea Rd. TW20 22 C6
Tinsey Clo. TW20 22 C4
Tite Hill. TW20 22 A4
Vicarage Av. TW20 22 C4
Vicarage Ct. TW20 22 C5
Vicarage Cres. TW20 22 C4
Vicarage Rd. TW20 22 C4
Wards Pl. TW20 22 D5
Warwick Av. TW20 22 D6
Wavendene Av. TW20 22 D6
Wendover Pl. TW20 22 D4
Wendover Rd. TW20 22 D4
Wesley Dri. TW20 22 B5
Wetton Pl. TW20 22 A4
Whitehall La. TW20 22 A6
Wickham La. TW20 22 C6
Windermere Clo. TW20 22 C5
Windsor Rd. TW20 22 A2
Woodhaw. TW20 22 C3
Wraysbury Rd. TW19 22 C1
Yardmead. TW20 22 B4

# EPSOM

Adelphi Rd. KT17 23 B2
Albert Rd. KT17 23 C3
Albert Villas. KT17 23 D4
Alexandra Rd. KT17 23 D3
Almond Rd. KT17 23 B1
Andrews Clo. KT17 23 C3
Ash Mews. KT18 23 C3
Ashdown Rd. KT17 23 D3
Ashley Av. KT18 23 B3
Ashley Ct. KT18 23 B3
Ashley Rd. KT18 23 B3
Aston Way. KT18 23 D5
Avenue Rd. KT18 23 B4
Axwood. KT18 23 A5
Barons Hurst. KT18 23 A6
Beaconsfield Pl. KT17 23 C2
Beech Rd. KT17 23 D5
Beech Walk. KT17 23 D1
Beechway. KT17 23 D5
Berkeley Pl. KT18 23 B5
Birches Clo. KT18 23 C3
Blenheim Rd. KT19 23 B1
Bridge Rd. KT17 23 D2
Bridle End. KT17 23 D3
Bridle Rd. KT17 23 D3
Burgh Heath Rd. KT17 23 C4
Burghfield. KT17 23 D5
Burnet Gro. KT19 23 A3
Caithness Dri. KT18 23 B4
Carters Rd. KT17 23 D5
Cedar Clo. KT17 23 D3
Cedar Hill. KT18 23 A5
Chalk La. KT18 23 B5
Chalk Paddock. KT18 23 B5
Chantry Hurst. KT18 23 B5
Chartwell Pl. KT18 23 C4
Chase End. KT19 23 B2
Chase Rd. KT19 23 B2
Chelwood Clo. KT17 23 D2
Church Rd. KT17 23 C3
Church St. KT17 23 C3
Chuters Gro. KT17 23 C1
Clayton Pl. KT17 23 C2
Cleves Ct. KT17 23 C2
College Av. KT17 23 D4
College Rd. KT17 23 C3
Conifer Park. KT17 23 C1
Copse Edge Av. KT17 23 D3
Court La. KT19 23 A2
Delaporte Clo. KT17 23 C2
Denham Rd. KT17 23 D2
Depot Rd. KT17 23 C3
Digdens Rise. KT18 23 A5
Dirdene Clo. KT17 23 D2
Dirdene Gdns. KT17 23 C2
Dirdene Gro. KT17 23 C2
Dorking Rd. KT18 23 A4
Dorling Dri. KT17 23 D2
Downs Av. KT17 23 C4
Downs Hill Rd. KT18 23 C4
Downs Rd. KT18 23 C4
Downs Way. KT18 23 C6
Downside. KT18 23 C3
Dudley Gro. KT18 23 A4
East St. KT17 23 C2
Eastway. KT19 23 A1
Elm Gro. KT18 23 A4
Elmslie Clo. KT19 23 A4
Epsom Rd. KT18 23 C1
Fairbriar Ct. KT18 23 B3
Fairview Rd. KT17 23 C1
Farriers Clo. KT17 23 C1
Farriers Rd. KT17 23 C1
Felstead Rd. KT19 23 B1
Gosfield Rd. KT19 23 B2
Grove Av. KT17 23 C3
Grove Rd. KT17 23 C3
Hambledon Hill. KT18 23 A6
Hambledon Vale. KT18 23 A6
Hamilton Clo. KT19 23 A1
Hampton Gro. KT17 23 D1
Hawthorne Pl. KT17 23 C2
Hazon Way. KT19 23 B2
Heathcote Rd. KT18 23 B3
Hereford Clo. KT18 23 B3
Hessle Gro. KT17 23 D1
High St. KT19 23 B3
Highridge Clo. KT18 23 C4
Hillcrest Clo. KT18 23 D5
Hook Rd. KT19 23 B1
Hookfield. KT19 23 A3
Horsley Clo. KT19 23 B2
Horton Gdns. KT19 23 A1
Horton Hill. KT19 23 A1
Hunters Clo. KT19 23 A3
Hurst Rd. KT19 23 B1
Hylands Clo. KT18 23 A5
Hylands Mews. KT18 23 A4
Hylands Rd. KT18 23 A5

INDUSTRIAL & RETAIL:
Longmead
    Ind Est. KT19 23 B1
Nonsuch
    Ind Est. KT17 23 C1

Jackson Clo. KT18 23 B4
Kendor Av. KT19 23 A1
Kiln La. KT17 23 C1
King Shades Wk. KT17 23 B3
Kingsdown Rd. KT17 23 D3
Laburnum Rd. KT18 23 B3
Ladbroke Rd. KT18 23 B4
Langlands Rise. KT19 23 A3
Langton Av. KT17 23 D1
Leighton Way. KT18 23 D3
Leith Rd. KT17 23 C2
Linden Pl. KT17 23 C2
Lindsay Clo. KT19 23 A3
Links Rd. KT17 23 D3
Lintons La. KT17 23 C2
Little Orchards. KT18 23 D3
Longdown Rd. KT17 23 D3
Longmead Rd. KT19 23 B1
Loop Rd. KT18 23 A5
Lower Court Rd. KT19 23 A3
Lynwood Av. KT17 23 D4
Lynwood Rd. KT17 23 D4
Madans Walk. KT18 23 B4
Maidenshaw Rd. KT19 23 B2
Malvern Ct. KT18 23 B4
Manor Green Rd. KT19 23 A1
Manor House Ct. KT18 23 A3
Marshalls Clo. KT19 23 A3
Mathias Clo. KT18 23 A3
Meadow Ct. KT18 23 A3
Meadway. KT19 23 A2
Middle Clo. KT17 23 C2
Middle La. KT17 23 C2
Milburn Walk. KT18 23 C5
Miles Rd. KT19 23 B1
Mill Rd. KT17 23 C2
Milton Gdns. KT18 23 C4
Mospey Cres. KT17 23 D4
Norman Av. KT17 23 D2
Oak Hill. KT18 23 A5
Oak Leaf Clo. KT19 23 A2
Oakmead Grn. KT18 23 A5
Orchard Gdns. KT18 23 A4
Park Hill Rd. KT17 23 D1
Pikes Hill. KT17 23 C3
Pine Hill. KT18 23 B5
Pitt Pl. KT17 23 C3
Pitt Rd. KT17 23 C3
Portland Pl. KT17 23 B1
Pound La. KT19 23 B1
Prospect Pl. KT17 23 C2
Providence Pl. KT17 23 C2
Randolph Rd. KT17 23 C4
Richmond Clo. KT18 23 A3
Ridgeway. KT19 23 A2
Rosebank. KT18 23 A3
Rosebery Av. KT17 23 A3
St Edith Clo. KT18 23 A4
St Elizabeth Dri. KT18 23 A4
St Georges Gdns. KT17 23 D4
St James Clo. KT18 23 B3
St Johns Av. KT17 23 D2
St Margarets Dri. KT18 23 A4
St Martins Av. KT18 23 C4
St Martins Clo. KT18 23 C3
St Theresa Clo. KT18 23 C5
Sharon Clo. KT19 23 A2
Shaw Clo. KT17 23 A2
Sheraton Dri. KT19 23 A2
South St. KT18 23 B3
Spread Eagle Wk. KT18 23 B3
Squirrels Way. KT18 23 B4
Station App. KT19 23 B3
Station Way. KT19 23 B3
Stevens Clo. KT17 23 B3
Stones Rd. KT17 23 C1
Sunny Bank. KT18 23 A6
Sweet Briar La. KT18 23 B1
Temple Rd. KT19 23 D1
The Green. KT17 23 D1
The Grove. KT17 23 C3
The Oaks. KT18 23 B3
The Parade. KT18 23 B3
The Ridings. KT18 23 C5
The Spinney. KT18 23 B3
Tintagel Clo. KT18 23 C3
Treadwell Rd. KT18 23 C5
Treemount Ct. KT17 23 C3
Upper Court Rd. KT19 23 A1
Upper High St. KT17 23 C3
Vancouver Clo. KT19 23 A1
Victoria Pl. KT17 23 C2
Wallace Fields. KT17 23 D2
Walnut Clo. KT18 23 C5
Warren Hill. KT18 23 B6
Waterloo Rd. KT19 23 B1

West Hill. KT19 23 A3
West Hill Av. KT19 23 A2
Westlands Ct. KT18 23 A4
West St. KT18 23 A4
Weston Rd. KT17 23 C1
Wheelers La. KT18 23 A3
White Horse Dri. KT18 23 A4
Whitmores Clo. KT18 23 A5
Wilmerhatch La. KT18 23 A6
Wimborne Clo. KT17 23 C3
Windmill Av. KT17 23 D1
Windmill Clo. KT17 23 D2
Windmill End. KT17 23 D2
Windmill La. KT17 23 D1
Woodcote Clo. KT18 23 B4
Woodcote End. KT18 23 B5
Woodcote Green Rd. KT18 23 A5
Woodcote Hurst. KT18 23 A6
Woodcote Hurst Ct. KT18 23 B5
Woodcote Pk Rd. KT18 23 A5
Woodcote Rd. KT18 23 B4
Woodstock Ct. KT17 23 B2
Wootton Clo. KT18 23 C5
Worlds End. KT18 23 B6
Worple Rd. KT18 23 B4
Wyeths Clo. KT17 23 C3
Wyeths Rd. KT17 23 C3
Yeomanry Clo. KT17 23 C2
Yew Tree Gdns. KT18 23 A5

## ESHER

Acorns Way. KT10 24 C4
Arbrook Chase. KT10 24 D5
Arbrook La. KT10 24 D5
Arran Way. KT10 24 C1
Ashburnham Pk. KT10 24 C3
Belvedere Dri. KT10 24 B4
Bracondale. KT10 24 C4
Brendon Clo. KT10 24 D5
Brendon Dri. KT10 24 D5
Brisson Clo. KT10 24 A4
Broom Clo. KT10 24 A4
Broomfields. KT10 24 D4
Carrick Gate. KT10 24 D2
Catos Hill. KT10 24 C3
Cedar Clo. KT10 24 A5
Chadworth Way. KT10 24 D4
Church St. KT10 24 C3
Clare Hill. KT10 24 B4
Claremont Av. KT10 24 A5
Claremont Dri. KT10 24 B5
Claremont End. KT10 24 C5
Claremont La. KT10 24 C3
Claremont Pk Rd. KT10 24 B5
Clive Rd. KT10 24 B3
Compton Clo. KT10 24 D4
Copsem Dri. KT10 24 C5
Copsem La. KT10 24 C5
Copsem Way. KT10 24 C5
Courtlands Av. KT10 24 A5
Cranford Rise. KT10 24 C4
D'Abernon Clo. KT10 24 B3
Dawes Ct. KT10 24 B3
Douglas Rd. KT10 24 B1
Drakes Clo. KT10 24 B4
Esher Clo. KT10 24 B4
Esher Grn. KT10 24 B3
Esher Park Av. KT10 24 C3
Esher Place Av. KT10 24 B3
Esher Rd. KT10 24 A3
Farm Rd. KT10 24 B1
Fir Tree Clo. KT10 24 C4
Grantley Pl. KT10 24 C4
Hare La. KT10 24 D4
Hawkshill Clo. KT10 24 A5
Hawkshill Way. KT10 24 A5
Haymeads Dri. KT10 24 C5
Heather Ct. KT10 24 B3
Heather Pl. KT10 24 B3
Heatherset Clo. KT10 24 A4
High Garth. KT10 24 C5
High St. KT10 24 B3
Hillbrow Rd. KT10 24 C3
Hillfield Ct. KT10 24 C4
Home Farm Clo. KT10 24 C5
Howitts Clo. KT10 24 A4
Hunting Clo. KT10 24 B3
INDUSTRIAL & RETAIL:
Sandown Ind Pk. KT10 24 A1
Joseph Locke Way. KT10 24 B1

Lakeside Dri. KT10 24 C5
Lammas La. KT10 24 A4
Latton Clo. KT10 24 B3
Little Mead. KT10 24 D3
Littleworth Av. KT10 24 D4
Littleworth Common Rd. KT10 24 D2
Littleworth La. KT10 24 D3
Littleworth Pl. KT10 24 D3
Littleworth Rd. KT10 24 D4
Lower Green Rd. KT10 24 B1
Lynne Walk. KT10 24 A3
Martineau Clo. KT10 24 D3
Meadway. KT10 24 B6
Milbourne La. KT10 24 C4
Milbrook. KT10 24 D5
Mill Rd. KT10 24 B1
More La. KT10 24 A5
Neville Clo. KT10 24 A5
New Rd. KT10 24 D2
Nightingale Rd. KT10 24 A4
Old Chestnut Av. KT10 24 B5
Orchard Way. KT10 24 C5
Orleans Clo. KT10 24 D1
Park Clo. KT10 24 A5
Park Rd. KT10 24 B3
Pelhams Clo. KT10 24 A3
Pelhams Walk. KT10 24 A2
Pemberton Pl. KT10 24 C2
Penates. KT10 24 D3
Portsmouth Rd. KT10 24 A6
Raleigh Dri. KT10 24 D4
Riverside Dri. KT10 24 A3
Rosebriars. KT10 24 D4
Sandown Av. KT10 24 C3
Sandown Gate. KT10 24 D1
Sandown Rd. KT10 24 C3
Station Rd. KT10 24 D1
Tellisford. KT10 24 B3
The Gardens. KT10 24 A3
The Mount. KT10 24 A5
Vincent Clo. KT10 24 B2
Warren Clo. KT10 24 C3
Wayneflete Tower Av. KT10 24 A2
West Acres. KT10 24 A5
West End Gdns. KT10 24 A4
West End La. KT10 24 A4
Westwood Clo. KT10 24 D2
Willowmere. KT10 24 A4
Winchester Clo. KT10 24 A2
Winterdown Rd. KT10 24 A5
Wolsey Gro. KT10 24 B3
Wolsey Rd. KT10 24 B3
Wood End. KT10 24 C1

## EWELL

Aragon Av. KT17 25 C4
Arundel Av. KT17 25 D4
Banstead Rd. KT17 25 D5
Beaufort Way. KT17 25 C3
Beech Walk. KT17 25 C5
Belfield Rd. KT19 25 A3
Bevan Park. KT17 25 B5
Bishopsmead Clo. KT19 25 A5
Bishopsmead Ct. KT19 25 A4
Blenheim Rd. KT19 25 A6
Bluegates. KT17 25 C2
Boleyn Av. KT17 25 C4
Bradford Dri. KT19 25 B1
Bradstock Rd. KT17 25 C1
Briarwood Rd. KT17 25 C1
Bridleway Clo. KT17 25 D5
Brook Mead. KT19 25 A2
Burford La. KT17 25 D5
Calverley Rd. KT17 25 C1
Carpenter Clo. KT17 25 B4
Castle Av. KT17 25 C4
Castle Par. KT17 25 C3
Castle Way. KT17 25 C3
Castlemaine Av. KT17 25 D3
Cedar Ct. KT17 25 C2
Chadacre Rd. KT17 25 C1
Chatsfield. KT17 25 C4
Cheam Rd. KT17 25 C4
Chelwood Clo. KT17 25 B6
Chessington Rd. KT19 25 A4
Chestnut Pl. KT17 25 B5
Chichester Ct. KT17 25 C3
Church St. KT17 25 C3
Chuters Gro. KT17 25 B6
Clandon Clo. KT17 25 B1
Cleves Av. KT17 25 D3

Conaways Clo. KT17 25 C4
Conifer Park. KT17 25 A6
Corbet Rd. KT17 25 A5
Courtlands Dri. KT17 25 A1
Cullerne Clo. KT17 25 B4
Cumberland Clo. KT19 25 A5
Cumnor Gdns. KT17 25 C2
Curvan Clo. KT17 25 B4
Dee Way. KT19 25 A4
Dell La. KT17 25 C1
Dell Rd. KT17 25 C1
Dirdene Clo. KT17 25 B6
Dirdene Gdns. KT17 25 B6
Dirdene Gro. KT17 25 A6
Dorling Dri. KT17 25 B6
East St. KT17 25 A6
Eastcroft Rd. KT19 25 A3
Elm Rd. KT17 25 B2
Elmstead Clo. KT19 25 A1
Elmwood Clo. KT17 25 C2
Elmwood Dri. KT17 25 C2
Epsom Rd. KT17 25 B5
Ernest Cotts. KT17 25 B5
Ewell By-Pass. KT17 25 C3
Ewell Court Av. KT19 25 A1
Ewell Downs Rd. KT17 25 C6
Ewell House Gro. KT17 25 B4
Ewell Park Gdns. KT17 25 B4
Ewell Park Way. KT17 25 C2
Fairfax Av. KT17 25 D4
Fairfield Way. KT17 25 A1
Fairview Rd. KT17 25 B6
Farriers Clo. KT17 25 A6
Farriers Rd. KT17 25 A6
Fennells Mead. KT17 25 B3
First Av. KT19 25 A3
Firswood Clo. KT19 25 A1
Garbrand Walk. KT17 25 B4
Gayfere Rd. KT17 25 C1
Gibraltar Cres. KT19 25 A4
Glenwood Rd. KT17 25 C1
Glyn Clo. KT17 25 C5
Green Lanes. KT19 25 A3
Hampton Gro. KT17 25 B5
Hazel Mead. KT17 25 C4
Hessle Gro. KT17 25 B5
High St. KT17 25 B3
Highfield Dri. KT19 25 B2
Hillside Rd. KT17 25 D4
Hollymoor La. KT19 25 A3
Holman Ct. KT17 25 C3
Howard Av. KT17 25 C4
INDUSTRIAL & RETAIL:
Nonsuch Ind Est. KT17 25 A5
Kenilworth Rd. KT17 25 B1
Kiln La. KT17 25 A6
Kingston Rd. KT17 25 A1
Kirby Clo. KT19 25 B1
Lakehurst Rd. KT19 25 A1
Lakeside. KT19 25 A1
Langton Av. KT17 25 B5
Larby Pl. KT17 25 A6
Leith Rd. KT17 25 A6
Lintons La. KT17 25 A6
London Rd. KT17 25 C2
Longmead Rd. KT19 25 B4
Lyncroft Gdns. KT17 25 B4
Manor Dri. KT19 25 A1
Marsh Av. KT19 25 B4
Masons Ct. KT17 25 B4
Meadow Walk. KT17 25 B2
Meadow Walk. KT19 25 A1
Meadowview Rd. KT19 25 A3
Middle Clo. KT17 25 A6
Middle La. KT17 25 A6
Mill La. KT17 25 B3
Mill Rd. KT17 25 B6
Mill View Clo. KT17 25 B3
Mongers La. KT17 25 B5
Mount Pleasant. KT17 25 B4
Nonsuch Ct Av. KT17 25 C4
Northcroft Rd. KT19 25 A2
Northfields. KT17 25 A5
Nursery Clo. KT17 25 A5
Oakland Way. KT19 25 A1
Old House Clo. KT17 25 B5
Old Schools La. KT17 25 B3
Ox La. KT17 25 C4
Park Av East. KT17 25 C2
Park Av West. KT17 25 C2
Park Hill Rd. KT17 25 B6
Parr Av. KT17 25 D4
Parry Clo. KT17 25 C2
Persfield Clo. KT17 25 B5
Portland Pl. KT17 25 A6

Portway. KT17 25 C4
Portway Cres. KT17 25 C4
Preston Dri. KT19 25 A1
Primrose Walk. KT17 25 B2
Purberry Gro. KT17 25 B3
Queensmead Av. KT17 25 D4
Reigate Rd. KT17 25 C5
Rembrandt Clo. KT19 25 B1
River Way. KT17 25 A3
Riverholme Dri. KT19 25 A3
Rosebery Par. KT17 25 B2
Rutherwyke Clo. KT17 25 C1
St James Av. KT17 25 B5
St Marys Clo. KT17 25 A1
St Normans Way. KT17 25 C5
Seaforth Gdns. KT19 25 B1
Seymour Av. KT17 25 D4
Seymour Mews. KT17 25 C4
Shaw Clo. KT17 25 B5
Shere Av. KT17 25 D5
Shortcroft Rd. KT17 25 B2
Somerset Clo. KT19 25 A4
South Mead. KT19 25 A2
Spring Ct. KT17 25 B3
Spring Mews. KT17 25 B3
Spring St. KT17 25 B4
Springfield Rd. KT17 25 D4
Stane Way. KT17 25 B4
Station App, Ewell East. KT17 25 C5
Station App, Stoneleigh. KT19 25 B1
Station Av. KT19 25 A3
Stoneleigh Broadway. KT17 25 C1
Stoneleigh Pk Rd. KT19 25 B1
Stones Rd. KT17 25 A6
Sunnymede Av. KT19 25 A3
Tayles Hill. KT17 25 B2
The Drive. KT19 25 B2
The Glade. KT17 25 C1
The Green. KT17 25 C6
The Grove. KT17 25 B4
The Hawthorns. KT17 25 B2
The Headway. KT17 25 B5
The Kingsway. KT17 25 B5
The Mount. KT17 25 B2
The Orchard. KT17 25 B2
The Ridings. KT17 25 B3
The Rise. KT17 25 C3
Vicarage La. KT17 25 C3
Victoria Pl. KT17 25 A6
Village Gdns. KT17 25 B4
Walsingham Gdns. KT19 25 B1
Waverley Rd. KT17 25 C1
Welbeck Clo. KT17 25 C3
West Gdns. KT17 25 A5
West Mead. KT19 25 A2
West St. KT17 25 A4
Westmorland Clo. KT19 25 A5
Weston Rd. KT17 25 A5
Willow Way. KT19 25 A1
Windmill Av. KT17 25 B6
Windmill End. KT17 25 B6
Windmill La. KT17 25 B6
Woodland Clo. KT19 25 A2
Woodstone Av. KT17 25 C1
Yeomanry Clo. KT19 25 A6

## FARNHAM

Abbey Ct. GU9 26 C3
Abbey St. GU9 26 C3
Acheulian Clo. GU9 26 C5
Adams Park Rd. GU9 26 D1
Alfred Rd. GU9 26 C4
Arthur Clo. GU9 26 C4
Arthur Rd. GU9 26 C4
*Aveley Clo, Aveley La. GU9 26 B6
Aveley La. GU9 26 B6
Avon Ct. GU9 26 C4
Avon Rd. GU9 26 C4
Babbs Mead. GU9 26 B3
Baldreys. GU9 26 B5
Bardsley Dri. GU9 26 A5
Barncroft. GU9 26 C4
Bear La. GU9 26 C3
Beaufort Rd. GU9 26 C4
Beavers Clo. GU9 26 A3
Beavers Hill. GU9 26 A2
Beavers Rd. GU9 26 A3
Beldham Rd. GU9 26 A6

Binfields. GU9 26 C1
Bishops Mead. GU9 26 B3
Black Pond La. GU9 26 C6
Borelli Mews. GU9 26 C3
*Borelli Yd, Borelli Mews. GU9 26 C3
Brambleton Av. GU9 26 B5
Bridgefield. GU9 26 D3
Brightwells Rd. GU9 26 C2
Brockhurst Lodge. GU9 26 B6
Brookmead Ct. GU9 26 B3
Broomleaf Cnr. GU9 26 D3
Broomleaf Rd. GU9 26 D3
Byworth Clo. GU9 26 A3
Cambridge Pl. GU9 26 C2
Castle Clo. GU9 26 B2
Castle Hill. GU9 26 B2
Castle St. GU9 26 B2
Cedarways. GU9 26 B6
Cherry Tree Clo. GU9 26 C2
Chestnut Av. GU9 26 A5
Cobbetts Way. GU9 26 A6
College Gdns. GU9 26 B3
Coopers Ter. GU9 26 C2
Coxbridge Mdws. GU9 26 A4
Crondall La. GU9 26 A3
Crosby Way. GU9 26 B3
Crundwell Clo. GU9 26 D1
Darvills La. GU9 26 D3
Deepdene. GU9 26 D3
Dogflud Way. GU9 26 C2
Dollis Dri. GU9 26 D2
Downing St. GU9 26 C2
East St. GU9 26 C2
Edward Rd. GU9 26 C5
Ernest Clo. GU9 26 C6
Fairholme Gdns. GU9 26 C4
Falkner Ct. GU9 26 C2
Falkner Rd. GU9 26 C3
Farnham By-Pass. GU9 26 A4
Fenns Yd. GU9 26 B3
Ferns Mead. GU9 26 B4
Firfield Rd. GU9 26 B6
Firgrove Ct. GU9 26 C3
Firgrove Hill. GU9 26 C3
Folly Hill. GU9 26 B1
Ford La. GU9 26 B6
Forge Clo. GU9 26 D1
Fox Rd. GU9 26 D6
Fox Yd. GU9 26 B3
Frensham Rd. GU9 26 C5
Garth Clo. GU9 26 B5
Great Austins. GU9 26 D4
Green La. GU9 26 A5
Greenfield Rd. GU9 26 A6
Greenhill Clo. GU9 26 A6
Greenhill Rd. GU9 26 D5
Greenhill Way. GU9 26 A6
Grove End Rd. GU9 26 B5
Guildford Rd. GU9 26 D2
Hale Rd. GU9 26 D1
Haven Way. GU9 26 D1
Hazell Rd. GU9 26 A3
High Park Rd. GU9 26 C2
Highfield Clo. GU9 26 B6
Highlands Clo. GU9 26 B6
Hill View Rd. GU9 26 A3
Hillary Clo. GU9 26 B5
Hillary Rd. GU9 26 C4
Hookstile La. GU9 26 C4
INDUSTRIAL & RETAIL:
*Farnham Business Centre, Dogflud Way. GU9 26 D2
Farnham Business Pk. GU9 26 B4
*Riverside Business Pk, Dogflud Way. GU9 26 D2
Ivy La. GU9 26 C3
Kimbers La. GU9 26 D2
Lancaster Av. GU9 26 D4
Langham Ct. GU9 26 C5
Lion & Lamb Yd. GU9 26 B2
Lion & Lamb Way. GU9 26 B2
Little Austins Rd. GU9 26 B4
Little Green La. GU9 26 A6
Lodge Hill Clo. GU9 26 D6
Lodge Hill Rd. GU9 26 D6
Long Bri. GU9 26 C3
*Long Garden Pl, Long Gdn Wk. GU9 26 B2
Long Garden Wk. GU9 26 B2
Long Garden Way. GU9 26 B2
Longley Rd. GU9 26 C2
Lower Church La. GU9 26 C3
Lower South View. GU9 26 C2

Lowndes Bldgs. GU9 26 B2
Lynch Rd. GU9 26 D3
Lynton Clo. GU9 26 A5
Marston Rd. GU9 26 A3
Mavins Rd. GU9 26 D5
Mead La. GU9 26 B3
Meadow Bank. GU9 26 B3
Menin Way. GU9 25 D4
Merlins Clo. GU9 26 C4
Middle Av. GU9 26 B4
Middle Bourne La. GU9 26 C6
Middle Church La. GU9 26 C3
Middlefield. GU9 26 A5
Middlefield Clo. GU9 26 A5
Mike Hawthorn Dri.
GU9 26 D2
Millgatae Ct. GU9 26 D2
Morley Rd. GU9 26 C4
Mount Pleasant. GU9 26 A3
Norman Ct. GU9 26 C3
Oak Ct. GU9 26 B4
Old Church La. GU9 26 D5
Old Farnham La. GU9 26 C4
Old Park La. GU9 26 A1
Osborn Rd. GU9 26 D1
Parfitts Clo. GU9 26 A3
Park Rd. GU9 26 D1
Park Row. GU9 26 C2
Pengilly Rd. GU9 26 B3
Pilgrims Clo. GU9 26 B5
Potters Gate. GU9 26 B3
Priory Ct. GU9 26 D5
Red Lion La. GU9 26 C5
Ridgway Hill Rd. GU9 26 C5
Ridgway Rd. GU9 26 C5
Romley Ct. GU9 26 D4
Ryle Rd. GU9 26 B5
St Cross Rd. GU9 26 C2
St Georges Rd. GU9 26 D3
St Georges Yd. GU9 26 C2
St James Av. GU9 26 D1
St James Ct. GU9 26 C2
St James Ter. GU9 26 C2
St Johns Gro. GU9 26 C5
St Johns Rd. GU9 26 C5
St Marys Pl. GU9 26 D2
Saxon Croft. GU9 26 C3
School La. GU9 26 D6
Searle Rd. GU9 26 C4
Selborne Gdns. GU9 26 A5
Sheephouse. GU9 26 C5
Shepherds Ct. GU9 26 C5
Shortheath Cres. GU9 26 A1
Shortheath Rd. GU9 26 B6
Snailslynch. GU9 26 D2
South St. GU9 26 C2
Southern Way. GU9 26 C3
Station Hill. GU9 26 C3
Stephendale Rd. GU9 26 D1
Stoke Hills. GU9 26 D1
Stream Farm Clo. GU9 26 D6
Stream Valley Rd. GU9 26 C5
Sumner Rd. GU9 26 C2
Sumner Rd. GU9 26 C2
Swingate Rd. GU9 26 D5
Talbot Rd. GU9 26 B4
The Borough. GU9 26 B3
The Buntings. GU9 26 A5
The Chantrys. GU9 26 A3
The Close. GU9 26 D4
The Drive. GU9 26 C5
The Fairfield. GU9 26 D3
The Hart. GU9 26 B2
The Hatches. GU9 26 A5
The Lindens. GU9 26 D4
The Old Orchard. GU9 26 A5
Thorold Rd. GU9 26 C2
Thurbans Rd. GU9 26 A6
Tilford Rd. GU9 26 D4
*Timber Clo,
The Hart. GU9 26 B3
Tor Rd. GU9 26 A3
Trafalgar Ct. GU9 26 C4
Trebor Av. GU9 26 D4
Underhill La. GU9 26 C6
Union Rd. GU9 26 C3
Upper Church La. GU9 26 C3
Upper South Vw. GU9 26 C2
Upper Way. GU9 26 B5
Valley La. GU9 26 B6
Vernon Ct. GU9 26 B3
Vicarage Hill. GU9 26 B3
Vicarage La. GU9
Vicarage La,
The Bourne. GU9 26 D6
Victoria Rd. GU9 26 C3

Waverley La. GU9 26 D3
Waynflete La. GU9 26 A3
Wayside. GU9 26 C3
Wells Cotts. GU9 26 A6
Wessex Pl. GU9 26 C4
West End Gro. GU9 26 A3
West St. GU9 26 A4
Weybank Clo. GU9 26 C2
Weydon Hill Clo. GU9 26 B4
Weydon Hill Rd. GU9 26 C4
Weydon La. GU9 26 A5
Weydon Mill La. GU9 26 B4
White Rose La. GU9 26 C6
Whitlet Clo. GU9 26 B3
Winton Rd. GU9 26 D1
Woodland Dri. GU9 26 B6
Woolmead Rd. GU9 26 C2
Wykeham Rd. GU9 26 C4
York Rd. GU9 26 C4

## FRIMLEY

Abbetts La. GU15 27 A2
Addison Rd. GU16 27 C5
*Albany Ct,
Albany Pk. GU16 27 A4
Albany Pk. GU16 27 A4
Alphington Av. GU16 27 C4
Alphington Grn. GU16 27 C4
Ansell Rd. GU16 27 C5
Apex Dri. GU16 27 B4
April Clo. GU15 27 A3
Armitage Dri. GU16 27 D4
Badgers Copse. GU15 27 C2
Badgerwood Dri. GU16 27 B3
Bailey Clo. GU16 27 B5
Balmoral Dri. GU16 27 C5
Banbury Clo. GU16 27 D6
Barnard Clo. GU16 27 C5
Barnes Rd. GU16 27 C5
Bassett Clo. GU16 27 C5
Bayfield Av. GU16 27 C3
Beaumaris Par. GU16 27 D5
Beech Av. GU15 27 B1
Belmont Mews. GU15 27 A2
Belmont Rd. GU15 27 A1
Belvoir Clo. GU16 27 D4
Bicknell Rd. GU16 27 C3
Birchfields. GU15 27 A1
Blackwater Valley Rd.
GU14 27 B6
Blythwood Dri. GU16 27 B3
Bowling Green Ct.
GU16 27 C6
Brackendale Clo. GU15 27 C2
Brackendale Rd. GU15 27 B1
Braemar Clo. GU16 27 D5
Bret Harte Rd. GU16 27 C4
Bridgemead. GU16 27 B5
Bristow Rd. GU15 27 A2
Broad Walk. GU16 27 C3
Broadlands. GU16 27 D5
Broughton Mews.
GU16 27 D4
Buckingham Way.
GU16 27 D4
Buckland Clo. GU14 27 A6
Burleigh Rd. GU16 27 B5
Burrel Rd. GU16 27 A5
Caernarvon. GU16 27 D5
Campbell Pl. GU16 27 D2
Carisbrooke. GU16 27 D5
Caroline Way. GU16 27 D4
Castle Clo. GU15 27 D1
Castle Rd. GU15 27 D1
Cedar La. GU16 27 B5
Chantry Ct. GU16 27 D4
Chilham Clo. GU16 27 D5
Chillingham Way.
GU15 27 A1
Chobham Rd. GU16 27 C4
Church Rd. GU16 27 C4
Coach House Clo. GU16 27 C2
Connop Way. GU16 27 D2
Conway Clo. GU16 27 D4
Coombe Clo. GU16 27 B5
Corfe Gdns. GU16 27 D4
Croft Way. GU16 27 D3
Cromwell Way. GU14 27 A6
Danebury Walk. GU16 27 D5
Dell Gro. GU16 27 D3
Denton Way. GU16 27 B3
Dorcas Ct. GU15 27 A2
Dunbar Rd. GU16 27 D6

Elgin Way. GU16 27 D5
Elmcroft Clo. GU16 27 D6
Evergreen Rd. GU16 27 D3
Fairfax Rd. GU14 27 A6
Fairfield Dri. GU16 27 C2
Falcon Ct. GU16 27 B4
Farm Ct. GU16 27 D3
Farm Rd. GU16 27 C3
Farnborough Rd. GU14 27 A6
Farrell Clo. GU15 27 A2
Felbridge Clo. GU16 27 D4
Ferniehurst. GU15 27 D1
Field La. GU16 27 B4
Forest Hills. GU15 27 A1
Frimley Grn Rd. GU16 27 C5
Frimley Grove Gdns.
GU16 27 B4
Frimley High St. GU16 27 A5
Frimley Rd. GU15 27 A2
Garfield Rd. GU15 27 A1
Garrick Way. GU16 27 C6
Gilbert Rd. GU15 27 A4
Glamis Clo. GU16 27 D6
Glencoe Clo. GU16 27 D5
Glynswood. GU15 27 D2
Goddards La. GU15 27 A2
Golf Dri. GU15 27 D1
Gordon Av. GU15 27 A1
Gordon Cres. GU15 27 A1
Gordon Rd. GU15 27 A1
Gorse Rd. GU16 27 C3
Greenbank Way. GU15 27 A3
Green Leas. GU16 27 C3
Grove Cross Rd. GU16 27 B4
Grovefields Av. GU16 27 C4
Hale Way. GU16 27 B4
Hanbury Way. GU15 27 A2
Hanover Clo. GU15 27 C4
Hawkswood Av. GU16 27 D3
Hawley La. GU14 27 A6
Hawthorn Rd. GU16 27 D3
Heather Mead. GU16 27 D3
Heather Mead Ct.
GU16 27 D3
Heatherdale Rd. GU15 27 A1
Heenan Clo. GU16 27 C6
Henley Dri. GU16 27 C6
Hermitage Clo. GU16 27 D4
High Beeches. GU16 27 B3
High Grove. GU14 27 A6
Hillside Cres. GU16 27 D6
Holly Hedge La. GU16 27 C3
Holly Hedge Rd. GU16 27 C3
Holly Tree Gdns. GU16 27 B5
Holt Clo. GU14 27 A6
Hope Fountain. GU15 27 D1

INDUSTRIAL & RETAIL:
Albany Pk Ind Est.
GU16 24 A4
Farnborough Gate
Retail Park. GU14 27 A6
Frimley Business Pk.
GU16 27 A5
Lyon Way Ind Est.
GU15 27 A4
Park Farm Ind Est.
GU16 27 A4
Ingle Dell. GU16 27 B1
James Rd. GU15 27 A3
James Way. GU15 27 A3
Kenmore Clo. GU16 27 B5
Kenton Clo. GU16 27 D3
Kilmartin Gdns. GU16 27 D4
Kingsclear Pk. GU15 27 B1
Kingsley Av. GU15 27 A1
Kingsmead. GU16 27 C6
Lakeland Dri. GU16 27 C4
Lanark Clo. GU16 27 C3
Lancaster Way. GU14 27 A6
Latham Av. GU16 27 C3
Lauder Clo. GU16 27 C3
Laurel Clo. GU15 27 B1
Le Marchant Hts. GU16 27 D2
Le Marchant Rd.
GU16 GU15 27 D2
Lendore Rd. GU16 27 B5
Leonard Clo. GU16 27 B5
Linkway. GU15 27 A2
Longmeadow. GU16 27 D2
Longford. GU15 27 B1
Lyon Way. GU16 27 A4
Mariners Dri. GU16 27 A6
Marston Dri. GU14 27 A6
Martin Way. GU16 27 C4
Maybury Clo. GU16 27 B5
Meadway. GU16 27 D3

Melville Av. GU16 27 D4
Merlin Ct. GU16 27 B4
Merrywood Pk. GU15 27 D1
Middlemoor Clo. GU16 27 D5
Middlemoor Rd. GU16 27 C5
Montrose Clo. GU16 27 C3
Moor Rd. GU16 27 D5
Morton Clo. GU16 27 D6
Mulgrave Rd. GU16 27 D3
Murrells La. GU15 27 A2
Nairn Clo. GU16 27 C3
Newlands Rd. GU15 27 A4
Norwich Av. GU15 27 C2
Oakway Dri. GU16 27 C4
Old Pasture Rd. GU16 27 D3
Old Pond Clo. GU15 27 A4
Oldbury Clo. GU16 27 D5
Oriel Hill. GU15 27 B1
Osborne Clo. GU16 27 C4
Overdale Rise. GU16 27 C2
Pans Gdns. GU16 27 D1
Park Av. GU15 27 A1
Park Rd. GU15 27 A2
Parkstone Dri. GU15 27 A1
Parkway. GU15 27 A2
Parsonage Way. GU16 27 C4
Partridge Clo. GU16 27 C4
Penshurst Rise. GU16 27 D5
Petworth Clo. GU16 27 D5
Petworth Ct. GU15 27 D1
Pevensey Way. GU16 27 D5
Pine Av. GU15 27 B1
Pine Mount Rd. GU15 27 B1
Portsmouth Rd.
GU16 GU15 27 B4
Prince Charles Cres.
GU14 27 A5
Purley Way. GU16 27 C5
Radcliffe Clo. GU16 27 D6
Raglan Clo. GU16 27 D5
Regent Way. GU16 27 D4
Richmond Clo. GU16 27 D4
Rideway Clo. GU15 27 A1
Ringwood Rd. GU14 27 A6
Robins Bow. GU16 27 A1
Rudd Hall Rise. GU15 27 C2
Russet Gdns. GU15 27 B2
Saddlewood. GU15 27 A1
St Andrews Way. GU16 27 D4
St Catherines Rd. GU16 27 D4
St Peters Way. GU16 27 D6
Sandown Dri. GU16 27 C3
Sandringham Way.
GU16 27 D5
Sayers Clo. GU16 27 C6
Scarlet Oaks. GU15 27 C2
Seaton Rd. GU15 27 A1
Shamrock Clo. GU16 27 B5
Sheridan Ct. GU16 27 B5
Sheridan Rd. GU16 27 B5
Sherwin Cres. GU14 27 A5
Stamford Av. GU16 27 D4
Station App. GU16 27 B5
Station Rd. GU16 27 A4
Stirling Clo. GU16 27 C3
Stonehouse Rise. GU16 27 C4
Stoneleigh Ct. GU16 27 D4
Sturdee Clo. GU16 27 C4
Sycamore Clo. GU16 27 C4
Sycamore Dri. GU16 27 C3
Tekels Av. GU15 27 B1
Tekels Clo. GU15 27 C1
Tekels Way. GU14 27 C2
The Cloisters. GU16 27 B4
The Close. GU16 27 B5
The Grove. GU16 27 B4
The Parade. GU16 27 B5
The Pavilions End.
GU15 27 B2
Tichborne Clo. GU16 27 D2
Tintagel Dri. GU16 27 D4
Tiverton Way. GU16 27 D4
Tomlins Av. GU16 27 D3
Trafford Rd. GU16 27 B5
Upper Verran Rd. GU15 27 B2
Verran Rd. GU15 27 B2
Walkers Ridge. GU15 27 C1
Wandsyke Clo. GU16 27 D5
Warren Rise. GU16 27 D3
Watchetts Dri. GU15 27 A3
Watchetts Lake Clo.
GU15 27 B2
Watchetts Rd. GU15 27 A2
Waverley Clo. GU15 27 A3
Ways End. GU15 27 C1
Well Clo. GU15 27 A1

Weller Dri. GU15 27 A2
Whins Clo. GU15 27 A1
Wilderness Rd. GU16 27 C3
Wilders Clo. GU16 27 C2
Willow Ct. GU16 27 B4
Wilmot Way. GU15 27 D2
Windsor Way. GU16 27 D5
Winterbourne Walk.
GU16 27 D5
Wood Rd. GU15 27 A4
Worsley Rd. GU16 27 C5
Yewtree Walk. GU16 27 C4

## GODALMING

Aarons Hill. GU7 28 A3
Allden Cotts. GU7 28 B3
Alvernia Clo. GU7 28 C5
Angel Ct. GU7 28 C5
Ashtead La. GU7 28 C6
Badgers Hollow. GU7 28 C1
Ball Field Rd. GU7 28 C1
Bargate Rise. GU7 28 B3
Beech Way. GU7 28 D4
Birchanger. GU7 28 C3
Borough Rd. GU7 28 C3
Braemar Clo. GU7 28 C4
Briarpatch. GU7 28 C1
Bridge Rd. GU7 28 D3
Bridge St. GU7 28 C3
Brighton Rd. GU7 28 D4
Busbridge La. GU7 28 D4
Butts La. GU7 28 C4
Carlos St. GU7 28 D3
Catteshall La. GU7 28 D3
Chalk Rd. GU7 28 C2
Charterhouse Rd. GU7 28 B1
Church St. GU7 28 C3
Cliffe Rise. GU7 28 B5
Cliffe Rd. GU7 28 B5
College Hill. GU7 28 B5
Coopers Rise. GU7 28 B4
Cow La. GU7 28 C4
Croft Rd. GU7 28 C3
Crownpits La. GU7 28 D4
Dean Rd. GU7 28 C1
Deanery Rd. GU7 28 C2
Dormers Clo. GU7 28 C5
Duncombe Rd. GU7 28 C4
Eashing La. GU7 28 A4
Farncombe St. GU7 28 D1
Fernden Rise. GU7 28 D1
Field View Cotts. GU7 28 B3
Filmer Gro. GU7 28 D2
Flambard Way. GU7 28 C3
Foxdene. GU7 28 B5
Franklyn Rd. GU7 28 A4
Frith Hill Rd. GU7 28 C1
Great George St. GU7 28 D3
Greenhill Clo. GU7 28 D4
Grosvenor Rd. GU7 28 D4
Grove Rd. GU7 28 B4
Harvest Hill. GU7 28 D3
Hawthorn Rd. GU7 28 A5
Heathfield Clo. GU7 28 C5
High Ridge. GU7 28 C5
High St. GU7 28 C3
Holloway Hill. GU7 28 C4
Holly La. GU7 28 B4
Huntsman La. GU7 28 C5
Ivybank. GU7 28 D1
Knoll Quarry. GU7 28 C1
Knoll Rd. GU7 28 C1
Ladywell Hill. GU7 28 C6
Latimer Rd. GU7 28 D4
Little Tumners Ct. GU7 28 D1
Lower Manor Rd. GU7 28 D2
Lower South St. GU7 28 C3
Manor Gdns. GU7 28 D1
Maple Hatch Clo. GU7 28 D5
Marshall Rd. GU7 28 D1
Mary Vale. GU7 28 C5
May Clo. GU7 28 A5
Mill La. GU7 28 A5
Miltons Cres. GU7 28 A5
Minster Rd. GU7 28 C4
Mint St. GU7 28 C5
Monteagle. GU7 28 C4
Moss La. GU7 28 C3
Nightingale Rd. GU7 28 D2
North St. GU7 28 C2
Oakdene Rd. GU7 28 B5
Ockford Rd. GU7 28 C4

ckford Dri. GU7 28 B4
ckford Ridge. GU7 28 A4
ckford Rd. GU7 28 B4
d Barn View. GU7 28 B5
d Lodge Clo. GU7 28 A4
d Station Way. GU7 28 D2
monde Rd. GU7 28 D1
rk Chase. GU7 28 D6
ark Rd. GU7 28 C5
arkfield. GU7 28 D5
perharow Rd. GU7 28 B2
illips Clo. GU7 28 C5
hillips Cotts,
  Aarons Hill. GU7 28 B3
rtsmouth Rd. GU7 28 A6
und Clo. GU7 28 D3
und La. GU7 28 D3
mrose Ridge. GU7 28 A5
llman Way. GU7 28 B5
arry Hill. GU7 28 A4
arter Mile Rd. GU7 28 D6
een St. GU7 28 D3
msden Rd. GU7 28 C4
chmond Rd. GU7 28 D1
ndy La. GU7 28 C1
lars Hill. GU7 28 C1
ymour Rd. GU7 28 A4
ackstead La. GU7 28 B4
adyhanger. GU7 28 D1
mmonds Cotts. GU7 28 A3
uth Hill. GU7 28 D3
uth St. GU7 28 D3
ation App. GU7 28 C3
ation Clo. GU7 28 C3
onepit Clo. GU7 28 B3
mmerhill. GU7 28 C1
mmerhouse Clo.
  GU7 28 C4
mmerhouse Rd. GU7 28 C4
e Avenue. GU7 28 D5
e Brambles. GU7 28 D5
e Burys. GU7 28 D3
e Drive. GU7 28 D5
e Horseshoe. GU7 28 B4
e Mint. GU7 28 D5
e Paddock. GU7 28 D5
ttenham Rd. GU7 28 D1
wn End Clo. GU7 28 D4
wn End Rd. GU7 28 D3
esley Corner. GU7 28 C5
esley La. GU7 28 C4
ycross Rd. GU7 28 C1
derhill Clo. GU7 28 D4
per Manor Rd. GU7 28 C3
per Queen St. GU7 28 C4
lley Vw. GU7 28 C4
arage Way. GU7 28 C3
toria Rd. GU7 28 B4
sterside La. GU7 28 B4
stbrook Rd. GU7 28 B2
ston Clo. GU7 28 D1
arf St. GU7 28 D3
ndy Wood. GU7 28 C5
lseley Rd. GU7 28 D2
olsack Way. GU7 28 D3

## GODSTONE

kers Mead. RH9 29 C2
y Path. RH9 29 C4
l Meadow. RH9 29 B5
tchingley Rd. RH9 29 A4
lbeggars La. RH9 29 C5
lin Gdns. RH9 29 B3
urch La. RH9 29 D4
yton Mead. RH9 29 B3
urt Rd. RH9 29 C4
whurst Mead. RH9 29 C3
vlands. RH9 29 C3
nville Dri. RH9 29 B3
tbourne Rd. RH9 29 C5
erdent Rd. RH9 29 C6
lyn Gdns. RH9 29 C3
ver La. RH9 29 D3
terdown. RH9 29 B2
gers Hill. CR3 29 D1
dstone By-Pass. RH9 29 C2
dstone Hill. RH9 29 C2
enwell Clo. RH9 29 B3
kmans Clo. RH9 29 B5
h St. RH9 29 B3
orow Cotts. RH9 29 C5
n Clo. RH9 29 B5

---

Ivy Mill La. RH9 29 A5
Leigh Place La. RH9 29 D5
Lindley Rd. RH9 29 C3
Love La. RH9 29 C5
North Park La. RH9 29 A4
Ockleys Mead. RH9 29 C3
Oxted Rd. RH9 29 C3
Quarry Rd. RH9 29 B1
Riders Way. RH9 29 C4
Rogers Mead. RH9 29 B5
Salisbury Rd. RH9 29 B3
Selbourne Sq. RH9 29 C2
The Green. RH9 29 B4
The Old Surrey Mews.
  RH9 29 B3
The Priory. RH9 29 B4
Tilburstow Hill Rd. RH9 29 C5
Tylers Clo. RH9 29 B3
Waterhouse La. RH1 29 A5
Willow Way. RH9 29 B5

## GREAT BOOKHAM/ LITTLE BOOKHAM

Admirals Rd. KT23 30 E4
Allen Rd. KT23 30 D3
Amey Dri. KT23 30 E2
Apple Tree Clo. KT22 30 E1
Ashdale. KT23 30 B3
Ashley Clo. KT23 30 B3
Atwood. KT23 30 A1
Barn Meadow La. KT23 30 B1
Barrett Rd. KT22 30 F2
Beales Rd. KT23 30 D4
Beattie Clo. KT23 30 B1
Beckley Par. KT23 30 E3
Beech Gro. KT23 30 D4
Bennetts Farm Pl. KT23 30 D4
Blackthorne Rd. KT23 30 F3
Bookham Gro. KT23 30 D3
Bracken Clo. KT23 30 C3
Broderick Gro. KT23 30 C3
Browning Rd. KT22 30 F2
Burney Clo. KT22 30 E2
Burnhams Rd. KT23 30 A1
Burrows Clo. KT23 30 B3
Camilla Clo. KT23 30 D2
Candy Croft. KT23 30 D1
Charlwood Clo. KT23 30 D1
Childs Hall Clo. KT23 30 B2
Childs Hall Dri. KT23 30 B2
Childs Hall Rd. KT23 30 B2
Chilmans Dri. KT23 30 D3
Christie Clo. KT23 30 D3
Chrystie La. KT23 30 D3
Church Clo. KT23 30 F1
Church Rd. KT23 30 B1
Cochrane Clo. KT23 30 C2
Crabtree Clo. KT23 30 E3
Crabtree La. KT23 30 F3
Dawnay Rd. KT23 30 E3
Dean Walk. KT23 30 D3
Dorking Rd. KT23 30 D3
Dowlans Clo. KT23 30 C4
Dowlans Rd. KT23 30 D4
Downs View Rd. KT23 30 E4
Downs Way. KT23 30 E3
Durleston Pk Dri. KT23 30 D3
East St. KT23 30 D3
Eastwick Dri. KT23 30 D1
Eastwick Park Av. KT23 30 D1
Eastwick Rd. KT23 30 D2
Edenside Rd. KT23 30 B1
Edgeley. KT23 30 A1
Elmswood. KT23 30 D3
Fairfield Clo. KT23 30 D3
Fairlawn. KT23 30 B2
Fernlea. KT23 30 D1
Fife Way. KT23 30 C2
Fiona Clo. KT23 30 C1
Flint Clo. KT23 30 E3
Fox Covert. KT22 30 F2
Fox La. KT23 30 B2
Gardeners Walk. KT23 30 D4
Gilmais. KT23 30 E3
Glebe Clo. KT23 30 C3
Goldstone Farm Vw.
  KT23 30 C4
Greathurst End. KT23 30 C1
Greenacres. KT23 30 C1
Greenway. KT23 30 D1
Greville Ct. KT23 30 D2
Griffin Way. KT23 30 C3

---

Groveside. KT23 30 C4
Groveside Clo. KT23 30 C4
Guildford Rd. KT23 30 B4
Halepit Rd. KT23 30 E3
Hales Oak. KT23 30 E3
Harecroft. KT22 30 E1
Hawkwood Dell. KT23 30 C3
Hawkwood Rise. KT23 30 C3
Hazel Way. KT22 30 E1
High St. KT23 30 D3
Highfields. KT22 30 F1
Hilltop Rise. KT23 30 E3
Howard Rd. KT23 30 E4
Huntsmans. KT23 30 F2
**INDUSTRIAL & RETAIL:**
  Bookham Ind Est.
  KT23 30 B1
Kennel Clo. KT23 30 E1
Kennel La. KT22 30 E1
Keswick Rd. KT23 30 D2
Kidborough Down.
  KT23 30 C4
Lang Clo. KT23 30 D1
Leatherhead Rd. KT23 30 E3
Lime Tree Clo. KT23 30 C1
Little Bookham St.
  KT23 30 B1
Long Copse Clo. KT23 30 C3
Long Meadow. KT23 30 B3
Longheath Dri. KT23 30 A2
Lower Rd. KT23 30 A4
Lower Shott. KT23 30 D3
Maddox La. KT23 30 A1
Maddox Rk. KT23 30 A1
Manor House La. KT23 30 A4
Maplehurst. KT22 30 F1
Mayfield Grn. KT23 30 C4
Mead Cres. KT23 30 C2
Meadowside. KT23 30 D4
Medefield. KT22 30 F1
Merrylands Rd. KT23 30 B1
Middlemead Clo. KT23 30 C3
Middlemead Rd. KT23 30 B2
Mill Clo. KT23 30 C2
Milton Way. KT22 30 E2
Murrells Walk. KT23 30 C1
Newenham Rd. KT23 30 C3
Norbury Way. KT23 30 E3
Oakbank. KT22 30 F1
Oakdene Clo. KT23 30 E4
Oakdene Rd. KT23 30 B2
Oaklands. KT22 30 F1
Orchard End. KT23 30 E2
Oveton Way. KT23 30 D3
Park Clo. KT22 30 E1
Park Grn. KT23 30 C1
Park Vw. KT23 30 C1
Park Way. KT23 30 C1
Parklands. KT23 30 C1
Pelham Way. KT23 30 E3
Pine Dean. KT23 30 D2
Pine Walk. KT23 30 D2
Polesden View. KT23 30 D4
Post House La. KT23 30 C1
Priors Mead. KT23 30 E3
Proctor Gdns. KT23 30 D3
Rectory La. KT23 30 B3
Richmond Clo. KT22 30 E1
Richmond Way. KT22 30 E1
Ridgelands. KT23 30 F1
Roger Simmons Ct.
  KT23 30 C1
St Nicholas Av. KT23 30 C1
Sayers Clo. KT23 30 E1
Sharon Clo. KT22 30 E1
Sheridans Rd. KT23 30 E3
Sole Farm Av. KT23 30 B2
Sole Farm Clo. KT23 30 B2
Sole Farm Rd. KT23 30 B2
Solecote. KT23 30 C2
South End. KT23 30 D3
Southey Clo. KT23 30 D2
Spring Gro. KT22 30 D1
Squirrels Grn. KT23 30 C1
Stone Hill Clo. KT23 30 B3
Styles End. KT23 30 D4
Sumner Clo. KT23 30 C1
Swanns Meadow. KT23 30 C2
Ten Acres. KT22 30 F2
Ten Acres Clo. KT22 30 F2
The Approach. KT23 30 B1
The Blackburn. KT23 30 C3
The Garstons. KT23 30 C2
The Green. KT22 30 D1
The Lorne. KT23 30 C3

---

The Moorings. KT23 30 C2
The Paddocks. KT23 30 D3
The Park. KT23 30 C1
The Ridge. KT22 30 F1
The Ridgeway. KT22 30 F1
The Spinney. KT23 30 D2
Timber Clo. KT23 30 E4
Townshott Clo. KT23 30 C3
Tudor Clo. KT23 30 C2
Turville Ct. KT23 30 D3
Twelve Acre Clo. KT23 30 B1
Vicarage Clo. KT23 30 C3
Vincent Clo. KT22 30 D1
Water La. KT23 30 A3
Wells Clo. KT23 30 E2
West Down. KT23 30 D4
White Way. KT23 30 D3

## GUILDFORD

Abbot Rd. GU1 31 C5
Acacia Rd. GU1 31 C2
Addison Rd. GU1 31 B4
Agraria Rd. GU2 31 A4
Alexandra Pl. GU1 31 D4
Alexandra Ter. GU1 31 D4
Angel Gate. GU1 31 C4
Annandale Rd. GU2 31 A5
Ardmore Av. GU2 31 A1
Ardmore Ho. GU2 31 A1
Ardmore Way. GU2 31 A1
Artillery Rd. GU1 31 B3
Artillery Ter. GU1 31 C3
Artington Walk. GU2 31 B6
Avington Clo. GU1 31 D3
Baillie Rd. GU1 31 D4
Bartholomews Ct. GU1 31 D4
Bedford Rd. GU1 31 B4
Beech La. GU2 31 B6
Beech Lawn. GU1 31 D3
Berkley Ct. GU1 31 D3
Bray Rd. GU2 31 A4
Bridge St. GU1 31 B4
Bright Hill. GU1 31 C4
Brodie Rd. GU1 31 C4
Burnham Gate. GU1 31 C3
Bury Fields. GU2 31 B5
Bury Mews. GU2 31 B5
Bury St. GU2 31 B5
Castle Hill. GU1 31 C5
Castle Sq. GU1 31 C4
Castle St. GU1 31 C4
Cathedral Clo. GU2 31 A1
Caxton Gdns. GU2 31 A1
Chantry View Rd. GU1 31 C6
Chapel St. GU1 31 C4
*Charlotte Ct,
  Addison Rd. GU1 31 D5
Chertsey St. GU1 31 C4
Cheselden Rd. GU1 31 D4
Chesham Mews. GU1 31 D4
Chesham Rd. GU1 31 D4
Chestnut Av. GU2 31 B6
Chestnut Rd. GU1 31 C2
Chevremont. GU1 31 C4
Church Rd. GU1 31 B3
Churchill Rd. GU1 31 D3
Clandon Rd. GU1 31 D3
*Clifford Manor Rd,
  Pilgrims Way. GU4 31 D6
Cline Rd. GU1 31 D4
College Rd. GU1 31 C4
Commercial Rd. GU1 31 B4
Cooper Rd. GU1 31 D4
Cross Lanes. GU1 31 D3
Crown Heights. GU1 31 C6
Dapdune Ct. GU1 31 B3
Dapdune Rd. GU1 31 B3
Deerbarn Rd. GU2 31 A1
Dene Rd. GU1 31 D3
Denmark Rd. GU1 31 C4
Denzil Rd. GU2 31 A4
Devon Bank. GU2 31 B5
Drummond Rd. GU1 31 B3
Dunsdon Av. GU2 31 A4
Eagle Rd. GU1 31 C3
Eastgate Gdns. GU1 31 C4
Echo Pit Rd. GU1 31 D5
Ennismore Av. GU1 31 D3
Epsom Rd. GU1 31 D4
Europa Park Rd. GU1 31 B1
Falcon Rd. GU1 31 C3
Farnham Rd. GU2 31 A5
*Ferndown Ct,
  Stocton Clo. GU1 31 B2

---

Ferry La. GU2 31 B6
Finch Rd. GU1 31 C3
Flower Walk. GU2 31 B5
Fort Rd. GU1 31 C5
Foxenden Rd. GU1 31 C3
Friary Br. GU1 31 B4
Friary St. GU1 31 B4
Friary Vw. GU1 31 B3
Gardner Rd. GU1 31 B3
Genyn Rd. GU2 31 A4
George Rd. GU1 31 C3
Glebe Ct. GU1 31 D3
Great Quarry. GU1 31 C5
Guildford Park Av. GU1 31 A4
Guildford Park Rd. GU2 31 A4
Guildown Av. GU2 31 A6
Guildown Rd. GU2 31 A6
Hamilton Gordon Ct.
  GU1 31 B2
Hanover Ct. GU1 31 C1
Harvey Rd. GU1 31 C4
Haydon Pl. GU1 31 C4
Heather Clo. GU2 31 A1
High Pewley. GU1 31 D5
High St. GU2 31 C4
Hillside Ct. GU1 31 D4
Hitherbury Clo. GU2 31 B6
Hunter Rd. GU1 31 D4
Hurst Croft. GU1 31 D6
**INDUSTRIAL & RETAIL:**
  Guildford Business Pk.
  GU2 31 A2
  Ladymead Retail
  Centre. GU1 31 B1
  Riverside Business
  Centre. GU1 31 B3
Iveagh Rd. GU2 31 A4
*Jefferies Pass,
  High St. GU1 31 C4
Jenner Rd. GU1 31 D4
Josephs Rd. GU1 31 B1
Kernel Ct. GU1 31 B3
Kings Rd. GU1 31 C3
Ladymead. GU1 31 B2
Langley Clo. GU1 31 B2
Laundry Rd. GU1 31 B4
Lawn Rd. GU2 31 B5
Leapale La. GU1 31 C4
Leapale Rd. GU1 31 C4
Leas Rd. GU1 31 B3
Lido Rd. GU1 31 C2
Linden Rd. GU1 31 D4
London Rd. GU1 31 D4
London Sq. GU1 31 D4
Ludlow Rd. GU2 31 A4
Lynwood. GU2 31 A4
Madrid Rd. GU2 31 A4
Manor Cres. GU2 31 A1
Manor Gdns. GU2 31 A1
Manor Rd. GU2 31 A1
Maple Gro. GU1 31 C1
Mareschal Rd. GU2 31 B5
Margaret Rd. GU1 31 B3
Markenfield Rd. GU1 31 B3
Market St. GU1 31 C4
Martyr Rd. GU1 31 C4
Mary Rd. GU1 31 B3
Mathion Ct. GU1 31 D3
Melville Ct. GU2 31 B6
Middleton Ind Est Rd.
  GU2 31 A2
Middleton Rd. GU2 31 A2
*Milkhouse Gate,
  Sydenham Rd. GU1 31 C4
Mill La. GU1 31 C4
Millbrook. GU1 31 B4
Millmead. GU2 31 B5
Millmead Ter. GU2 31 B5
Minster Gdns. GU1 31 C3
Mount Pl. GU2 31 B5
Mount Pleasant. GU2 31 B5
Mountside. GU2 31 A5
Nethermount. GU2 31 A5
Nettles Ter. GU1 31 C3
Nightingale Rd. GU1 31 C3
North St. GU1 31 B4
Northdown La. GU1 31 D6
Old Palace Rd. GU2 31 A4
Onslow Rd. GU1 31 C3
Onslow St. GU1 31 B4
Oxford Rd. GU1 31 C4
Oxford Ter. GU1 31 C4
Pannells Ct. GU1 31 C4
Park Chase. GU1 31 D3
Park Rd. GU1 31 C3
Park St. GU1 31 B4

Parkhurst Rd. GU12 31 A1
Parkway. GU1 31 C2
Percy Rd. GU2 31 A1
Pewley Bank. GU1 31 D4
Pewley Hill. GU1 31 C5
Pewley Point. GU1 31 D5
Pewley Way. GU1 31 D4
Phoenix Ct. GU1 31 B4
Pilgrims Way. GU4 31 C6
Poltimore Rd. GU2 31 A4
Portsmouth Rd. GU2 31 B6
Poundfield. GU1 31 C2
Poyle Rd. GU1 31 C5
Priory Ct. GU2 31 B6
Quarry St. GU1 31 C4
Queens Rd. GU1 31 C3
Recreation Rd. GU1 31 B2
Ridgemount. GU2 31 A3
Rivermount Gdns. GU2 31 B6
Riverside. GU1 31 C1
Riverview. GU1 31 B2
*Riverwood Ct, Weyside Rd. GU1 31 B1
Rookwood Ct. GU2 31 B5
Rupert Rd. GU2 31 A4
St Catherines Dri. GU2 31 A6
St Catherines Pk. GU1 31 D4
St Lukes Sq. GU1 31 D4
*St Saviours Pl, Leas Rd. GU1 31 B3
Sandalwood. GU2 31 A4
Sandfield Ter. GU1 31 C4
Sandy La. GU3 31 B6
Scholars Wk. GU2 31 A3
Semaphore Rd. GU1 31 D5
Shalford Rd. GU4 31 C5
South Hill. GU1 31 C5
Springfield Rd. GU1 31 C3
Springside Ct. GU1 31 B2
Station App. GU1 31 D3
Station Vw. GU1 31 B4
Stocton Clo. GU1 31 B2
Stocton Rd. GU1 31 B2
Stoke Fields. GU1 31 C3
Stoke Gro. GU1 31 C3
Stoke Mews. GU1 31 C3
Stoke Park Ct. GU1 31 C3
Stoke Rd. GU1 31 C2
Stoughton Rd. GU1 31 B1
Stratford Pl. GU1 31 C6
Swan La. GU1 31 C4
Sycamore Ct. GU1 31 D4
Sycamore Rd. GU1 31 C2
Sydenham Rd. GU1 31 C4
Tenniel Clo. GU2 31 A1
Testard Rd. GU2 31 B4
The Bars. GU1 31 C4
The Friary. GU1 31 B4
The Meadows. GU2 31 B6
The Mews. GU1 31 B3
The Mount. GU2 31 A5
The Piccards. GU2 31 B6
*The Shambles, Quarry St. GU2 31 C4
*Tilehouse Rd, Pilgrims Way. GU4 31 D6
Turnham Clo. GU2 31 B6
Tunsgate. GU1 31 C4
Tunsgate Sq. GU1 31 C4
Upper Guildown Rd. GU2 31 A6
Upperton Rd. GU2 31 A4
Victoria Rd. GU1 31 D3
Walnut Tree Clo. GU1 31 B3
Walnut Tree Park. GU1 31 B3
Ward St. GU1 31 C4
Warren Rd. GU1 31 D4
Warwicks Bench. GU1 31 C5
Warwicks Bench La. GU1 31 D6
Warwicks Bench Rd. GU1 31 D6
Waterden Clo. GU1 31 D3
Waterden Rd. GU1 31 D3
Waterside Mews. GU1 31 B1
Wendy Cres. GU1 31 A1
West Mount. GU2 31 B5
West Rd. GU1 31 D4
Weston Rd. GU2 31 A2
Wey View Ct. GU1 31 B3
Weyside Gdns. GU1 31 B1
Weyside Rd. GU1 31 A1
Weyview Clo. GU1 31 B1
Wharf Rd. GU1 31 B3
Wherwell Rd. GU2 31 B4
William Rd. GU1 31 B3
Wodeland Av. GU2 31 A5
Woking Rd. GU1 31 C1
Woodbridge Hill. GU2 31 A1
Woodbridge Mdws. GU1 31 B2
Woodbridge Rd. GU1 31 B2
Woodcote. GU2 31 A6
Worplesdon Rd. GU2 31 A1
Wych Elm Rise. GU1 31 D5
York Rd. GU1 31 C3

## HASLEMERE

Azalea Dri. GU27 32 B1
Bartholomew Clo. GU27 32 E1
Beaufield Gate. GU27 32 F2
Beech Rd. GU27 32 E2
Border Rd. GU27 32 A3
Braeside Clo. GU27 32 B1
Bridge Rd. GU27 32 E2
Buffbeards La. GU27 32 A2
Bunch La. GU27 32 C2
Bunch Way. GU27 32 C2
Camelsdale Rd. GU27 32 A4
Cedar Ct. GU27 32 D3
Chatsworth Av. GU27 32 E1
Cherrimans Orchard. GU27 32 A3
Cherry Tree Av. GU27 32 B2
Chestnut Av. GU27 32 E2
Chilcroft Rd. GU27 32 B2
Chiltern Clo. GU27 32 D4
Church La. GU27 32 E2
Church Rd, Haslemere. GU27 32 E2
Church Rd, Shottermill. GU27 32 B3
Cobden La. GU27 32 E2
Collards La. GU27 32 E3
College Hill. GU27 32 E3
College Hill Ter. GU27 32 E3
Courts Hill Rd. GU27 32 D3
Courts Mount Rd. GU27 32 D3
Critchmere Hill. GU27 32 A2
Critchmere La. GU27 32 A3
Critchmere Vale. GU27 32 A3
Dale Vw. GU27 32 B3
Deepdene. GU27 32 A3
Dell Clo. GU27 32 C2
Denbigh Rd. GU27 32 F4
Dene Clo. GU27 32 E3
Derby Rd. GU27 32 D2
Dolphin Clo. GU27 32 A2
Eliot Dri. GU27 32 A3
Farnham La. GU27 32 B1
Field Path. GU27 32 E2
Field Way. GU27 32 E2
Fox Rd. GU27 32 A3
George Denyer Clo. GU27 32 E2
Grayswood Rd. GU27 32 F2
Hales Field. GU27 32 E3
Halfmoon Hill. GU27 32 E3
Hasle Dri. GU27 32 D3
Haste Hill. GU27 32 F4
Hedgehog La. GU27 32 C3
Herondale. GU27 32 A3
High La. GU27 32 D1
High St. GU27 32 E3
Highbury Gro. GU27 32 E1
Highercombe Rd. GU27 32 F2
Hill Ct. GU27 32 D3
Hill Rd. GU27 32 E3
Hillside Rd. GU27 32 B4
Hindhead Rd. GU27 32 A2
Holly Ridge. GU27 32 D3
**INDUSTRIAL & RETAIL:**
Weydown Ind Est. GU27 32 D2
Junction Pl. GU27 32 B3
Kemnal Pk. GU27 32 F2
Kiln Fields. GU27 32 E1
Kings Rd. GU27 32 B3
Linchmere Rd. GU27 32 A4
Lion Clo. GU27 32 B2
Lion Grn. GU27 32 B3
Lion La. GU27 32 B2
Lion Mead. GU27 32 B3
Liphook Rd. GU27 32 A3
Longdene Rd. GU27 32 C3
Lower St. GU27 32 D3
Lucas Field. GU27 32 A3
Mallard Clo. GU27 32 A3
Manor Clo. GU27 32 A3
Manor Cres. GU27 32 A3
Manor Lea. GU27 32 A3
Marley Combe Rd. GU27 32 B4
Marley La. GU27 32 A4
Mead Way. GU27 32 B3
Meadow Vale. GU27 32 C3
Midhurst Rd. GU27 32 C4
Mill Clo. GU27 32 A3
Moorfield Rd. GU27 32 B4
Museum Hill. GU27 32 E3
New Rd. GU27 32 B4
Nutcombe La. GU26 32 A1
Oaklands. GU27 32 E2
Old Haslemere Rd. GU27 32 E4
Old Mill Pl. GU27 32 B2
Orchard Clo. GU27 32 B4
Park Rd. GU27 32 E3
Parsons Clo. GU27 32 E1
Parsons Grn. GU27 32 E1
Pathfields Clo. GU27 32 E2
Penwith Dri. GU27 32 A4
Peperham Rd. GU27 32 E1
Petworth Rd. GU27 32 E3
Pine View Clo. GU27 32 E1
Pitfold Clo. GU27 32 A3
Polecat Hill. GU27 32 B1
Polecat Valley. GU27 32 B1
Popes Mead. GU27 32 E2
Priors Wood. GU27 32 B3
Puckshott Way. GU27 32 E1
Roe Deer Copse. GU27 32 A3
Rosemary Ct. GU27 32 E2
St Christophers Grn. GU27 32 C3
St Christophers Rd. GU27 32 C3
St Stephens Clo, Haslemere. GU27 32 E2
St Stephens Clo, Shottermill. GU27 32 B3
Sandrock. GU27 32 D3
School Rd. GU27 32 B4
Scotland La. GU27 32 D4
Scotlands Clo. GU27 32 D4
Scotlands Hill. GU27 32 E4
Shepherds Hill. GU27 32 E3
Shottermill Pk. GU27 32 A2
Shottermill Rd. GU27 32 A3
Sickle Mill Rd. GU27 32 B3
Sickle Rd. GU27 32 B3
Springfarm Rd. GU27 32 A4
Station App. GU27 32 D3
Stile Gdns. GU27 32 B3
Stoatley Hollow. GU27 32 C1
Stoatley Rise. GU27 32 C1
Sturt Av. GU27 32 B4
Sturt Rd. GU27 32 B3
Sun Brow. GU27 32 B3
Swan Barn Rd. GU27 32 F3
Tanners La. GU27 32 E2
Tennysons La. GU27 32 F4
Tennysons Ridge. GU27 32 F4
The Avenue. GU27 32 B2
The Meads. GU27 32 B3
The Millstream. GU27 32 A3
The Paddock. GU27 32 C1
The Spinney. GU27 32 E1
Three Gates La. GU27 32 F2
Timber Mill Ct. GU27 32 B3
Trout Rd. GU27 32 A3
Underwood Rd. GU27 32 B2
Uplands Clo. GU27 32 F1
Vicarage La. GU27 32 B3
Well La. GU27 32 E2
West St. GU27 32 E2
Weyhill. GU27 32 B3
Weycombe Rd. GU27 32 E1
Weydown Rd. GU27 32 D2
Weysprings. GU27 32 C2
Whitfield Clo. GU27 32 E1
Whitfield Rd. GU27 32 E1
Woodlands La. GU27 32 B2

## HORLEY

*Abinger Keep, Langshott La. RH6 33 D2
Airport Way. RH6 33 B6
Albert Rd. RH6 33 C2
*Albury Keep, Langshott La. RH6 33 D2
Apperlie Dri. RH6 33 D5
Arne Gro. RH6 33 A1
Arrivals Rd. RH6 33 A6
Ashleigh Clo. RH6 33 B3
Aurum Clo. RH6 33 D4
Avenue Gdns. RH6 33 D4
Avondale Clo. RH6 33 B1
Baden Dri. RH6 33 A2
Bakehouse Rd. RH6 33 B1
Balcombe Gdns. RH6 33 D4
Balcombe Rd. RH6 33 C2
Barley Mead. RH6 33 D2
Bayfield Rd. RH6 33 A2
Bayhorne La. RH6 33 D5
Benhams Clo. RH6 33 C1
Benhams Dri. RH6 33 C1
Birchwood Clo. RH6 33 D2
Blundell Av. RH6 33 A2
Bolters Rd. RH6 33 B1
Bonehurst Rd. RH6 33 C1
Brackenside. RH6 33 D2
Bremner Av. RH6 33 A2
Briarswood. RH6 33 D2
Brighton Rd. RH6 33 A4
*Brockham Keep, Langshott La. RH6 33 D2
Brookwood. RH6 33 D2
Bullfinch Clo. RH6 33 A2
Burton Clo. RH6 33 C4
Carlton Ct. RH6 33 C1
Carters Meade Clo. RH6 33 D2
Castle Dri. RH6 33 D4
Chaffinch Way. RH6 33 A2
Chantry Clo. RH6 33 B2
Charlesfield Rd. RH6 33 B2
Chatelet Clo. RH6 33 C2
Chequers Clo. RH6 33 B2
Chequers Dri. RH6 33 B2
Chesters. RH6 33 A1
Chestnut Rd. RH6 33 C1
Cheyne Walk. RH6 33 B5
Church Rd. RH6 33 B4
Church Rd. RH6 33 B3
Church Walk. RH6 33 B4
Churchview Clo. RH6 33 A4
Cloverfields. RH6 33 D2
Collingwood Clo. RH6 33 D1
Consort Way. RH6 33 C3
Consort Way East. RH6 33 C4
Court Lodge Rd. RH6 33 A2
Cranbourne Clo. RH6 33 C1
Crescent Way. RH6 33 B5
Crewdson Rd. RH6 33 D3
Deepfields. RH6 33 B1
Delta Dri. RH6 33 C4
Dene Clo. RH6 33 A1
Departures Rd. RH6 33 A6
Downe Clo. RH6 33 A1
Drake Rd. RH6 33 A3
Eastway. RH6 33 D6
Elizabeth Ct. RH6 33 C3
*Elmtree Clo, Horley Row. RH6 33 C1
Emlyn Rd. RH6 33 A2
Ewelands. RH6 33 D2
Fairfield Av. RH6 33 C4
Fairlawns. RH6 33 D4
Fairstone Ct. RH6 33 D2
Fallowfield Way. RH6 33 D2
Ferndown. RH6 33 B1
Fieldview. RH6 33 D2
Firlands. RH6 33 D2
Fishers. RH6 33 D2
Fuel Farm Rd. RH6 33 A6
Furlong Way. RH6 33 B6
Gatwick Way. RH6 33 B6
Gower Rd. RH6 33 A3
Granary Clo. RH6 33 B1
Grassmere. RH6 33 D2
Greatlake Ct. RH6 33 C2
Greenfields Clo. RH6 33 A1
Greenfields Rd. RH6 33 A1
Grendon Clo. RH6 33 B1
Grove Rd. RH6 33 A2
Grovelands. RH6 33 D4
Hardy Clo. RH6 33 A3
Haroldslea Dri. RH6 33 D5
Harrowsley Ct. RH6 33 D2
Harvestside. RH6 33 D2
Hatchgate. RH6 33 B4
Hayfields. RH6 33 D2
Heatherlands. RH6 33 D2
Hedingham Clo. RH6 33 D2
Heritage Lawn. RH6 33 D2
Heronswood Ct. RH6 33 D2
Hevers Av. RH6 33 B2
High St. RH6 33 C3
*Holmbury Keep, Langshott La. RH6 33 D2
Homefield Clo. RH6 33 C2
Horley Row. RH6 33 B2
Hurst Rd. RH6 33 A2
Hutchins Way. RH6 33 B1
Hyperion Walk. RH6 33 C5
Kelsey Clo. RH6 33 B3
Kenya Ct. RH6 33 B1
Kidworth Clo. RH6 33 B1
Kiln La. RH6 33 B1
Kimberley Clo. RH6 33 A3
Kings Rd. RH6 33 C3
Kingsley Rd. RH6 33 A1
Ladbroke Rd. RH6 33 C1
Lake La. RH6 33 D1
Landen Pk. RH6 33 A1
Langshott. RH6 33 D1
Langshott La. RH6 33 D2
Larkfield. RH6 33 D2
Le May Clo. RH6 33 C2
Lechford Rd. RH6 33 B4
Lee St. RH6 33 A2
Limes Av. RH6 33 D4
Lincoln Clo. RH6 33 B4
London Rd. RH6 33 A4
Longbridge Rd. RH6 33 B4
Longbridge Rd. RH6 33 A5
Longbridge Wk. RH6 33 B5
Longbridge Way. RH6 33 B5
Lumley Ct. RH6 33 C2
Lumley Rd. RH6 33 C2
Magnolia Ct. RH6 33 B3
Mallard Clo. RH6 33 B1
Manor Clo. RH6 33 B3
Manor Dri. RH6 33 B3
Massetts Rd. RH6 33 B4
Maizecroft. RH6 33 D2
Meadowcroft Clo. RH6 33 D5
Meadowside. RH6 33 D2
Meathgreen Av. RH6 33 A1
Meathgreen La. RH6 33 A1
Michael Cres. RH6 33 C5
Mill Clo. RH6 33 A2
Mosford Clo. RH6 33 B1
Newlands Clo. RH6 33 B1
Norfolk Clo. RH6 33 B4
North Terminal Approach Rd. RH6 33 B6
North Way. RH6 33 B6
Oakwood Rd. RH6 33 C2
Oatlands. RH6 33 D2
Oldfield Clo. RH6 33 B4
Oldfield Rd. RH6 33 B4
Orchard Clo. RH6 33 B2
Parklawn Av. RH6 33 B1
Park View. RH6 33 B1
Parkhurst Gro. RH6 33 A
Parkhurst Rd. RH6 33 A
Parkway. RH6 33 B
Parsons Clo. RH6 33 A
Perimeter Rd Nth. RH6 33 A
Pine Gdns. RH6 33 B
Povey Cross Rd. RH6 33 A
Powell Clo. RH6 33 A
Primrose Av. RH6 33 C
Priory Clo. RH6 33 B
Queens Gate. RH6 33 C
Queens Rd. RH6 33 B
Racecourse Way. RH6 33 B
Ramsey Clo. RH6 33 B
Raymer Walk. RH6 33 D
Regents Mews. RH6 33 C
Rickwood. RH6 33 D
Ring Road Nth. RH6 33 D
Ringley Av. RH6 33 B
Riverside. RH6 33 B
Roffey Clo. RH6 33 B
Rosemary Ct. RH6 33 A
Rosemary La. RH6 33 D
Roslan Ct. RH6 33 D
*Rudgwick Keep, Langshott La. RH6 33 D
Russells Cres. RH6 33 C
Rutherwick Clo. RH6 33 A
Ryelands. RH6 33 D
St Georges Clo. RH6 33 D
St Hildas Clo. RH6 33 C
Sangers Dri. RH6 33 B
Sarel Way. RH6 33 C
Silverlea Gdns. RH6 33 D
Smallfield Rd. RH6 33 D
Smallmead. RH6 33 D
Smithbarn Clo. RH6 33 D

Green La. KT22 35 D3
Guildford Rd. KT22 35 A5
Harriots Clo. KT21 35 D2
Harriotts La. KT21 35 C1
Hatherwood. KT22 35 D3
Hawks Hill. KT22 35 A5
Hawks Hill Clo. KT22 35 A5
Hawks Hill Ct. KT22 35 A5
Hazelmere Clo. KT22 35 B1
Headley Rd. KT22 35 D4
Heymede. KT22 35 C5
High St. KT22 35 B4
Highfields. KT21 35 D1
Highlands Av. KT22 35 C4
Highlands Clo. KT22 35 C4
Highlands Pk. KT22 35 D5
Highlands Rd. KT22 35 C4
Highwoods. KT22 35 C3
Hilltop Clo. KT22 35 C5
Holly Ct. KT22 35 A4
Homefield Clo. KT22 35 C3
Homelands. KT22 35 C3
Howard Clo. KT22 35 C5
Hulton Clo. KT22 35 C5
INDUSTRIAL & RETAIL:
Mole Business Pk.
KT22 35 A3
Research Area. KT22 35 A2
Ryebrook Business Pk.
KT22 35 B2
Kingscroft Rd. KT22 35 B2
Kingslea. KT22 35 B2
Kingston Av. KT22 35 B3
Kingston House Gdns.
KT22 35 B3
Kingston Rd. KT22 35 B1
Leach Gro. KT22 35 C4
Leatherhead By-Pass.
KT22 35 C2
Leatherhead Rd. KT22 35 D3
Leret Way. KT22 35 B3
Levett Rd. KT22 35 C2
Linden Ct. KT22 35 C3
Linden Gdns. KT22 35 C3
Linden Pit Path. KT22 35 B3
Linden Rd. KT22 35 B3
Longshaw. KT22 35 A1
Magazine Pl. KT22 35 B4
Mayell Clo. KT22 35 C5
Mayfield. KT22 35 C3
Melvin Shaw. KT22 35 C5
Middle Rd. KT22 35 B3
Mill La. KT22 35 A4
Minchin Clo. KT22 35 B4
Mole Valley Pl. KT21 35 D1
North St. KT22 35 A1
Oak Rd. KT22 35 B3
Oaks Clo. KT22 35 B3
Old Station App. KT22 35 A3
Orchard Dri. KT21 35 D2
Orchard Leigh. KT22 35 C1
Ottways La. KT21 35 D1
Owen Pl. KT22 35 B4
Park Clo. KT22 35 B3
Park Rise. KT22 35 B3
Parr Clo. KT22 35 A2
Poplar Av. KT22 35 C4
Poplar Rd. KT22 35 C4
Quarry Clo. KT22 35 D3
Queen Annes Gdns.
KT22 35 B3
Queen Annes Ter. KT22 35 B3
Randalls Cres. KT22 35 A2
Randalls Farm La. KT22 35 B2
Randalls Park Av. KT22 35 A2
Randalls Park Dri. KT22 35 A3
Randalls Rd. KT22 35 A2
Randalls Way. KT22 35 A2
Reigate Rd. KT22 35 D5
Russell Ct. KT22 35 B4
St Johns Av. KT22 35 C2
St Johns Clo. KT22 35 B3
St Johns Rd. KT22 35 C2
St Marys Rd. KT22 35 B4
St Nicholas Hill. KT22 35 C4
Salvation Pl. KT22 35 A6
Shires Clo. KT21 35 B1
South View Rd. KT21 35 D1
Station App. KT22 35 A3
Station Rd. KT22 35 A3
Summerfield. KT21 35 D1
Sunmead Clo. KT22 35 A4
Swan Ct. KT22 35 B3
Taleworth Clo. KT21 35 D2
Taleworth Pk. KT21 35 D2
Taleworth Rd. KT21 35 D2

Tanners Dean. KT22 35 D4
Tate Clo. KT22 35 C5
The Crescent. KT22 35 B4
The Driftway. KT22 35 C5
The Knoll. KT22 35 C3
The Limes. KT22 35 C4
The Murreys. KT21 35 D1
The Priors. KT21 35 D1
The Withies. KT22 35 C2
Thorncroft Dri. KT22 35 B5
Tregarthen Pl. KT22 35 C3
Tudor Walk. KT22 35 A2
Uplands. KT21 35 D1
Upper Fairfield Rd.
KT22 35 B3
Vicarage La. KT22 35 B4
Wallis Mews. KT22 35 A4
Waterfields. KT22 35 B1
Waterway Rd. KT22 35 A4
Waverley Pl. KT22 35 B4
West Farm Av. KT21 35 D1
West Farm Clo. KT21 35 C1
West Farm Dri. KT21 35 D1
Windfield. KT22 35 C3
Windmill Dri. KT22 35 C5
Wood End. KT22 35 D6
Woodvill Rd. KT22 35 B2
Worple Rd. KT22 35 C5
Yarm Ct Rd. KT22 35 C5
Yarm Way. KT22 35 D5
Young St. KT22 35 A6

Ash Clo. RH7 36 C3
Bakers Clo. RH7 36 C2
Bakers La. RH7 36 C2
Blackberry La. RH7 36 B5
Camden Rd. RH7 36 C3
Church Rd. RH7 36 C3
College Clo. RH7 36 B3
Crowhurst Rd. RH7 36 B1
Deacons Ct. RH7 36 A3
Drivers Mead. RH7 36 B4
East Grinstead Rd. RH7 36 B4
Edenbrook. RH7 36 C3
Felcourt Rd. RH7 36 B6
Godstone Rd. RH7 36 A2
Green La. RH7 36 A4
Grove Rd. RH7 36 C2
Gunpit Rd. RH7 36 B3
Haxted Rd. RH7 36 C1
Haywardens. RH7 36 B3
Headland Way. RH7 36 B3
High St. RH7 36 B3
Jenners Clo. RH7 36 B3
Jenny La. RH7 36 B3
Lincolns Mead. RH7 36 A4
Lingfield Common Rd.
RH7 36 A1
Little Lullenden. RH7 36 C2
Mount Pleasant Rd.
RH7 36 A3
New Place Gdns. RH7 36 C3
Newchapel Rd. RH7 36 A3
Old School Pl. RH7 36 B3
Orchard Mead. RH7 36 B4
Paddock Clo. RH7 36 A4
Park La. RH7 36 C2
Pauls Mead. RH7 36 B3
Plaistow St. RH7 36 B3
Racecourse Rd. RH7 36 C4
Ray Clo. RH7 36 A2
Ray La. RH7 36 A1
Rushfords. RH7 36 C2
St Piers La. RH7 36 D4
Saxbys La. RH7 36 C3
Selbys. RH7 36 C2
Stanfords Pl. RH7 36 B4
Station Rd. RH7 36 C2
Talbot Rd. RH7 36 B4
The Square. RH7 36 A3
Town Hill. RH7 36 C3
Vicarage Clo. RH7 36 B3
Vicarage La. RH7 36 B3

Amberley Rd. GU8 37 B1
Badgers Cross. GU8 37 C2
Bannister Clo. GU8 37 C5
Busdens Clo. GU8 37 C3

Busdens La. GU8 37 C3
Busdens Way. GU8 37 C3
Chapel Clo. GU8 37 C1
Chapel La. GU8 37 C1
Cherry Tree Rd. GU8 37 B2
Chichester Clo. GU8 37 B6
Church Clo. GU8 37 C2
Church Rd. GU8 37 C2
Cramhurst La. GU8 37 B5
Croft Rd. GU8 37 B5
Dorlcote. GU8 37 B6
Eashing La. GU7 37 C1
East Fields. GU8 37 C6
Elmside. GU8 37 C2
Flitwick Grange. GU8 37 C2
Gasden Copse. GU8 37 A5
Gasden Dri. GU8 37 A5
Gasden La. GU8 37 A5
George Elliot Clo. GU8 37 C6
George Rd. GU8 37 C1
Green La. GU8 37 B3
Guildford & Godalming
By-Pass. GU8 37 C2
Haslemere Rd. GU8 37 A5
Heathview Rd. GU8 37 B4
Highcroft. GU8 37 C3
Hurst Farm Clo. GU8 37 C1
Keswick Rd. GU8 37 A5
Khartoum Rd. GU8 37 B5
Ladycross. GU8 37 C3
Leehurst. GU8 37 B2
Little London. GU8 37 B5
Lower Moushill La.
GU8 37 A2
Lower Manor Rd. GU8 37 C2
Malthouse Mead. GU8 37 C6
Manor Fields. GU8 37 B1
Manor Grn. GU8 37 B2
Manor Lea Clo. GU8 37 B1
Manor Lea Rd. GU8 37 B1
Martins Wood. GU8 37 B4
Meadow Clo. GU8 37 D2
Merryacres. GU8 37 B4
Middlemarch. GU8 37 B6
Midleton Clo. GU8 37 C1
Milford Heath Rd. GU8 37 B3
Milford Lodge. GU8 37 C3
Milford Rd. GU8 37 A1
Mill La. GU8 37 C2
Moushill La. GU8 37 B3
New Rd. GU8 37 B2
Oak Tree Rd. GU8 37 C2
Ockfields. GU8 37 C2
Old Elstead Rd. GU8 37 B2
Oxted Grn. GU8 37 B4
Petworth Rd. GU8 37 C4
Portsmouth Rd. GU8 37 A4
Potters Clo. GU8 37 C1
Rake La. GU8 37 C4
Roke Clo. GU8 37 B6
Roke La. GU8 37 B6
Sandy La. GU8 37 B3
Springwood. GU8 37 D2
Station La. GU8 37 D2
Sunny Down. GU8 37 B6
Sunny Hill. GU8 37 B6
Swallow Clo. GU8 37 B4
The Cedars. GU8 37 B3
The Lawns. GU8 37 C2
The Manor. GU8 37 C2
Upper Manor Rd. GU8 37 C2
Webb Rd. GU8 37 A5
Wheeler La. GU8 37 B5
Wildcroft Wood. GU8 37 B5
Willow Mead. GU8 37 C6
Willow Mews. GU8 37 C6
Woodpeckers. GU8 37 B4
Yew Tree Rd. GU8 37 A5

Arnewood Clo. KT22 38 B4
Beech Clo. KT11 38 A2
Beech Close Ct. KT11 38 A2
Beechwood Dri. KT11 38 A2
Birch Vale. KT11 38 B3
Birchwood La. KT22 38 D1
Birds Hill Dri. KT22 38 D4
Birds Hill Rise. KT22 38 D4
Birds Hill Rd. KT22 38 D3
Blundel La. KT11 38 A6
Bracken Hill. KT11 38 B2
Briars Ct. KT22 38 D4

Broom Hall. KT22 38 C5
Broomfield Ride. KT22 38 D3
Burn Clo. KT22 38 D6
Canterbury Mws. KT22 38 C4
Charlwood Dri. KT22 38 D6
Chatsworth Pl. KT22 38 D3
Clockhouse Mead.
KT22 38 B4
Copsem La. KT22 38 C1
Courtleas. KT11 38 A3
Courtney Pl. KT11 38 A2
Danes Clo. KT22 38 C5
Danes Way. KT22 38 D5
Danesmead. KT11 38 A2
Englemere Pk. KT22 38 B4
Esher By-Pass. KT11 38 A1
Fairmile Heights. KT11 38 A4
Fairmile Park Rd. KT11 38 A3
Fairoak Clo. KT22 38 D2
Fairoak La. KT22 38 C3
Falconhurst. KT22 38 D5
Fernhill. KT22 38 D5
Furze Field. KT22 38 D3
Goldrings Rd. KT22 38 C4
Hardwick Clo. KT22 38 C6
Hawkhurst. KT11 38 A5
Hawksview. KT11 38 A3
Heath Ridge Grn. KT11 38 A4
Heath Rd. KT22 38 C2
Heathfield. KT22 38 A5
High Dri. KT22 38 D4
High St. KT22 38 D4
Highfield Clo. KT22 38 D2
Hill Clo. KT11 38 A2
Holtwood Rd. KT22 38 B4
Irene Rd. KT11 38 A5
Kimberley Ride. KT11 38 B4
Kings Warren. KT22 38 C2
Leatherhead Rd. KT22 38 D5
Lebanon Dri. KT11 38 A3
Leys Rd. KT22 38 D3
Links Green Way. KT11 38 A4
Littleheath La. KT11 38 A4
Lyfield. KT22 38 B5
Manor Way. KT22 38 C6
Meadway. KT22 38 D5
Midgarth Clo. KT22 38 C4
Moles Hill. KT22 38 D2
Montrose Gdns. KT22 38 D3
Northcote. KT22 38 C4
Oakshade Rd. KT22 38 C4
Old Farmhouse Dri.
KT22 38 D5
Oxdowne Clo. KT11 38 B4
Parkfields. KT22 38 D1
Percival Clo. KT22 38 B1
Pond Piece. KT22 38 B4
Pony Chase. KT11 38 A4
Queens Dri. KT22 38 C1
Randolph Clo. KT11 38 A4
Richards Rd. KT11 38 B5
Roundhill Way. KT11 38 B2
Sandringham Pk. KT11 38 A2
Sandroyd Way. KT11 38 A3
Sandy Dri. KT11 38 A2
Sandy La. KT11 38 A2
Sandy Way. KT11 38 A3
Sheath La. KT22 38 B4
Silverdale Av. KT22 38 B4
Somerville Rd. KT11 38 A4
Spicers Field. KT22 38 D3
Spinney Clo. KT11 38 A2
Spinneycroft. KT22 38 C6
Station App. KT22 38 D6
Steels La. KT22 38 B4
Stokesheath Rd. KT22 38 C1
The Chase. KT22 38 C6
The Gables. KT22 38 C3
The Knoll. KT11 38 A4
The Ridgeway. KT22 38 C5
The Ridings. KT11 38 A3
The Rythe. KT11 38 B1
The Spinney. KT22 38 C2
The Starlings. KT22 38 C4
The Warren. KT22 38 C3
Torland Rd. KT22 38 D4
Tudor Clo. KT11 38 A4
Twinoaks. KT11 38 A4
Uplands Dri. KT22 38 D4
Warren La. KT22 38 C1
Waverley Rd. KT22 38 B5
Wellington Pl. KT11 38 A3
Woodside Rd. KT11 38 B4
Woodsway. KT22 38 D4
Wrens Hill. KT22 38 C5

Amy Rd. RH8 39 B2
Barnfield Way. RH8 39 D6
Barrow Green Rd. RH8 39 A1
Beadles La. RH8 39 A3
Beatrice Rd. RH8 39 B2
Blind La. RH8 39 B3
Bluehouse Gdns. RH8 39 C1
Bluehouse La. RH8 39 B2
Boulthurst Way. RH8 39 D5
Brassey Rd. RH8 39 C5
Broadham Grn Rd. RH8 39 A6
Broadham Pl. RH8 39 A6
Bromford Clo. RH8 39 C6
Central Way. RH8 39 A4
Chalkpit La. RH8 39 A3
Chalkpit Wood. RH8 39 A1
Chestnut Copse. RH8 39 D6
Chichele Rd. RH8 39 B7
Church La. RH8 39 A3
Church Way. RH8 39 C5
Coldshott. RH8 39 C6
Comforts Farm Av. RH8 39 C6
Culver Dri. RH8 39 B3
Detillens La. RH8 39 D2
Downs Way. RH8 39 B7
East Hill. RH8 39 B3
East Hill Ct. RH8 39 B3
East Hill Rd. RH8 39 B3
Eastlands Wy. RH8 39 A3
Ellice Rd. RH8 39 B3
Farley Pk. RH8 39 A3
Field Ct. RH8 39 B3
Gibbs Brook La. RH8 39 A6
Gordons Way. RH8 39 B3
Granville Rd. RH8 39 C1
Green Acres. RH8 39 B7
Greenhurst La. RH8 39 C5
Gresham Clo. RH8 39 C2
Gresham Rd. RH8 39 C1
Hall Hill. RH8 39 A3
Hallsland Way. RH8 39 D6
Haywain. RH8 39 A3
Hazelwood Heights.
RH8 39 D3
Hazelwood Rd. RH8 39 D6
High St,
Limpsfield. RH8 39 D2
High St,
Oxted. RH8 39 A2
Holland Cres. RH8 39 D6
Holland La. RH8 39 D6
Holland Rd. RH8 39 D6
Home Park. RH8 39 D6
Hookwood Cnr. RH8 39 D6
Hoskins Rd. RH8 39 B5
Hoskins Walk. RH8 39 B5
Hurst Green Clo. RH8 39 C5
Hurst Green Rd. RH8 39 C5
Hurstlands. RH8 39 C5
Icehouse Wood. RH8 39 B6
INDUSTRIAL & RETAIL:
Fairview Ind Est. RH8 39 D1
Johnsdale. RH8 39 C2
Laurel Dri. RH8 39 C6
Master Clo. RH8 39 B6
Meadow Brook. RH8 39 A6
Meldrum Clo. RH8 39 C5
Mill La. RH8 39 B3
Mill Shaw. RH8 39 A6
Neb La. RH8 39 A6
New Lodge Dri. RH8 39 C5
New Rd. RH8 39 B5
Napppleton Way. RH8 39 D5
Oak Shaw. RH8 39 A3
Oast Rd. RH8 39 B3
Old La. RH8 39 B3
Orchard Way. RH8 39 A3
Oxted By-Pass. RH8 39 A4
Padbrook. RH8 39 C1
Padbrook Clo. RH8 39 C1
Paddock Clo. RH8 39 C1
Paddock Way. RH8 39 C1
Park Rd. RH8 39 C5
Parklands. RH8 39 A3
Peter Av. RH8 39 A3
Pollards Oak Cres. RH8 39 C1
Pollards Oak Rd. RH8 39 C1
Pollards Wood Hill.
RH8 39 D1
Pollards Wood Rd. RH8 39 D1
Popes La. RH8 39 C5

est Hill. RH8 — 39 D2
arry Clo. RH8 — 39 B4
arry Rd. RH8 — 39 B4
ckfield Clo. RH8 — 39 C4
ckfield Rd. RH8 — 39 C3
seacre. RH8 — 39 D6
semary Clo. RH8 — 39 D6
Clair Clo. RH8 — 39 A4
Marys Clo. RH8 — 39 B2
kham Rd. RH8 — 39 A1
atts Hill. RH8 — 39 C2
uthlands La. RH8 — 39 A6
ring La. RH8 — 39 A4
ringfield. RH8 — 39 A4
anhopes. RH8 — 39 D2
ation App. RH8 — 39 B2
ation Rd East. RH8 — 39 B2
ation Rd West. RH8 — 39 B2
vlvan Clo. RH8 — 39 D2
nhouse Rd. RH8 — 39 A5
sters Clo. RH8 — 39 D5
ie Greenway. RH8 — 39 D6
ie Hawthorns. RH8 — 39 D6
ie Maltings. RH8 — 39 B4
ie Waldrons. RH8 — 39 C5
tsey Rd. RH8 — 39 D1
vedale Rd. RH8 — 39 C3
ater La. RH8 — 39 D1
est Hill. RH8 — 39 A3
est Hill Bank. RH8 — 39 A3
esterham Rd. RH8 — 39 C2
estlands Way. RH8 — 39 A1
heeler Av. RH8 — 39 A2
Vilderness Rd. RH8 — 39 A3
Volfs Hill. RH8 — 39 D4
Volfs Rd. RH8 — 39 D3
Volfs Row. RH8 — 39 D3
Volfs Wood. RH8 — 39 D5
Voodhurst La. RH8 — 39 B4
Voodhurst Park. RH8 — 39 B3
Voodland Ct. RH8 — 39 A1
Voodland Rise. RH8 — 39 B3
Vynnstow Park. RH8 — 39 C4

## REIGATE/ REDHILL

bbotts Rise. RH1 — 41 H1
binger Dri. RH1 — 41 F6
lbany Clo. RH2 — 40 B1
lbert Rd North. RH2 — 40 A2
lbert Rd South. RH2 — 40 A3
lbion Rd. RH2 — 40 C4
lders Rd. RH2 — 40 C2
llingham Rd. RH2 — 40 B6
lma Rd. RH2 — 40 C2
lpine Rd. RH1 — 41 H1
lthorne Rd. RH1 — 41 G5
rbutus Clo. RH1 — 40 D6
rbutus Rd. RH1 — 40 D6
rdshiel Dri. RH1 — 41 F5
ash Dri. RH1 — 41 H5
ancroft Ct. RH2 — 40 C4
ancroft Rd. RH2 — 40 B4
assett Rd. RH2 — 40 B3
atts Hill. RH1 — 41 F2
axter Av. RH1 — 41 F3
eaufort Clo. RH2 — 40 A3
eaufort Rd. RH2 — 40 A3
eech Dri. RH1 — 41 E3
eech Rd. RH2 — 40 B1
ell St. RH2 — 40 B5
elmont Rd. RH2 — 40 D5
everley Heights. RH2 — 40 C1
irchway. RH1 — 41 H5
irkheads Rd. RH2 — 40 B2
lackborough Clo. RH2 — 40 D4
lackborough Rd. RH2 — 40 D4
lackstone Clo. RH1 — 41 E4
lackstone Hill. RH1 — 41 E4
lackthorn Clo. RH2 — 40 D6
lackthorn Rd. RH2 — 40 D6
lanford Rd. RH2 — 40 D4
ox Tree Wk. RH1 — 40 D6
ramble Clo. RH1 — 41 H5
*Bramble Walk,
  Bramble Clo. RH1 — 41 H5
Brambletye Park Rd.
  RH1 — 41 G5
ramley Clo. RH1 — 41 G5
rightlands Rd. RH2 — 40 D2
righton Rd. RH1 — 41 G4
roadhurst Gdns. RH2 — 40 C6


Brokes Cres. RH2 — 40 B1
Brokes Rd. RH2 — 40 B2
Brook Rd. RH1 — 41 G4
Brooklands Ct. RH2 — 40 C2
Brooklands Way. RH1 — 41 F2
Brownlow Rd. RH1 — 41 E3
Buckhurst Clo. RH1 — 41 F2
Budgen Dri. RH1 — 41 G1
Burlington Pl. RH2 — 40 B3
Burnham Dri. RH2 — 40 B3
Burwood Clo. RH2 — 40 D4
Caberfeigh Pl. RH1 — 41 E3
Canons Clo. RH2 — 40 A2
Carlton Green. RH1 — 41 E1
Carlton Rd. RH1 — 41 E1
Carrington Clo. RH1 — 41 F3
Cartmel Clo. RH1 — 41 E2
Castlefield Rd. RH2 — 40 B3
Cavendish Gdns. RH1 — 41 H3
Cavendish Rd. RH1 — 41 H3
Caxton Rise. RH1 — 41 H3
Cedar Clo. RH2 — 40 D6
Chaldon Clo. RH1 — 41 F6
Chanctonbury Chase.
  RH1 — 41 H4
Chapel Rd. RH1 — 41 G3
Charman Rd. RH1 — 41 F3
Chart La. RH2 — 40 C4
Chart Way. RH1 — 40 D5
Chartfield Rd. RH2 — 40 D5
Cherry Green Clo. RH1 — 41 H5
Chestnut Clo. RH1 — 41 H5
*Chestnut Mead,
  Oxford Rd. RH1 — 41 F3
Chipstead Clo. RH1 — 41 G5
Church Ct. RH2 — 40 C3
Church Rd,
  Redhill. RH1 — 41 F5
Church Rd,
  Reigate. RH2 — 40 B6
Church St. RH2 — 40 B3
Church Walk. RH2 — 40 C4
Churchfield Rd. RH2 — 40 A3
Clarence Rd. RH1 — 40 D6
Clarence Walk. RH1 — 41 F1
Clarendon Rd. RH1 — 41 G3
Clarendon Rd Sth. RH1 — 41 G2
Clayhall La. RH2 — 40 A6
Cleeves Ct. RH1 — 41 H2
Clyde Rd. RH1 — 41 H3
Cockshott Hill. RH2 — 40 C5
Cockshott Rd. RH2 — 40 C5
Colebrook Rd. RH1 — 41 F2
Colesmead Rd. RH1 — 41 G1
Colman Way. RH1 — 41 F1
Common Rd. RH1 — 41 F6
Conifer Clo. RH2 — 40 B2
Coniston Way. RH1 — 41 E2
Copley Clo. RH1 — 41 F1
Coppice La. RH2 — 40 A1
Copse Rd. RH1 — 40 D6
Cornfield Rd. RH2 — 40 D5
Cotland Acres. RH1 — 41 E6
Crakell Rd. RH2 — 40 D4
Cranston Clo. RH1 — 40 C5
Crescent Rd. RH2 — 40 B6
Cromwell Rd. RH1 — 41 G3
Cronks Hill. RH1 — 40 D5
Cronks Hill Clo. RH1 — 41 E6
Cronks Hill Rd. RH1 — 41 E5
Crossland Rd. RH1 — 41 H3
Croydon Rd. RH2 — 40 C3
Cygnets Clo. RH1 — 41 G1
Daneshill. RH1 — 41 F2
Daneshill Clo. RH1 — 41 F2
Deerings Rd. RH2 — 40 C3
Dennis Clo. RH1 — 41 F1
Devon Cres. RH1 — 41 E4
Diamond Ct. RH1 — 41 H5
Dome Way. RH1 — 41 F3
Doods Park Rd. RH2 — 40 D3
Doods Rd. RH2 — 40 D3
Doods Way. RH2 — 41 E3
Doran Dri. RH1 — 41 H5
Douglas Rd. RH2 — 40 C3
Downswood. RH2 — 41 H5
Duncroft Clo. RH2 — 40 A3
Dunottar Clo. RH1 — 41 E6
Durfold Dri. RH2 — 40 D3
Eastbrook Rd. RH1 — 41 G5
Earlswood Rd. RH1 — 41 G5
East Rd. RH2 — 40 A3
East Walk. RH1 — 41 H5
Eastnor Rd. RH2 — 40 B6
Effingham Rd. RH2 — 40 C4
Eldersley Clo. RH1 — 41 F1


Eldersley Gdns. RH1 — 41 F2
Elm Rd. RH1 — 41 F4
Emlyn Rd. RH1 — 41 G5
Eversfield Rd. RH2 — 40 C3
Evesham Clo. RH2 — 40 A3
Evesham Rd. RH2 — 40 A3
Evesham Rd Nth. RH2 — 40 A3
Fairfax Av. RH1 — 41 F3
Fairford Clo RH2 — 40 D2
Fairlawn Dri. RH1 — 41 E5
Fengates Rd. RH1 — 41 F3
Fenton Clo. RH1 — 41 G3
Fenton Rd. RH1 — 41 G3
Fir Tree Walk. RH2 — 40 D3
Flint Clo. RH1 — 41 F2
Fountain Rd. RH1 — 41 F5
Frenches. RH1 — 41 G1
Frenches Ct. RH1 — 41 G1
Frenches Rd. RH1 — 41 G1
Friths Dri. RH2 — 40 C1
Fulbourne Clo. RH1 — 41 F1
Furze Clo. RH1 — 41 F3
Furze Hill. RH1 — 41 F3
Furzefield Cres. RH2 — 40 D5
Furzefield Rd. RH2 — 40 D5
Gable Ct. RH1 — 41 H2
Garibaldi Rd. RH1 — 41 F4
Garlands Rd. RH1 — 41 F4
Gatton Clo. RH2 — 40 D1
Gatton Park Rd. RH2 — 41 E1
Gatton Rd. RH2 — 40 D1
Gloucester Rd. RH1 — 41 G2
Glovers Rd. RH2 — 40 C5
Goodwood Rd. RH1 — 41 H2
Gordon Rd. RH1 — 41 H1
Green La,
  Redhill. RH1 — 41 F1
Green La,
  Reigate. RH2 — 40 A4
Green Way. RH1 — 41 F2
Greenhayes Clo. RH2 — 40 D3
Greenstones Clo. RH1 — 40 D6
Greystones Dri. RH2 — 40 D1
Grovehill Rd. RH2 — 41 F3
Gurneys Clo. RH1 — 41 G4
Haigh Cres. RH1 — 41 H5
Hardwick Rd. RH1 — 40 D6
Hardwicke Rd. RH2 — 40 B3
Harewood Clo. RH2 — 40 D1
Harrison Clo. RH2 — 40 C5
Hartington Pl. RH2 — 40 B2
Hartspiece Rd. RH1 — 41 H5
Hatchlands Rd. RH1 — 41 E3
Hawthorn Way. RH1 — 41 H5
Hazel Clo. RH2 — 40 C6
Hazel Rd. RH2 — 40 D6
Hethersett Clo. RH2 — 40 D1
High St, Redhill. RH1 — 41 G3
High St, Reigate. RH2 — 40 B4
High Trees Rd. RH2 — 40 D5
Highlands Rd. RH2 — 41 E3
Hill House Dri. RH2 — 40 C6
Hillfield Clo. RH1 — 41 H3
Hillfield Rd. RH1 — 41 H3
Hilltop Rd. RH2 — 40 C5
Hillview Dri. RH1 — 41 H5
Hitherwood Clo. RH1 — 41 E1
Holland Rd. RH1 — 41 F3
Holly Rd. RH2 — 40 C6
Holmesdale Rd. RH2 — 40 B3
Holmethorpe Av. RH1 — 41 H1
Hooley La. RH1 — 41 G5
Horley Rd. RH1 — 41 F6
Hornbeam Rd. RH2 — 40 C6
Howard Pl. RH2 — 40 B2
Howard Rd. RH2 — 40 C4
Huntersfield Clo. RH2 — 40 C1
Huntingdon Rd. RH1 — 41 G3
Hurstleigh Clo. RH1 — 41 F2
Hurstleigh Dri. RH1 — 41 G2
Ifield Clo. RH1 — 41 F6
Ifold Rd. RH1 — 41 G5
INDUSTRIAL & RETAIL:
  Kingswood Business Pk.
  RH1 — 41 G4
Isbells Dri. RH2 — 40 C5
Juniper Clo. RH2 — 40 D6
Juniper Rd. RH2 — 40 D6
Keats Av. RH1 — 41 H2
Kendal Clo. RH1 — 41 E2
Kilmarnock Pk. RH2 — 40 C1
Kingfisher Rd. RH1 — 41 H1
Kings Av. RH1 — 41 F5
Knighton Clo. RH1 — 41 G5
Knights Pl. RH1 — 41 H3
Knightwood Clo. RH2 — 40 B6


Ladbroke Gro. RH1 — 41 G3
Ladbroke Rd. RH1 — 41 G2
Lakeside. RH1 — 41 H1
Langlands Clo. RH2 — 40 D1
Larch Clo. RH2 — 40 D6
Ledbury Rd. RH2 — 40 B3
Lennox Ct. RH1 — 41 H3
Lesbourne Rd. RH2 — 40 C4
Lime Clo. RH2 — 40 C6
Linkfield Gdns. RH1 — 41 E3
Linkfield La. RH1 — 41 F2
Linkfield St. RH1 — 41 F3
Linnell Rd. RH1 — 41 H5
London Rd,
  Redhill. RH1 — 41 G2
London Rd,
  Reigate. RH2 — 40 B3
Lorian Dri. RH2 — 40 D3
Lower Bridge Rd. RH1 — 41 F3
Lower Rd. RH2 — 40 D6
Lymden Gdns. RH2 — 40 C5
Lynwood Rd. RH1 — 41 G2
Mackrells. RH1 — 40 D6
Madeira Walk. RH2 — 41 E3
Mallard Clo. RH1 — 41 H1
Manor Rd. RH2 — 40 A2
Mark St. RH2 — 40 C3
Marketfield Rd. RH1 — 41 G3
Marketfield Way. RH1 — 41 G3
Mead Clo. RH1 — 41 G1
Merrywood Park. RH2 — 40 C1
Mill St. RH1 — 41 F4
Mill Way. RH2 — 41 E4
Millview Clo. RH2 — 41 E1
Monks Walk. RH2 — 40 C4
Monson Rd. RH1 — 41 G1
Mostyn Ter. RH1 — 41 H5
Mount Dri. RH2 — 40 D1
Mount Rise. RH1 — 41 E6
Mountview Clo. RH1 — 41 E6
Mountview Dri. RH1 — 41 E6
Nash Dri. RH1 — 41 G2
Nash Gdns. RH1 — 41 G2
New North Rd. RH2 — 40 A6
*Nightingale Ct
  St Annes Mnt. RH1 — 41 H2
Noke Dri. RH1 — 41 H3
Norbury Rd. RH1 — 40 A3
North Rd. RH2 — 40 A6
North St. RH1 — 41 F2
Nutfield Rd. RH1 — 41 H4
Nutley Clo. RH2 — 40 B3
Nutley La. RH2 — 40 A2
Oak Rd. RH2 — 40 C2
Oak Way. RH2 — 41 E4
Oakdene Rd. RH1 — 41 F3
Oakfield Dri. RH2 — 40 B2
Oakhill Rd. RH1 — 41 F4
Oaklands Dri. RH1 — 41 H5
Oaks Rd. RH2 — 40 D2
Oakwood Glo. RH1 — 41 H4
Old Pottery Clo. RH2 — 40 C6
Old Redstone Dri. RH1 — 41 H5
Orchard Rd. RH2 — 40 C3
Orewell Gro. RH2 — 40 C5
Osborne Rd. RH1 — 41 H1
Oxford Rd. RH1 — 41 F3
Palmer Clo. RH1 — 41 H4
Park Hall Rd. RH2 — 40 B2
Park House Rd. RH2 — 40 A6
Park La. RH2 — 40 A5
Park La East. RH2 — 40 A6
Parkgate Rd. RH2 — 40 C5
Pendleton Clo. RH1 — 41 F5
Pendleton Rd. RH1 — 41 E6
Penrith Clo. RH1 — 41 E2
Philanthropic Rd. RH1 — 41 H5
Pilgrims Pl. RH2 — 40 B2
Pilgrims Way. RH2 — 40 A2
Princes Clo. RH2 — 41 G6
Princess Way. RH1 — 41 G3
Priory Ct. RH2 — 40 A4
Priory Dri. RH2 — 40 B6
Priory Rd. RH2 — 40 B6
Quarry Hill Pk. RH2 — 40 C1
Queens Ct. RH1 — 41 H2
Queensway. RH1 — 41 G3
Radnor Ct. RH1 — 41 F4
Raglan Clo. RH2 — 40 D2
Raglan Rd. RH2 — 40 C1
Randal Cres. RH2 — 40 B6
Ranelagh Rd. RH1 — 41 F3
Ravens Clo. RH2 — 41 F2
Reading Arch Rd. RH1 — 41 G3
Redstone Hill. RH1 — 41 G3


Redstone Hollow. RH1 — 41 H4
Redstone Manor. RH1 — 41 G4
Redstone Park. RH1 — 41 H3
Redstone Rd. RH1 — 41 G5
Redwood Mt. RH2 — 40 B1
Regent Cres. RH1 — 41 G2
Reigate Hill. RH2 — 40 B2
Reigate Hill Clo. RH2 — 40 B1
Reigate Rd. RH2 — 40 C3
Rennie Ter. RH1 — 41 H5
Ridgegate Clo. RH2 — 41 E1
Ridgemount Way. RH1 — 41 E5
Ridgeway Ct. RH1 — 41 F4
Ridgeway Rd. RH1 — 41 F4
Ringley Park Av. RH2 — 41 E4
Ringley Park Rd. RH2 — 40 D3
Robin Gdns. RH1 — 41 H1
Roebuck Clo. RH1 — 40 B4
Rosemead Clo. RH1 — 41 E6
Rowan Clo. RH2 — 40 D6
Rural Way. RH1 — 41 H4
Rushworth Rd. RH2 — 40 B3
Rutland Clo. RH1 — 41 F2
St Albans Rd. RH2 — 40 C5
St Andrews Clo. RH2 — 40 C5
St Annes Blvd. RH1 — 41 H1
St Annes Dri. RH1 — 41 H2
St Annes Mnt. RH1 — 41 H2
St Annes Rise. RH1 — 41 H2
St Annes Way. RH1 — 41 H2
St Clair Clo. RH2 — 40 D3
St Davids Clo. RH2 — 40 D2
St Johns. RH1 — 41 F6
St Johns Rd. RH1 — 41 G5
St Johns Ter Rd. RH1 — 41 G5
St Lawrence Way. RH2 — 40 B4
St Marys Rd. RH2 — 40 D3
St Mathews Rd. RH1 — 41 G3
Sandcross La. RH2 — 40 A6
Sandhills Rd. RH2 — 40 B5
Sandpit Rd. RH1 — 41 F4
Saxon Way. RH2 — 40 A3
Schroders Av. RH1 — 41 H1
Seale Hill. RH2 — 40 B6
Sheep Walk. RH2 — 40 A1
Sheldon Clo. RH2 — 40 C5
Sheridan Dri. RH2 — 40 C2
Shire Pl. RH1 — 41 G5
Shrewsbury Rd. RH1 — 41 E3
Silverstone Clo. RH1 — 41 F2
Sincots Rd. RH1 — 41 G3
Slipshoe St. RH2 — 40 B3
Smith Rd. RH2 — 40 B6
Smoke La. RH2 — 40 C5
Somers Clo. RH2 — 40 B2
Somers Rd. RH2 — 40 B2
Somerset Rd. RH1 — 41 E6
South Rd. RH2 — 40 C4
South Walk. RH2 — 40 C3
Southmead. RH1 — 41 G1
Sparrows Mead. RH1 — 41 H1
Springcopse Rd. RH2 — 40 C5
Spruce Clo. RH1 — 41 F2
Station App. RH1 — 41 G6
Station Rd,
  Earlswood. RH1 — 41 G6
Station Rd,
  Redhill. RH1 — 41 F3
Summerly Av. RH2 — 40 B3
Sussex Clo. RH1 — 41 E4
Sycamore Wk. RH2 — 40 C6
Sylvan Way. RH1 — 41 H4
Talbot Clo. RH2 — 40 C5
The Belfry. RH1 — 41 F3
The Bield. RH2 — 40 B5
The Cedars. RH2 — 40 D3
The Chase. RH2 — 41 E4
The Clears. RH2 — 40 A1
The Close. RH2 — 40 C4
The Crescent,
  Earlswood. RH1 — 41 E6
The Crescent,
  Reigate. RH2 — 40 C3
The Cutting. RH1 — 41 F5
The Dell. RH2 — 40 B2
The Fairways. RH1 — 41 E6
The Frenches. RH1 — 41 G1
The Mews. RH2 — 40 C3
The Ridings. RH2 — 41 E1
The Tannery. RH1 — 41 F3
The Way. RH1 — 41 E2
Timperley Gdns. RH1 — 41 G3
Tree Way. RH2 — 40 C1
Trehaven Parade. RH2 — 40 C6
Trentham Rd. RH1 — 41 H5
Tunnel Rd. RH2 — 40 B3

Underhill Park Rd. RH2 40 B1
Upper Bridge Rd. RH1 41 F4
Upper West St. RH2 40 A3
Utterton Way. RH1 41 E6
Vandyke Clo. RH1 41 F1
Victoria Rd. RH1 41 G5
Vogan Clo. RH2 40 C6
Warren Rd. RH2 40 C2
Warrenne Heights. RH1 41 E6
Warrenne Way. RH2 40 B3
Warwick Rd. RH1 41 G2
Washington Clo. RH2 40 B1
Waterlow Rd. RH2 40 D5
Waterslade. RH1 41 F3
Wesley Clo. RH2 40 A4
West Rd. RH2 40 C4
West St. RH2 40 A3
Westfield. RH2 40 C1
Westview Clo. RH1 41 F6
Whitebeam Dri. RH2 40 C6
Whitepost Hill. RH1 41 E4
Wiggie La. RH1 41 H1
Willow Rd. RH1 40 D6
Willow Walk. RH1 41 H6
Wilmots Clo. RH2 40 D3
Wilton Rd. RH1 41 G4
Windemere Way. RH2 41 E2
Windmill Clo. RH2 41 E2
Windmill Dri. RH2 41 E2
Windmill Way. RH2 41 E1
Woodcrest Walk. RH2 41 E1
Woodfield Clo. RH1 41 F2
Woodfield Way. RH1 41 F2
Woodlands Av. RH1 41 G5
Woodlands Rd. RH1 41 F5
Woodside Way. RH1 41 H4
Worcester Rd. RH2 40 B3
Wordsworth Mead. RH1 41 H2
Wray Common Rd. RH2 .40 D2
Wray La. RH2 41 E1
Wray Park Rd. RH2 40 C2
Wrayfield Av. RH2 40 D2
Wraylands Dri. RH2 41 E2
Wraymead Pl. RH2 40 C2
Yardley Clo. RH2 40 C2
Yeats Clo. RH1 40 D6
Yew Tree La. RH2 40 C1
Yorke Gdns. RH2 40 B3
Yorke Rd. RH2 40 B3

# RICHMOND

Adelaide Rd. TW9 42 D2
Albany Pass. TW10 42 C3
Albany Rd. TW10 42 C3
Albert Rd. TW10 42 C3
Alexandra Rd. TW1 42 A4
Alton Rd. TW9 42 C2
Arlington Clo. TW1 42 A4
Arlington Rd. TW1 42 A4
Arosa Rd. TW1 42 B4
Ashley Rd. TW9 42 C1
Audley Rd. TW10 42 C2
Austin Clo. TW1 42 A3
Bardolph Rd. TW9 42 D2
Beatrice Rd. TW10 42 C3
Beaufort Rd. TW1 42 A5
Beaulieu Clo. TW1 42 B5
Beaumont Av. TW9 42 C2
*Benns Wk,
  Kew Rd. TW9 42 C2
Beresford Av. TW1 42 A4
Braddon Rd. TW9 42 D1
Brewers La. TW9 42 B3
Bridge St. TW9 42 B4
Broadhurst Clo. TW10 42 D4
Budds Alley. TW1 42 A3
Burdett Rd. TW9 42 D1
Calvert Ct. TW9 42 D2
Cambrian Rd. TW10 42 C4
Cambridge Pk. TW1 42 A5
Cambridge Pk Ct. TW1 42 A5
Cambridge Rd. TW1 42 B4
Caplan Ct. TW10 42 D4
Cardigan Rd. TW10 42 C4
Carrington Rd. T10W 42 D2
Castle Yd. TW10 42 B3
Castlegate. TW9 42 D1
Catherine Dri. TW9 42 C2
Cedar Heights. TW10 42 C6
Cedar Ter. TW9 42 C2
Charlotte Sq. TW10 42 D4

Charmouth Ct. TW10 42 D3
Chester Av. TW10 42 C4
Chilton Rd. TW9 42 D1
Chisholm Rd. TW10 42 C5
Chislehurst Rd. TW10 42 C4
Cholmondeley Walk. TW9 42 A3
Church Ct. TW9 42 B3
Church Rd. TW9 42 C2
Church Rd. TW10 42 C3
Church Ter. TW10 42 B3
Church Walk. TW9 42 B3
Clarence St. TW9 42 B2
Clevedon Rd. TW1 42 B4
Compass Hill. TW10 42 B4
Connaught Rd. TW10 42 C3
Courtlands. TW10 42 D3
Cresswell Rd. TW1 42 B4
Crofton Ter. TW9 42 C2
Crown Ter. TW9 42 D2
Dancer Rd. TW9 42 D1
Darell Rd. TW9 42 D1
Dee Rd. TW9 42 D2
Denbigh Gdns. TW10 42 C4
Denton Rd. TW1 42 A4
Dorchester Mews. TW1 42 A5
Downe Ter. TW10 42 C5
Drummonds Pl. TW9 42 B3
Ducks Walk. TW1 42 A3
Duke St. TW9 42 B3
Duncan Rd. TW9 42 C2
Dunstable Rd. TW9 42 C2
Dynevor Rd. TW10 42 C3
Ellerker Gdns. TW10 42 B4
Ellesmere Rd. TW1 42 A4
Eton St. TW9 42 B3
Evelyn Gdns. TW9 42 C2
Evelyn Rd. TW9 42 C2
Evelyn Ter. TW9 42 C1
Fairlawns. TW1 42 A4
Farrer Ct. TW1 42 A5
Fitzwilliam Av. TW9 42 D1
Fitzwilliam Ho. TW9 42 B2
Friars La. TW9 42 A3
Friars Stile Pl. TW10 42 C4
Friars Stile Rd. TW10 42 C4
Gainsborough Rd. TW9 42 D1
Garrick Clo. TW9 42 A3
Gaston Bell Clo. TW9 42 C1
George St. TW9 42 B3
Golden Ct. TW9 42 B3
Gordon Rd. TW9 42 D1
Greenside. TW9 42 B3
Grena Gdns. TW9 42 D2
Grena Rd. TW9 42 D2
Greville Rd. TW10 42 D4
Grosvenor Av. TW10 42 C3
Grosvenor Rd. TW10 42 C3
Grove Rd. TW10 42 D4
Halford Rd. TW10 42 B3
Haversham Clo. TW1 42 B5
Heathcote Rd. TW1 42 A4
Heron Sq. TW9 42 B3
Hill Rise. TW10 42 B4
Hill St. TW9 42 B3
Hobart Pl. TW10 42 C5
*Holbrook Pl,
  Hill Rise. TW10 42 B4
Houblon Ct. TW10 42 C3
Howson Ter. TW10 42 B4
Hyde Rd. TW10 42 C3
Jocelyn Rd. TW9 42 C1
Jones Walk. TW10 42 D4
Kew Foot Rd. TW9 42 B2
Kew Rd. TW9 42 C2
King George Sq. TW10 42 D4
King St. TW9 42 B3
Kings Farm Rd. TW10 42 D2
Kings Mead. TW10 42 D4
Kings Rd. TW10 42 C3
*Lancaster Mews,
  Richmond Hill. TW10 42 B4
Lancaster Pk. TW10 42 B4
Larkfield Rd. TW9 42 C2
Lenton Rise. TW9 42 B1
Lewis Rd. TW10 42 C2
Lichfield Gdns. TW9 42 C3
Lion Gate Gdns. TW9 42 C1
Lorne Rd. TW10 42 C4
Lower George St. TW9 42 B3
Lower Grove Rd. TW10 42 D4
Lower Mortlake Rd. TW9 42 C2
Lower Richmond Rd. TW9 42 D1
Maids of Honour Row. TW9 42 B3

Manning Pl. TW10 42 D4
Manor Gdns. TW9 42 D2
Manor Gro. TW9 42 D2
Manor Pk. TW9 42 D2
Manor Rd. TW9 42 D2
Marchmont Rd. TW10 42 C3
Marlborough Rd. TW10 42 C4
Meadow Clo. TW10 42 B6
Meadowside. TW1 42 B5
Michels Row. TW9 42 B2
*Michelsdale Dri,
  Rosedale Rd. TW9 42 C2
Montague Rd. TW10 42 C4
Morley Rd. TW1 42 A4
Mount Ararat Rd. TW10 42 C3
Nightingale La. TW10 42 C5
North Rd. TW9 42 D1
Northumberland Pl. TW10 42 B4
Old Deer Park Gdns. TW9 42 C1
Old House Gdns. TW1 42 A4
Old Palace La. TW9 42 A3
Old Palace Yd. TW9 42 A3
Onslow Av. TW10 42 C4
Onslow Rd. TW10 42 C4
Orchard Rd. TW9 42 D1
Ormond Av. TW10 42 B3
Ormond Rd. TW10 42 B3
Pagoda Av. TW 42 C1
Paradise Rd. TW9 42 B3
Park House Gdns. TW1 42 A3
Park La. TW9 42 B2
Park Rd,
  Richmond. TW10 42 C4
Park Rd,
  Twickenham. TW1 42 A4
Parkshot. TW9 42 B2
Patten Alley. TW10 42 B3
Paved Ct. TW9 42 B3
Peldon Av. TW10 42 D3
Peldon Pass. TW10 42 D3
Pembroke Villas. TW9 42 B3
*Perseverance Pl,
  Kew Rd. TW9 42 C2
Petersham Rd. TW10 42 B4
Portland Ter. TW9 42 B4
Powers Ct. TW1 42 B5
Preston Rd. TW10 42 C3
Princes Rd. TW10 42 B3
Princes St. TW9 42 B3
Pyrland Rd. TW10 42 D4
Quadrant Rd. TW9 42 B3
Queens Ct. TW10 42 D4
Queens Cres. TW10 42 D3
Queens Keep. TW1 42 A4
Queens Rise. TW10 42 D4
Queens Rd. TW10 42 C5
Queensberry Pl. TW9 42 A3
Raleigh Rd. TW9 42 D1
Ravensbourne Rd. TW1 42 A4
Red Lion St. TW9 42 B3
Retreat Rd. TW9 42 B3
Reynolds Pl. TW10 42 C5
Richmond Bri. TW1 42 B4
Richmond Hill. TW10 42 B4
Richmond Hill Ct. TW10 42 C4
Richmond Rd. TW1 42 A5
River La. TW10 42 B6
Riverdale Gdns. TW1 42 A4
Riverdale Rd. TW1 42 A4
Riverside. TW9 42 A6
Rosedale Rd. TW9 42 C2
Roseleigh Clo. TW1 42 B5
Rosemont Rd. TW10 42 C4
Rosslyn Rd. TW1 42 A4
Royston Rd. TW10 42 C3
Russell Walk. TW10 42 D4
Rutland Dri. TW10 42 B6
Ryde Pl. TW1 42 A4
St Georges Rd. TW9 42 D2
St John's Gro. TW9 42 C2
St John's Rd. TW9 42 C2
St Margaret's Rd. TW1 42 A4
St Mary's Gro. TW9 42 C1
St Paul's Rd. TW9 42 C1
St Stephen's Gdns. TW1 42 A5
St Stephen's Pass. TW1 42 A5
Salisbury Rd. TW9 42 C2
Sandycombe Rd,
  Richmond. TW9 42 D1
Sandycombe Rd,
  Twickenham. TW1 42 A5

Sawyers Hill. TW10 42 D5
Sayers Walk. TW10 42 C5
Selwyn Av. TW9 42 C2
Shaftesbury Rd. TW9 42 C2
Sheen Pk. TW9 42 C2
Sheen Rd. TW9 42 C2
Sheendale Rd. TW9 42 C2
Spring Gro Rd. TW10 42 D3
Spring Ter. TW9 42 C3
Stafford Pl. TW10 42 C5
Stanmore Gdns. TW9 42 D1
Stanmore Rd. TW9 42 C1
Star & Garter Hill. TW10 42 C6
Sun Alley. TW9 42 B2
Sydney Rd. TW9 42 C2
Temple Rd. TW9 42 D1
Terrace La. TW10 42 C5
The Avenue. TW9 42 A3
The Green. TW9 42 B3
The Hermitage. TW10 42 B3
The Quadrant. TW9 42 B3
The Square. TW9 42 B3
The Vineyard. TW10 42 B4
The Wardrobe. TW9 42 A3
Topiary Sq. TW9 42 C1
Tower Rise. TW9 42 C1
Townshend Rd. TW9 42 C2
Townshend Ter. TW9 42 C2
Tree Clo. TW10 42 B6
*Trinity Cotts,
  Bardolph Rd. TW9 42 D2
Trinity Rd. TW9 42 D2
Twickenham Br. TW9 42 A3
Twickenham Rd. TW9 42 A2
Victoria Villas. TW9 42 D2
Vineyard Pass. TW9 42 B3
Vivienne Clo. TW1 42 A5
Wakefield Rd. TW10 42 B3
Warren Ftpth. TW1 42 B5
Warrington Rd. TW10 42 A4
Water La. TW9 42 B3
Waterloo Pl. TW9 42 B3
Wayside Ct. TW1 42 A4
West Sheen Vale. TW9 42 C2
Whittaker Av. TW9 42 B3
Willoughby Rd. TW1 42 A4
Wilton Av. TW9 42 D2
Windham Rd. TW9 42 D1
Winter Box Walk. TW10 42 D3
Worple Way. TW10 42 C3
York Rd. TW10 42 C3

# STAINES

Allyn Clo. TW18 43 C5
Annie Brookes Clo. TW18 43 A2
Argosy Gdns. TW18 43 C5
Aspen Clo. TW18 43 C4
Augur Clo. TW18 43 C4
Avenue Rd. TW18 43 A4
Avondale Av. TW18 43 C6
Baden Clo. TW18 43 D6
Barons Way. TW20 43 A5
Beehive Rd. TW18 43 B4
Berkeley Clo. TW19 43 A1
Billet Rd. TW18 43 D2
Birch Grn. TW18 43 D3
Bishops Way. TW20 43 A5
Boleyn Clo. TW18 43 B4
Bowes Rd. TW18 43 B4
Bremer Rd. TW18 43 D2
Bridge Clo. TW18 43 B3
Bridge St. TW18 43 B3
Broad Acre. TW18 43 D4
Budebury Rd. TW18 43 C4
Bundys Way. TW18 43 B5
Burges Way. TW18 43 D4
Carlyle Rd. TW18 43 C6
Chandos Rd. TW18 43 A4
Cherry Orchard. TW18 43 C4
Chertsey La. TW18 43 B4
Chestnut Manor Clo. TW18 43 D4
Chiltern Clo. TW18 43 D4
Church St. TW18 43 A3
Claremont Rd. TW18 43 A4
Clarence St. TW18 43 B3
Colnbridge Clo. TW18 43 B4
Commercial Rd. TW18 43 C5
Coopers Clo. TW18 43 D4
Cornwall Way. TW18 43 B5
Cotswold Clo. TW18 43 D4
Crossways. TW20 43 A5

Cumberland St. TW18 43 A4
*Curlew Ct,
  Leacroft Clo. TW18 43 D3
Devils La. TW20 43 A6
Dolphin Ct Nth. TW18 43 D2
Drake Av. TW18 43 C4
Duncan Gdns. TW18 43 C4
Edgell Rd. TW18 43 C4
Eton Ct. TW18 43 C4
Fairfield Av. TW18 43 C3
Farm Clo. TW18 43 B4
Farm Rd. TW18 43 D5
Farmers Rd. TW18 43 B4
Farnell Rd. TW18 43 D2
Ferry Av. TW18 43 B6
Florence Gdns. TW18 43 D6
Garrick Clo. TW18 43 C6
George St. TW18 43 C3
Georgian Clo. TW18 43 D3
Gloucester Dri. TW18 43 A3
Goodman Pl. TW18 43 B3
Gordon Clo. TW18 43 D3
Goring Rd. TW18 43 A4
*Grebe Ct,
  Leacroft Clo. TW18 43 D3
Green Pk. TW18 43 B3
Greenlands Rd. TW18 43 D3
Gresham Rd. TW18 43 C4
Grosvenor Rd. TW18 43 D6
Grovebarns. TW18 43 C5
Guildford St. TW18 43 C5
Hale St. TW18 43 B3
Hawks Way. TW18 43 C3
*Heron Ct,
  Leacroft Clo. TW18 43 D3
High St. TW18 43 B3
Huntingfield Way. TW20 43 A5
Hythe Park Rd. TW20 43 A5
Hythe Rd. TW18 43 A4
Hythefield Av. TW20 43 A5
INDUSTRIAL & RETAIL:
  Pine Trees Business Pk. TW18 43 B4
  Two Rivers Shopping Centre. TW18 43 B3
Island Clo. TW18 43 A3
Jamnagar Clo. TW18 43 C5
Kestrel Av. TW18 43 C2
Kingfisher Dri. TW18 43 D2
Kingsbury Cres. TW18 43 A3
Kingston Rd. TW18 43 A3
Knights Clo. TW20 43 A5
Knightsbridge Cres. TW18 43 D5
Knowle Grn. TW18 43 D4
Knowle Park Av. TW18 43 D4
Lacey Clo. TW20 43 A6
Laleham Rd. TW18 43 C4
Lammas Clo. TW18 43 B2
Lammas Dri. TW18 43 A3
Langley Rd. TW18 43 C5
Langton Way. TW20 43 A5
Lansdowne Rd. TW18 43 D6
Lark Av. TW18 43 C2
Leacroft. TW18 43 D3
Leacroft Clo. TW18 43 D3
London Rd. TW18 43 C3
Manor Pk. TW18 43 A2
Manor Pl. TW18 43 D4
Market Sq. TW18 43 B4
Matthews La. TW18 43 B4
Mayfield Gdns. TW18 43 B5
Meadow Ct. TW18 43 B2
Meadow Gdns. TW18 43 A4
Meadway. TW18 43 C6
Meadway Clo. TW18 43 C6
Midway Clo. TW18 43 D2
Millmead. TW18 43 C3
Monsell Gdns. TW18 43 B4
Moor La. TW18 43 A1
Moormede Cres. TW18 43 C2
Murdoch Clo. TW18 43 C4
Mustard Mill Rd. TW18 43 B3
New St. TW18 43 C3
Norris Rd. TW18 43 B3
Nursery Gdns. TW18 43 D6
Octavia Way. TW18 43 D5
Park Av. TW18 43 C5
Penton Hook Rd. TW18 43 C6
Penton Rd. TW18 43 C6
Pine Wood Dri. TW18 43 D4
Plover Clo. TW18 43 D4
Priory Grn. TW18 43 D4
Prospect Pl. TW18 43 C4
Pullmans Pl. TW18 43 C3

ailway Ter. TW18 43 A4
aleigh Ct. TW18 43 D3
chmond Cres. TW18 43 C4
chmond Rd. TW18 43 C4
ver Bank. TW18 43 C5
ver Park Av. TW18 43 A3
verfield Rd. TW18 43 C5
verside Dri. TW18 43 B4
verside Rd. TW18 43 C6
obin Way. TW18 43 C2
ochester Rd. TW18 43 A5
osefield Rd. TW18 43 D3
uskin Rd. TW18 43 C5
t Olaves Clo. TW18 43 C6
t Pauls Rd. TW18 43 A4
t Peters Clo. TW18 43 C5
idney Rd. TW18 43 C3
ilverdale Rd. TW18 43 D3
immons Pl. TW18 43 B4
outh St. TW18 43 C4
taines Bridge. TW18 43 B3
taines By-Pass. TW18 43 A2
tanwell Moor Rd. TW19 43 D2
tanwell New Rd. TW18 43 D2
tation Path. TW18 43 C3
wallow Clo. TW18 43 C3
hames St. TW18 43 B4
he Beeches. TW18 43 D4
he Causeway. TW18 43 A3
he Cygnets. TW18 43 C4
he Fernery. TW18 43 B4
he Hythe. TW18 43 B4
he Maltings. TW18 43 B3
he Oaks. TW18 43 C4
horpe Lea Rd. TW20 43 A5
horpe Rd. TW18 43 A4
illys La. TW18 43 B3
imsway. TW18 43 B4
Vicarage Rd. TW18 43 A2
Victoria Rd. TW18 43 B2
Vapshott Rd. TW18 43 B4
Vaters Dri. TW18 43 B2
Vendover Pl. TW18 43 A4
Vendover Rd. TW18 43 A4
Vestbourne Rd. TW18 43 D6
Vestbrook Rd. TW18 43 C4
Vheatsheaf La. TW18 43 C6
Vitheygate Av. TW18 43 D5
Vraysbury Gdns. TW18 43 B3
Vraysbury Rd. TW18 43 A2
Vyatt Rd. TW18 43 C4
Veoveney Clo. TW18 43 A1

## SUNBURY

Allen Clo. TW16 44 D4
Allen Rd. TW16 44 D4
Annett Clo. TW17 44 A6
Anvil Rd. TW16 44 C6
Aragon Clo. TW16 44 A2
Ashridge Way. TW16 44 B1
Avon Rd. TW16 44 B1
Barnard Clo. TW16 44 C2
Batavia Clo. TW16 44 D4
Batavia Rd. TW16 44 C4
*Beauclerc Ct,
  French St. TW16 44 D5
Beechwood Av. TW16 44 B1
Beechwood Ct. TW16 44 C1
Belgrave Cres. TW16 44 D3
Belgrave Rd. TW16 44 B3
Benwell Ct. TW16 44 B3
Berkeley Mews. TW16 44 D5
Beverley Rd. TW16 44 B4
Bingley Rd. TW16 44 B1
Bracken Clo. TW16 44 C3
Brackenwood. TW16 44 C3
Bridgefoot. TW16 44 B3
Bridle Clo. TW16 44 C6
Broad Oak. TW16 44 A1
Brook Dri. TW16 44 A1
Brooklands Clo. TW16 44 A3
Broomfield. TW16 44 A3
Bryan Clo. TW16 44 B2
Bryony Way. TW16 44 B1
Burgoyne Rd. TW16 44 A1
Cadbury Clo. TW16 44 A2
Cadbury Rd. TW16 44 A2
Camilla Clo. TW16 44 A1
Camilla Ct. TW16 44 A1
Cardinals Walk. TW16 44 A2
Carlton Rd. TW16 44 B2

Castle Clo. TW16 44 A2
*Castle Walk,
  Elizabeth Gdns. TW16 44 D5
Catherine Dri. TW16 44 A2
Cavendish Clo. TW16 44 B1
Cavendish Ct. TW16 44 A1
Cavendish Rd. TW16 44 A1
Cedar Way. TW16 44 A2
Chaplin Cres. TW16 44 A1
Chertsey Rd. TW16 44 A1
Chestnut Clo. TW16 44 A1
Churchill Way. TW16 44 C1
Church St. TW16 44 C6
Claremont Av. TW16 44 D4
Cleves Way. TW16 44 A1
Crayonne Clo. TW16 44 A3
Croysdale Av. TW16 44 C5
Cumberland Pl. TW16 44 C6
Dale Rd. TW16 44 A2
Downside. TW16 44 B3
Elizabeth Gdns. TW16 44 D5
Elm Dri. TW16 44 D4
Elmbrook Clo. TW16 44 C3
Evelyn Cres. TW16 44 B4
Evelyn Way. TW16 44 B4
Fairlawns. TW16 44 B5
Falcon Way. TW16 44 A4
Farrier Clo. TW16 44 C5
Fordbridge Rd. TW16 44 C6
Forest Dri. TW16 44 C5
Forge La. TW16 44 C5
Freeman Clo. TW17 44 A6
French St. TW16 44 D4
Furzewood. TW16 44 C3
Grangewood Dri. TW16 44 A3
Green La. TW16 44 B2
Green Leas. TW16 44 B2
Green Leas Clo. TW16 44 B2
Green St. TW16 44 B3
Green Way. TW16 44 B6
Griffin Way. TW16 44 C4
Halliford Rd. TW16 44 B6
Hamilton Pl. TW16 44 C3
Hanworth Rd. TW16 44 C2
Harris Way. TW16 44 A3
Hawkewood Rd. TW16 44 C5
Heath Gro. TW16 44 B2
Heathcroft Av. TW16 44 B2
Heatherlands. TW16 44 B1
Heathlands Clo. TW16 44 B4
Helgiford Gdns. TW16 44 A2
Holmbank Clo. TW16 44 A6
Homewaters Av. TW16 44 B3
Howard Clo. TW16 44 D4
Ilex Clo. TW16 44 D4

INDUSTRIAL & RETAIL:
Dolphin Ind Est.
  TW16 44 A4
Windmill Business
  Village. TW16 44 A3
Kelly Clo. TW17 44 A4
Kempton Av. TW16 44 D3
Kempton Ct. TW16 44 D3
Kenyngton Dri. TW16 44 B1
Keywood Dri. TW16 44 C1
Kings Av. TW16 44 D3
Kingsmead Av. TW16 44 D5
Laburnum Cres. TW16 44 C3
Laytons La. TW16 44 D4
Lime Cres. TW16 44 D4
Loudwater Clo. TW16 44 C6
Lyndhurst Av. TW16 44 B5
Manor Dri. TW16 44 B4
Manor Gdns. TW16 44 B4
Manor La. TW16 44 C4
Marlin Clo. TW16 44 A1
Martingale Clo. TW16 44 B6
Maryland Way. TW16 44 C4
Meadhurst Pk. TW16 44 A2
Meadows End. TW16 44 B3
Mill Farm Av. TW16 44 A3
Minsterley Av. TW17 44 A6
Montford Rd. TW16 44 C6
Nursery Gdns. TW16 44 B4
Nursery Rd. TW16 44 A4
Oak Gro. TW16 44 C2
Oakington Dri. TW16 44 D4
Old Orchard. TW16 44 D5
Orchard Rd. TW16 44 B4
Park Rd. TW16 44 C2
Parke Rd. TW16 44 C6
Parkwood Gro. TW16 44 B5
Percy Bryant Rd. TW16 44 A3
Peregrine Rd. TW16 44 A4
Pinewood. TW16 44 C3

Priory Clo. TW16 44 C3
Queensway. TW16 44 C4
Ravendale Rd. TW16 44 B4
Ravenscourt. TW16 44 B4
Rooksmead Rd. TW16 44 B5
Rope Walk. TW16 44 D5
Saddlebrook Pk. TW16 44 A2
St Marys Clo. TW16 44 B6
Salix Clo. TW16 44 C2
Saxonbury Av. TW16 44 D5
Scotts Av. TW16 44 A2
Scotts Way. TW16 44 A2
Seymour Way. TW16 44 A2
Shire Ct. TW16 44 C6
Silverdale Dri. TW16 44 C4
Spelthorne Gro. TW16 44 A3
Springfield Gro. TW16 44 B3
Staines Rd East. TW16 44 C3
Staines Rd West. TW16 44 A2
Station App. TW16 44 C3
Station Rd. TW16 44 B3
Stile Path. TW16 44 A6
Stratton Rd. TW16 44 B4
Summer Trees. TW16 44 C3
Sunbury Cross. TW16 44 B3
Sunmead Rd. TW16 44 B5
Sunna Gdns. TW16 44 D4
Sutherland Av. TW16 44 B4
Sutherland Gdns.
  TW16 44 B4
Thames St. TW16 44 C6
The Avenue. TW16 44 D3
The Chase. TW16 44 A6
The Crofts. TW17 44 A6
The Green. TW16 44 A6
The Haven. TW16 44 B2
The Parade. TW16 44 B2
The Pines. TW16 44 C5
The Ridings. TW16 44 B1
The Rowans. TW16 44 A1
The Spinney. TW16 44 C3
The Vale. TW16 44 C1
The Vineyards. TW16 44 C6
The Walk. TW16 44 B2
Upper Halliford Grn.
  TW17 44 A6
Upper Halliford Rd.
  TW17 44 A5
Vereker Dri. TW16 44 C5
Vicarage Rd. TW16 44 B1
Windmill Rd. TW16 44 A3
Windmill Rd West.
  TW16 44 A4
Windsor Ct. TW16 44 B2
Windsor Rd. TW16 44 B2
Wolsey Rd. TW16 44 B2
Woodberry Clo. TW16 44 C2
Wychwood Clo. TW16 44 B2

## SUTTON

Albany Mews. SM1 45 A4
Albert Rd. SM1 45 D4
Albion Rd. SM2 45 D6
Albury Ct. SM1 45 C3
Alexandra Av. SM1 45 A2
Alfred Rd. SM1 45 D4
All Saints Rd. SM1 45 C1
Ambleside Gdns. SM2 45 D5
Angel Hill. SM1 45 B1
Angel Hill Dri. SM1 45 C1
Anton Cres. SM1 45 A1
Ashton Clo. SM1 45 A3
Avon Clo. SM1 45 D3
Avondale Ct. SM1 45 C1
Banbury Ct. SM1 45 B6
Beauchamp Rd. SM1 45 A3
Bedford Ter. SM1 45 D5
Beech Tree Pl. SM1 45 B6
Beggars Roost La. SM1 45 A5
Belsize Gdns. SM1 45 C2
Benfleet Clo. SM1 45 D1
Benhill Av. SM1 45 D1
Benhill Rd. SM1 45 D1
Benhill Wood Rd. SM1 45 D1
Benhilton Gdns. SM1 45 C1
Betchworth Clo. SM1 45 D3
Beulah Rd. SM1 45 A3
Bishops Clo. SM1 45 D2
Blackbush Clo. SM2 45 C5
Blenheim Rd. SM1 45 B3
Brambleacres Clo. SM2 45 A6
Bramley Rd. SM1 45 A1
Brandon Rd. SM1 45 B3

Brandy Way. SM2 45 A6
Bridge Rd. SM2 45 B5
Bridgefield Rd. SM1 45 A5
Brighton Rd. SM2 45 C5
Brunswick Ct. SM1 45 C2
Brunswick Rd. SM1 45 C3
Bryanstone Ct. SM1 45 C2
Burgess Rd. SM1 45 B3
Burnell Rd. SM1 45 B2
Bushey La. SM1 45 B2
Bushey Rd. SM1 45 B2
Cadogan Ct. SM2 45 B5
Calthorpe Gdns. SM1 45 C1
Camborne Rd. SM2 45 B6
Camden Gdns. SM1 45 B4
Camden Rd. SM1 45 B4
Carshalton Rd. SM1 45 C4
Cavendish Rd. SM2 45 C6
Cedar Gdns. SM1 45 C5
Cedar Rd. SM2 45 C5
Chalcot Clo. SM2 45 A6
Chalk Pit Rd. SM1 45 C4
Chaucer Gdns. SM1 45 A2
Chaucer Rd. SM1 45 A2
Cheam Rd. SM1 45 A5
Chilworth Gdns. SM1 45 C1
Christchurch Pk. SM2 45 C6
Chudleigh Gdns. SM1 45 D1
Clarence Rd. SM1 45 B3
*Cliffe Walk,
  Greyhound Rd. SM1 45 D4
Clowser Clo. SM1 45 D4
Clyde Rd. SM1 45 B3
Collingwood Rd. SM1 45 A1
Compton Ct. SM1 45 C2
Coniston Gdns. SM2 45 D5
Constance Rd. SM1 45 D3
Coombe Walk. SM1 45 B1
Copse Hill. SM2 45 C6
Cranford Ct. SM1 45 C2
Cressingham Gro. SM1 45 C1
Crown Rd. SM1 45 B3
Cumnor Rd. SM2 45 D5
Deans Rd. SM1 45 B2
Devonshire Rd. SM2 45 D6
Dibdin Clo. SM1 45 A1
Dibdin Rd. SM1 45 A1
Dovercourt La. SM1 45 C2
Duchess Clo. SM1 45 D2
Duke St. SM1 45 D2
Eaton Rd. SM2 45 D5
Elgin Rd. SM1 45 D1
Elm Gro. SM1 45 B3
Erskine Rd. SM1 45 D2
Evesham Clo. SM2 45 A6
Falcourt Clo. SM1 45 B4
Ferndown Clo. SM2 45 C5
Forest Dene Ct. SM2 45 C5
Frampton Clo. SM2 45 A6
Gibson Rd. SM1 45 B4
Glena Mount. SM1 45 C2
Godstone Rd. SM1 45 D2
Goosens Clo. SM1 45 D4
Grampian Clo. SM2 45 D6
Grange Rd. SM2 45 A6
Grange Vale. SM2 45 C6
Greenford Rd. SM1 45 B3
Grennell Rd. SM1 45 D1
Greyhound Rd. SM1 45 C4
Grove Av. SM1 45 A5
Grove Rd. SM1 45 A5
Haddon Rd. SM1 45 B3
Hallmead Rd. SM1 45 B1
Heather Gdns. SM1 45 A6
Henry Hatch Wk. SM2 45 B2
High St. SM1 45 B2
High St. SM1 45 C4
Hill Rd. SM1 45 C4
Hillcroome Rd. SM1 45 D5
Hillview Rd. SM1 45 D1
Homefield Park. SM1 45 B3
Hope Clo. SM1 45 D3
Hunting Gate Mews.
  SM1 45 C1
Ivydene Clo. SM1 45 C3
Jengar Clo. SM1 45 C3
Keswick Clo. SM1 45 C2
Kirk Rise. SM1 45 C1
Landseer Rd. SM1 45 A5
Langley Park Rd. SM1 45 C3
Lavender Rd. SM1 45 D2
Lenham Rd. SM1 45 D1
Leslie Gdns. SM2 45 B6
Lewis Rd. SM1 45 B4
Lind Rd. SM1 45 D3
Litchfield Rd. SM1 45 C3

Lodge Pl. SM1 45 C3
Lower Rd. SM1 45 D3
Magnolia Ct. SM2 45 B6
Manor Ct. SM1 45 C3
Manor La. SM1 45 C3
Manor Park Rd. SM1 45 C4
Manor Pl. SM1 45 C3
Marian Ct. SM1 45 B4
Marlins Clo. SM1 45 D4
Marshalls Rd. SM1 45 B3
Mason Rd. SM1 45 C3
Mayfield Rd. SM2 45 D5
Milestone Clo. SM2 45 D6
Milford Gro. SM1 45 C2
Milton Rd. SM1 45 A2
Mitre Clo. SM2 45 D6
Monksdene Gdns. SM1 45 C1
Montana Gdns. SM1 45 D4
Montpelier Rd. SM1 45 D3
Montrose Gdns. SM1 45 C1
Morland Rd. SM1 45 D4
Mulgrave Rd. SM2 45 A6
Munslow Gdns. SM1 45 D2
Myrtle Rd. SM1 45 D3
Nash Clo. SM1 45 D1
Norman Rd. SM1 45 A3
Northspur Rd. SM1 45 A1
Nursery Rd. SM1 45 C3
Oakhill Rd. SM1 45 C2
Oakwood Ct. SM1 45 C2
Oldfields Rd. SM1 45 A1
Oliver Rd. SM1 45 D3
Orchard Gdns. SM1 45 A3
Orchard Rd. SM1 45 A3
Orme Rd. SM1 45 C4
Osborne Pl. SM1 45 D4
Overton Rd. SM2 45 A6
Palmerston Rd. SM1 45 D3
Parkhurst Rd. SM1 45 D2
Petersham Clo. SM1 45 A4
Princes St. SM1 45 D3
Pylbrook Rd. SM1 45 B1
Reading Rd. SM1 45 D4
Rectory Rd. SM1 45 B2
Ripley Gdns. SM1 45 C3
Robin Hood La. SM1 45 A4
Rose Hill. SM1 45 B1
Rosebery Gdns. SM1 45 C2
Russell Way. SM1 45 B4
Rutherford Clo. SM2 45 D5
St Barnabas Rd. SM1 45 A3
St James Rd. SM1 45 A3
St James Rd. SM1 45 A3
St Nicholas Centre.
  SM1 45 B3
St Nicholas Rd. SM1 45 C4
St Nicholas Way. SM1 45 B3
Sherwood Pk Rd. SM1 45 B4
Shott Clo. SM1 45 D4
Sorrento Rd. SM1 45 B1
Stanley Rd. SM2 45 B6
Stanmore Gdns. SM1 45 C2
Stayton Rd. SM1 45 A1
Strathearne Rd. SM1 45 B3
Sunnyhurst Clo. SM1 45 A1
Sutton Common Rd.
  SM1 45 B1
Sutton Court Rd. SM1 45 C5
Sutton Park Rd. SM1 45 B4
Sydney Rd. SM1 45 A3
Tapestry Clo. SM2 45 B6
Tate Rd. SM1 45 A4
The Green. SM1 45 B2
The Quadrant. SM1 45 C5
Thicket Cres. SM1 45 D3
Thicket Rd. SM1 45 D3
Thorncroft Rd. SM1 45 B3
Throwley Rd. SM1 45 C4
Throwley Way. SM1 45 C4
Times Sq. SM1 45 C4
Tormead Clo. SM1 45 A5
Town Sq. SM1 45 C4
Turnpike La. SM1 45 D4
Upper Vernon Rd. SM1 45 D4
Upton Dene. SM2 45 B6
Vale Rd. SM1 45 B2
Vermont Rd. SM1 45 B1
Vernon Rd. SM1 45 C4
Vicarage Rd. SM1 45 B2
Victoria Rd. SM1 45 B2
Village Row. SM2 45 A6
Vine Clo. SM1 45 C1
Walnut Mews. SM2 45 C6
Warwick Rd. SM1 45 C5
Waterloo Rd. SM1 45 D3
Wellesley Rd. SM2 45 C5

West St. SM1 45 B4
Western Rd. SM1 45 A4
Weymouth Ct. SM2 45 B6
White Lodge Clo. SM2 45 D6
Wilcox Rd. SM1 45 B3
William Rd. SM1 45 D3
Wings Clo. SM1 45 A3
Woodend. SM1 45 C1
Woodside Rd. SM1 45 C2
Worcester Rd. SM2 45 A6
York Rd. SM2 45 A5

# TADWORTH/ BURGH HEATH

*Abbotts,
  Harendon. KT20 46 B5
Acres Gdns. KT20 46 C3
Alcocks Clo. KT20 46 D3
Alcocks La. KT20 46 D4
Allum Gro. KT20 46 A4
Ashcombe Ter. KT20 46 A4
Ashurst Rd. KT20 46 A4
Avenue Clo. KT20 46 A5
Ballards Grn. KT20 46 D2
Bayeux. KT20 46 C5
Beechdene. KT20 46 A5
Bidhams Cres. KT20 46 B4
Birchgate Mews. KT20 46 B4
Bonsor Dri. KT20 46 D5
Brier Rd. KT20 46 A2
Brighton Rd. KT20 46 D4
Broad Walk. KT18 46 C2
Broadfield Clo. KT20 46 B3
Campion Dri. KT20 46 A3
Can Hatch. KT20 46 D2
Canons La. KT20 46 D2
Cedar Walk. KT20 46 D4
Chapel Gro. KT18 46 B2
Chapel Rd. KT20 46 B6
Chapel Way. KT18 46 B2
Cheam Clo. KT20 46 A4
Chetwode Dri. KT18 46 C2
Chetwode Rd. KT20 46 B3
Christopher Ct. KT20 46 B6
Church La. SM7 46 C1
Copleigh Dri. KT20 46 D3
Copley Way. KT20 46 C3
Copt Hill La. KT20 46 D4
Corner Farm Clo. KT20 46 B5
Coxdean. KT18 46 B2
Croffets. KT20 46 C4
Cross Rd. KT20 46 B5
Cuddington Clo. KT20 46 C
De Burgh Gdns. KT20 46 C3
Delves. KT20 46 C5
Derby Clo. KT18 46 A2
Dorking Rd. KT20 46 C6
Downland Clo. KT18 46 A1
Downland Gdns. KT18 46 A1
Downland Way. KT18 46 A1
Downs View. KT20 46 A4
Downs Way. KT20 46 A4
Downs Way Clo. KT20 46 A4
Downs Wood. KT18 46 A1
Duncan Rd. KT20 46 D2
Egmont Way. KT20 46 D2
Elm Gdns. KT18 46 C4
Emily Davison Dri. KT18 46 A1
Epsom La Nth. KT18 46 B4
Epsom La Sth. KT20 46 B5
Fairacres. KT20 46 B4
Ferriers Way. KT18 46 C2
Fleetwood Clo. KT20 46 C4
Garlichill Rd. KT18 46 B1
Glen Clo. KT20 46 D6
Gorse Clo. KT20 46 A3
Great Tattenhams.
  KT18 46 A1
Harendon. KT20 46 B5
Harpurs. KT20 46 C5
Hatch Gdns. KT20 46 C3
Hawes Rd. KT20 46 C3
Headley Dri. KT18 46 A2
Headley Gro. KT20 46 B3
Heathcote. KT20 46 C5
Heathdene. KT20 46 D2
Heather Clo. KT20 46 D6
Heathlands. KT20 46 C5
Heathside Ct. KT20 46 B6
Henbit Clo. KT20 46 A2
Hewers Way. KT20 46 B3
High St. KT20 46 B6
Hill La. KT20 46 D4

Hillview Clo. KT20 46 B4
Home Farm Clo. KT20 46 C1
Homefield Gdns. KT20 46 B3
Hudsons. KT20 46 C4
Killasser Ct. KT20 46 B6
Kings Ct. KT20 46 B5
Kingsdene. KT20 46 A5
Kingswood Rd. KT20 46 A5
Kipings. KT20 46 C5
Long Walk. KT18 46 C2
Longfield Cres. KT20 46 C3
Longmere Gdns. KT20 46 C2
Lordsgrove Clo. KT20 46 A3
Lothian Wood. KT20 46 A6
Lynden Clo. KT20 46 C4
Lywood Clo. KT20 46 B5
*Mabbotts,
  Harendon. KT20 46 B5
Mallow Clo. KT20 46 A2
Marbles Way. KT20 46 C2
Maybury Clo. KT20 46 D2
Meadow Way. KT20 46 D1
Meare Clo. KT20 46 B6
Meon Clo. KT20 46 A5
Merefield Gdns. KT20 46 C3
Merland Clo. KT20 46 B3
Merland Grn. KT20 46 B3
Merland Rise. KT20 46 B2
Merton Gdns. KT20 46 C4
Micheham Gdns. KT20 46 B4
Mill Rd. KT20 46 C6
Milstead Clo. KT20 46 A6
Morden Clo. KT20 46 C3
Morston Clo. KT20 46 A3
Morton. KT20 46 C4
Motts Hill La. KT20 46 A6
New Rd. KT20 46 B6
Norman Clo. KT18 36 A2
North View Cres. KT18 46 B1
Oakdene. KT20 46 D3
Oaklands Way. KT20 46 B5
Oaks Way. KT18 46 A4
Oatfield Rd. KT20 46 A4
Oatlands Rd. KT20 46 D2
Parthia Clo. KT20 46 A2
Petersmead Clo. KT20 46 B6
Pit Wood Grn. KT20 46 B3
Preston La. KT20 46 B4
Prossers. KT20 46 C4
Radolphs. KT20 46 C5
Reigate Rd. KT20 46 C1
Rowan Mead. KT20 46 A2
Royal Dri. KT18 46 A2
Ruffets Way. KT20 46 D2
Russells. KT20 46 C5
St Leonards Rd. KT18 46 B2
St Marks Rd. KT18 46 B1
Saxons. KT20 46 C4
Shawley Cres. KT18 46 C1
Shawley Way. KT18 46 A1
Shelvers Grn. KT20 46 B4
Shelvers Hill. KT20 46 B4
Shelvers Spur. KT20 46 B4
Shelvers Way. KT20 46 B4
Sherbourne Clo. KT18 46 B1
Somerfield Clo. KT20 46 D2
Spindlewoods. KT20 46 A6
Staithes Way. KT20 46 B3
Station App Rd. KT20 46 B6
Stewarts. KT20 46 C4
Stokes Ridings. KT20 46 C6
Summerlay Clo. KT20 46 D4
Tadorne Rd. KT20 46 B4
Tadworth St. KT20 46 B6
Tangier Way. KT20 46 D1
Tangier Wood. KT20 46 D1
Tattenham Cres. KT18 46 A1
Tattenham Gro. KT18 46 A1
Tattenham Way. KT20 46 C1
The Avenue. KT20 46 A6
The Dell. KT20 46 B4
The Green. KT20 46 D2
The Hoppety. KT20 46 C6
The Knowle. KT20 46 B4
The Lye. KT20 46 B6
The Ridings. KT20 46 B4
The Rise. KT20 46 B4
The Spinney. KT20 46 A2
The Walled Garden.
  KT20 46 C5
The Warren. KT20 46 D6
Thurnham Way. KT20 46 B6
Tower Rd. KT20 46 B6
Trittons. KT20 46 C4
Troy Clo. KT20 46 A3
Tulyar Clo. KT20 46 A3

Upland Way. KT18 46 B1
Vernon Walk. KT20 46 C3
Walkfield Dri. KT18 46 A1
Waterer Gdns. KT20 46 D1
Waterfield. KT20 46 A3
Waterfield Grn. KT20 46 A4
Waterhouse La. KT20 46 D4
Watermead. KT20 46 A4
Watts Clo. KT20 46 C6
Watts La. KT20 46 C5
Watts Mead. KT20 46 C6
Wessels. KT20 46 C4
West Dri. KT20 46 C1
Whitebeam Way. KT20 46 A4
Whitegate Way. KT20 46 A3
Willow Bank Gdns.
  KT20 46 B5
Wilsons. KT20 46 C5
Woodland Way. KT20 46 D6

# VIRGINIA WATER

Abbey Rd. GU25 47 E2
Abbots Dri. GU25 47 C2
Badgers Hill. GU25 47 D2
Beechmont Av. GU25 47 E3
Blacknest Rd. GU25 47 A1
Bourne Rd. GU25 47 E3
Bourneside. GU25 47 B4
Bridge La. GU25 47 F3
Brock Way. GU25 47 D2
Cabrera Av. GU25 47 D3
Cabrera Clo. GU25 47 D3
Callow Hill. GU25 47 C1
Chapel Sq. GU25 47 F1
Chestnut Av. GU25 47 A2
Christchurch Rd. GU25 47 B1
*Connolly Ct,
  Holloway Dri. GU25 47 F2
*Crossland Ho,
  Holloway Dri. GU25 47 F2
Crown La. GU25 47 D4
Crown Rd. GU25 47 D4
East Dri. GU25 47 B4
Edgell Clo. GU25 47 F1
Friars Rd. GU25 47 E2
Furnival Clo. GU25 47 E4
*Gillespie ho,
  Holloway Dri. GU25 47 F2
Gorse Hill La. GU25 47 E2
Gorse Hill Rd. GU25 47 E2
Harpesford Av. GU25 47 C3
Heath Clo. GU25 47 E1
Heath Rise. GU25 47 E2
Heatherside Dri. GU25 47 B4
Hillside. GU25 47 D3
Hollow La. GU25 47 D1
Holloway Dri. GU25 47 F2
Home Clo. GU25 47 E3
Irvine Pl. GU25 47 F2
Keepers Walk. GU25 47 E3
Knowle Gro. GU25 47 D4
Knowle Gro Clo. GU25 47 D4
Lake Rd. GU25 47 C2
Lambly Hill. GU25 47 F1
Lime Tree Wk. GU25 47 F2
Lindale Clo. GU25 47 A2
London Rd. GU25 47 A2
Lyne Rd. GU25 47 E4
Mereside. GU25 47 A3
Monks Rd. GU25 47 D2
Morella Clo. GU25 47 C1
Nuns Walk. GU25 47 E2
Oak Tree Clo. GU25 47 E4
Oakwood Rd. GU25 47 D3
Pinel Clo. GU25 47 F2
Pinewood Rd. GU25 47 B4
Pipers End. GU25 47 E1
Portnall Clo. GU25 47 A3
Portnall Rise. GU25 47 A3
Portnall Rd. GU25 47 A3
Quentin Way. GU25 47 C1
Sandhills Ct. GU25 47 B2
Sandhills La. GU25 47 F3
Sandy La. GU25 47 C2
Spring Woods. GU25 47 C2
Station App. GU25 47 E2
Station Par. GU25 47 E2
Stayne Rd. GU25 47 B2
Stroude Rd. GU25 47 F1
Stuart Way. GU25 47 B1
Sundon Cres. GU25 47 C3
The Close. GU25 47 D3

*The Grange,
  Holloway Dri. GU25 47 F2
The Lane. GU25 47 F1
The Mount. GU25 47 E4
The Mount Clo. GU25 47 E4
The Orchard. GU25 47 F3
Tithe Clo. GU25 47 E4
Tithe Mdws. GU25 47 E4
Trotsworth Av. GU25 47 E2
Trotsworth Ct. GU25 47 E2
Trumps Grn Av. GU25 47 E3
Trumps Grn Clo. GU25 47 F3
Trumps Grn Rd. GU25 47 E3
Upper Walk. GU25 47 F2
Virginia Av. GU25 47 D2
Virginia Beeches. GU25 47 D1
Virginia Dri. GU25 47 D2
Waterfall Clo. GU25 47 A1
Waverley Dri. GU25 47 B1
Wellington Av. GU25 47 C2
Wentworth Dri. GU25 47 A2
West Drive. GU25 47 A4
Whitehill Pl. GU25 47 F3
Woodlands Rd. GU25 47 D1
Woodlands Rd East.
  GU25 47 D1
Woodlands Rd West.
  GU25 47 D1
Woodshore Clo. GU25 47 C3
Woodside Way. GU25 47 C1

# WALTON- on-THAMES

Abbotswood. KT13 48 B4
Adelaide Rd. KT12 48 D4
Alexandra Clo. KT12 48 D3
Alpine Rd. KT12 48 D1
Annett Rd. KT12 48 C1
Apex Clo. KT13 48 A4
Ardesley Wood. KT13 48 B5
Ashley Clo. KT12 48 B2
Ashley Dri. KT12 48 C4
Ashley Park Av. KT12 48 C3
Ashley Park Cres. KT12 48 C2
Ashley Park Rd. KT12 48 C3
Ashley Rise. KT12 48 C4
Ashley Rd. KT12 48 C4
Beech Rd. KT13 48 A5
Beechcroft Manor.
  KT13 48 A4
Beechwood Av. KT13 48 A5
Beechwood Clo. KT13 48 B5
Beechwood Manor.
  KT13 48 B5
Belgrave Clo. KT12 48 D5
Berkeley Clo. KT13 48 A3
Berkeley Gdns. KT12 48 C1
Beverley Clo. KT13 48 A3
Bishops Hill. KT12 48 C1
Bowes Rd. KT12 48 D3
Brackley. KT13 48 A6
Bridge Clo. KT12 48 B1
Bridge St. KT12 48 B1
Broadwater Clo. KT12 48 C6
Broadwater Rd Nth.
  KT12 48 C6
Broadwater Rd Sth.
  KT12 48 C6
Brockley Combe. KT13 48 A5
Broom Way. KT13 48 A5
Burwood Park Rd. KT13 48 D5
Carlton Rd. KT12 48 D1
Castle Green. KT13 48 A4
Castle Rd. KT13 48 A4
Charlton Av. KT12 48 D5
Charlton Kings. KT12 48 C5
Chiltern Ct. KT12 48 C5
Church St. KT12 48 C1
Church Walk. KT12 48 C2
Churchfield Rd. KT12 48 C2
Cleves Wood. KT12 48 B5
Colby Rd. KT12 48 C5
Collingwood Pl. KT12 48 D4
Conifers. KT13 48 B5
Copenhagen Way. KT12 48 D4
Cottimore Av. KT12 48 D1
Cottimore La. KT12 48 D1
Cottimore Ter. KT12 48 D1
Cranley Rd. KT12 48 B6
Cricket Way. KT13 48 A5
Crossway. KT12 48 D3
Crutchfield La. KT12 48 D3
Culverden Ct. KT13 48 A4

Dale Rd. KT12 48 C
Dovehouse Grn. KT13 48 A
Drynham Pk. KT13 48 A
Dudley Rd. KT12 48 C
Dunally Pk. TW17 48 A
Eastwick Rd. KT12 48 D
Egmont Rd. KT12 48 D
Ellesmere Pl. KT13 48 B
Eriswell Rd. KT12 48 C
Esher Av. KT12 48 D
Fairlawn. KT13 48 A
Farmleigh Gro. KT12 48 B
Felix La. TW17 48 B
Fir Clo. KT12 48 D
Fisher Clo. KT12 48 C
Fox Clo. KT13 48 A
Foxholes. KT13 48 A
Gainsborough Ct. KT12 48 C
Grange Ct. KT12 48 C
Grove Cres. KT12 48 D
Haddon Clo. KT13 48 A
Halfway Grn. KT12 48 C
Hall Place Dri. KT13 48 B
Hanover Walk. KT13 48 A
Harvey Rd. KT12 48 C
Hepworth Way. KT12 48 C
Hersham Rd. KT12 48 C
High St. KT12 48 C
Highfield Rd. KT12 48 C
Hillrise. KT12 48 C
Holly Grn. KT13 48 A
Horvath Clo. KT13 48 A
Hungerford Sq. KT13 48 A
Hurley Clo. KT12 48 D.
Hurst Gro. KT12 48 B:
Ireton Av. KT12 48 B:
Kenwood Dri. KT12 48 D(
Kilrue La. KT12 48 D:
Kings Clo. KT12 48 D:
Kings Rd. KT12 48 C
Kingsbridge Rd. KT12 48 D
Lakeside. KT13 48 A`
Lancaster Ct. KT12 48 D
Linden Gro. KT12 48 C:
Mallards Reach. KT13 48 C`
Manor Pl. KT12 48 C`
Manor Rd. KT12 48 C`
Marrowells. KT13 48 B4
Mayfield Clo. KT13 48 DE
Mayfield Gdns. KT12 48 C5
Mayfield Rd. KT12 48 CE
Mayo Rd. KT12 48 C`
Mere Rd. KT12 48 A4
Midway. KT12 48 D3
Millbrook. KT13 48 B5
Montague Clo. KT12 48 D1
Moorlands. KT12 48 D4
Mount Felix. KT12 48 B1
Nelson Clo. KT12 48 D2
Netherby Rd. KT13 48 A6
New Zealand Av. KT12 48 C5
Oakfields. KT12 48 B2
Oakhill Gdns. KT13 48 A3
Oatlands Av. KT13 48 A6
Oatlands Chase. KT13 48 A4
Oatlands Dri. KT13 48 A4
Oatlands Grn. KT13 48 A4
Oatlands Mere. KT13 48 A4
Old School Mews. KT13 48 A4
Onslow Rd. KT12 48 C5
Orchard End. KT13 48 B3
Osborne Rd. KT12 48 D2
Pantile Rd. KT13 48 A5
Park Clo. KT12 48 B3
Pennington Dri. KT13 48 B4
Penny La. TW17 48 A1
Priory Clo. KT12 48 C4
Priory Pl. KT12 48 C4
Queens Rd. KT12 48 A6
Red House La. KT12 48 C3
Ridge Mt. KT12 48 B3
Ridgeway. KT12 48 B1
River Mount. KT13 48 B1
Riverside. TW17 48 B1
Ronneby Clo. KT13 48 A4
Rosslyn Pk. KT13 48 A4
Rowan Grn. KT13 48 A5
Roydon Ct. KT12 48 B4
Royston Clo. KT12 48 D2
St Georges Lodge.
  KT13 48 A6
St Mary's Rd. KT13 48 A5
St Vincent Rd. KT12 48 D4
Sandy Way. KT12 48 B2
Sarum Grn. KT13 48 B4
Sherbourne Gdns.
  TW17 48 A1

Shewens Rd. KT13 48 A5
Sidney Rd. KT12 48 D1
Silver Tree Clo. KT12 48 C4
Silverdale Av. KT12 48 B3
Stafford Sq. KT13 48 A5
Station Av. KT12 48 C5
Stompond La. KT12 48 C3
Stonebanks. KT12 48 C1
Sullivans Reach. KT12 48 C1
Swan Wk. TW17 48 A1
Sycamore Ct. KT13 48 B4
Templemere. KT13 48 A4
Terrace Rd. KT12 48 C1
Thames Meadow.TW17 48 A2
Thames St. KT12 48 C1
The Chestnuts. KT12 48 D2
The Crescent. KT12 48 B1
The Glebe. KT12 48 C6
The Grange. KT12 48 D3
The Grove. KT12 48 D1
The Laurels. KT12 48 A4
The Links. KT12 48 C3
The Mount. KT13 48 B3
The Paddocks. KT13 48 B4
The Quillot. KT12 48 B6
Tower Gro. KT13 48 B3
Trafalgar Dri. KT12 48 D4
Vale Rd. KT13 48 A4
Vicarage Wlk, Mayo Rd. KT12 48 C1
Victoria Clo. KT13 48 A4
Victoria Rd. KT13 48 A4
Victoria Way. KT13 48 A4
Village Clo. KT13 48 A4
Walton Bri. TW17 48 A1
Walton Bri Rd. TW17 48 A1
Walton Centre. KT12 48 C2
Walton La. KT13 48 A1
Wellington Clo. KT12 48 C2
West Gro. KT12 48 D5
Westcar La. KT12 48 D6
Westdene Way. KT13 48 B4
Willowhayne Dri. KT12 48 D1
Winchester Rd. KT12 48 C2
Woodland Gro. KT13 48 A5
Woodside. KT12 48 C2
Woodside Av. KT12 48 D5
Wynton Gro. KT12 48 D4


## WARLINGHAM


lbert Rd. CR6 49 C3
lexandra Av. CR6 49 D3
lexandra Rd. CR6 49 C3
shwood. CR6 49 A5
udley Dri. CR6 49 A1
adgers La. CR6 49 A5
eechwood La. CR6 49 B5
eulah Walk. CR3 49 C6
irch Way. CR6 49 B4
lanchmans Rd. CR6 49 C4
ond Rd. CR6 49 B4
oxwood Way. CR6 49 B3
roadlands Dri. CR6 49 A5
ug Hill. CR3 49 A6
urfield Dri. CR6 49 A5
utlers Dene Rd. CR3 49 D5
utterfly Walk. CR6 49 A6
amp Rd. CR3 49 B6
edar Clo. CR6 49 C4
hapel Rd. CR6 49 B4
helsham Clo. CR6 49 C4
helsham Rd. CR6 49 C4
hurch La. CR6 49 B3
hurch Rd. CR6 49 A3
hurchill Clo. CR6 49 A3
ranmer Clo. CR6 49 C3
ranmer Gdns. CR6 49 C3
rewes Av. CR6 49 A2
rewes Clo. CR6 49 A2
rewes Farm La. CR6 49 B3
rewes La. CR6 49 A2
rowborough Clo. CR6 49 C4
rowborough Dri. CR6 49 C4
ane Rd. CR6 49 B3
aniels La. CR6 49 D1
ukes Hill Rd. CR3 49 C6
den Way. CR6 49 C4
glise Rd. CR6 49 C3
m Clo. CR6 49 B3
m Rd. CR6 49 B3
arleigh Rd. CR6 49 B3
arm Rd. CR6 49 C4
ern Clo. CR6 49 C4
Glebe Rd. CR6 49 B3
Green Hill La. CR6 49 C3
Green La. CR6 49 C2
Gresham Av. CR6 49 C4
Hamsey Green Gdns. CR6 49 A2
Harewood Gdns. CR2 49 A1
Harrow Gdns. CR6 49 C1
Harrow Rd. CR6 49 C1
High La. CR6 49 D4
High Pines. CR6 49 A5
Hillbury Clo. CR6 49 A4
Hillbury Gdns. CR6 49 A4
Hillbury Rd. CR6 49 A4
Hilltop Walk. CR3 49 C6
Homefield Rd. CR6 49 A5
Huntsman Clo. CR6 49 A5
Kingswood Av. CR3 49 A1
Kingswood La. CR6 49 A1
Landscape Rd. CR6 49 A5
Larch Clo. CR6 49 C4
Leas La. CR6 49 B4
Leas Rd. CR6 49 B4
Lime Gro. CR6 49 C4
Limpsfield Rd. CR6 49 A2
Linden Gro. CR6 49 B4
Lunghurst Rd. CR3 49 D6
Manor Clo. CR6 49 C3
Marks Rd. CR6 49 C4
Marston Dri. CR6 49 C4
Mayes Clo. CR6 49 B4
Meadway. CR6 49 A1
Mint Walk. CR6 49 B3
Old Farleigh Rd. CR6 49 C1
Old Westhall Clo. CR6 49 A5
Overhill. CR6 49 A5
Park Ley Rd. CR3 49 B6
Parsonage Clo. CR6 49 C2
Plantation La. CR6 49 B6
Redvers Rd. CR6 49 A4
Ridley Rd. CR6 49 A4
Shelton Av. CR6 49 A3
Shelton Clo. CR6 49 A3
Slines New Rd. CR3 49 B6
Stuart Rd. CR6 49 A6
Sunnybank. CR6 49 C3
Tandridge Rd. CR6 49 B5
The Court. CR6 49 C4
The Green. CR6 49 B3
The Meadows. CR6 49 B3
Trenham Dri. CR6 49 A2
Tydcombe Rd. CR6 49 A5
Verdayne Gdns. CR6 49 A2
Ward La. CR6 49 A2
Warren Park. CR6 49 B4
Waterfield Dri. CR6 49 A5
Westhall Park. CR6 49 A5
Westhall Rd. CR6 49 A4
Woldingham Rd. CR3 49 A6


## WEYBRIDGE


Addlestone Rd. KT13 50 A2
*Agnes Scott Ct, Palace Dri. KT13 50 C2
Albany Ct. KT13 50 C2
Anderson Rd. KT13 50 D2
Arlington Lodge. KT13 50 C2
Aspen Sq. KT13 50 D2
Baker St. KT13 50 B2
Balfour Rd. KT13 50 A2
Barham Clo. KT13 50 D2
Barrington Lodge. KT13 50 C3
Beales La. KT13 50 B1
Belvedere Clo. KT13 50 B3
Bentley Dri. KT13 50 B6
Bridge Rd. KT13 50 A2
Bridgeham Clo. KT13 50 B3
Brooklands La. KT13 50 A4
Brooklands Rd. KT13 50 B6
Broomfield Ct. KT13 50 B4
Brumana Clo. KT13 50 B4
Caenshill Rd. KT13 50 B5
Caenwood Clo. KT13 50 B5
Campbell Rd. KT13 50 B5
Castle View Rd. KT13 50 C2
*Catherine Howard Ct, Palace Dri. KT13 50 C2
Cavendish Rd. KT13 50 C6
Cedar Gro. KT13 50 D2
Cedar Rd. KT13 50 B2
Chartfield Pl. KT13 50 C4
Chaucer Av. KT13 50 B5
Chestnut Av. KT13 50 D5
Chestnut La. KT13 50 C3
Church La. KT13 50 B2
Church St. KT13 50 B2
Church Walk. KT13 50 B1
Churchfield Rd. KT13 50 B2
Churchfields Av. KT13 50 C3
Churchill Dri. KT13 50 D2
Clevedon. KT13 50 D4
Cobbetts Hill. KT13 50 C5
Cranmer Clo. KT13 50 B5
Cricket Vw. KT13 50 C3
Crossfield Pl. KT13 50 C5
Curzon Clo. KT13 50 B3
Curzon Rd. KT13 50 B3
Daneswood Clo. KT13 50 C3
Darnley Pk. KT13 50 B1
*Denmark Ct, Grotto Rd. KT13 50 C2
Devonshire Rd. KT13 50 B2
Dorchester Rd. KT13 50 B1
Dovecote Clo. KT13 50 C1
Dresden Way. KT13 50 C3
East Rd. KT13 50 D5
Edge Clo. KT13 50 B6
Egerton Pl. KT13 50 D4
Egerton Rd. KT13 50 D4
Elgin Rd. KT13 50 B4
Elmgrove Rd. KT13 50 B2
Farnell Mews. KT13 50 B1
Finnart Clo. KT13 50 C2
Fir Grange Av. KT13 50 C4
Firfields. KT13 50 C5
Fortescue Rd. KT13 50 A3
Gascoigne Rd. KT13 50 B2
*Gate Ct, Gate Way. KT13 50 C2
Gate Way. KT13 50 C2
Glencoe Rd. KT13 50 B1
Godolphin Rd. KT13 50 D5
Golf Club Rd. KT13 50 C6
Gower Rd. KT13 50 D4
Granville Clo. KT13 50 C4
Granville Rd. KT13 50 C5
Greenlands Rd. KT13 50 C1
Greenside Rd. KT13 50 C1
Grotto Rd. KT13 50 C1
Grove Pl. KT13 50 C3
Hadley Pl. KT13 50 B5
Haines Ct. KT13 50 D3
Hamm Ct. KT13 50 A2
Hanger Hill. KT13 50 C4
Heath Rd. KT13 50 B3
Heathbridge. KT13 50 B5
Heathbridge App. KT13 50 B5
Heathside. KT13 50 C4
Herons Croft. KT13 50 D4
High Pine Clo. KT13 50 D3
High Point. KT13 50 B4
High St. KT13 50 B2
Hill Brook Gdns. KT13 50 B5
Hillcrest. KT13 50 C3
Holme Chase. KT13 50 C4
Holstein Av. KT13 50 B2
Ikona Ct. KT13 50 D4
**INDUSTRIAL & RETAIL:**
The Heights Business Pk. KT13 50 B6
Jason Clo. KT13 50 C4
Jessamy Rd. KT13 50 B1
John Cobb Rd. KT13 50 B5
Julian Hill. KT13 50 B5
Kenwood Pk. KT13 50 D4
Kingswood Clo. KT13 50 C5
Lakeside Grange. KT13 50 D2
Latymer Clo. KT13 50 C2
Layton Ct. KT13 50 C2
Leavesden Rd. KT13 50 C3
Limes Rd. KT13 50 B3
Linden Rd. KT13 50 D6
Locke King Clo. KT13 50 B6
Locke King Rd. KT13 50 B6
Lonsdale Rd. KT13 50 B5
Lucas Clo. KT13 50 D4
Manor Chase. KT13 50 C3
Manor Ct. KT13 50 C2
Manor Walk. KT13 50 B3
Mansfield Clo. KT13 50 B4
March Rd. KT13 50 B3
Marlborough Dri. KT13 50 C2
Mayfield Rd. KT13 50 A3
Meadows Leigh Clo. KT13 50 C2
Melrose Rd. KT13 50 B3
Minorca Rd. KT13 50 B2
Molyneux Rd. KT13 50 B3
Montrose Walk. KT13 50 B1
Monument Grn. KT13 50 B2
Monument Hill. KT13 50 C2
Monument Rd. KT13 50 C2
Mount Pleasant. KT13 50 B1
Mulberry Clo. KT13 50 C2
New Rd. KT13 50 C3
North Common. KT13 50 C3
Northfield Pl. KT13 50 B5
Oakdale Rd. KT13 50 B2
Oakfield Glade. KT13 50 D2
Oatlands Av. KT13 50 D3
Oatlands Clo. KT13 50 D3
Oatlands Dri. KT13 50 C2
Old Avenue. KT13 50 D5
Old Palace Rd. KT13 50 C2
Old Wharf Way. KT13 50 A2
Outram Pl. KT13 50 D4
Palace Dri. KT13 50 C2
*Palace Way, Palace Dri. KT13 50 C2
Park Dri. KT13 50 B4
Park Lawn Rd. KT13 50 C2
Park Way. KT13 50 D2
Pine Ct. KT13 50 D3
Pine Gro. KT13 50 C3
Pine Gro Mews. KT13 50 D3
Portmore Pk Rd. KT13 50 A2
Portmore Quays. KT13 50 A2
Portmore Way. KT13 50 B2
Princes Rd. KT13 50 C3
Pyrcroft La. KT13 50 C3
Quadrant Way. KT13 50 A2
Queens Rd. KT13 50 C3
Radnor Rd. KT13 50 B1
*Rede Ct, Old Palace Rd. KT13 50 C2
Round Oak Rd. KT13 50 A2
St Albans Av. KT13 50 B1
St Charles Pl. KT13 50 B3
St Georges Av. KT13 50 C4
St Georges Clo. KT13 50 D4
St Georges Lodge. KT13 50 D3
St James Mews. KT13 50 B3
St Michaels Ct. KT13 50 D3
Segrave Clo. KT13 50 B5
Seven Arches App. KT13 50 A5
Sorbie Clo. KT13 50 D4
South Rd, St Georges Hill. KT13 50 C6
South Rd, Weybridge. KT13 50 D3
Southerland Clo. KT13 50 D2
Southfield Pl. KT13 50 C6
Spenser Av. KT13 50 B6
Springfield La. KT13 50 B2
Springfield Meadows. KT13 50 B2
Station App. KT13 50 B5
Stoneleigh Pk. KT13 50 C4
Stroudwater Pk. KT13 50 C4
*Stuart Ct, Grotto Rd. KT13 50 C2
Thames St. KT13 50 B1
The Crescent. KT13 50 B2
The Meades. KT13 50 D4
The Square. KT13 50 D3
The Willows. KT13 50 B1
Towers Walk. KT13 50 C4
Trelawney Gro. KT13 50 B4
Tudor Walk. KT13 50 C1
Vaillant Rd. KT13 50 C2
Vale Clo. KT13 50 D1
Vale Rd. KT13 50 D1
Virginia Clo. KT13 50 D4
Warpole Park. KT13 50 B5
Warren Ct. KT13 50 B4
Warren Way. KT13 50 C4
Warreners La. KT13 50 D6
Waverley Rd. KT13 50 B3
Wentworth Dene. KT13 50 C4
West Palace Gdns. KT13 50 C1
West Rd. KT13 50 C6
Wey Rd. KT13 50 A2
Weybridge Pk. KT13 50 B3
Weybridge Rd. KT13 50 A2
White Knights Rd. KT13 50 D5
Windsor Walk. KT13 50 C3
Winterbourne Gro. KT13 50 D4
Wood La. KT13 50 D6
Woodland Way. KT13 50 D3
Woodsome Lodge. KT13 50 C4
York Rd. KT13 50 D3


## WOKING


Abbey Rd. GU22 51 A3
Abbotsford Clo. GU22 51 E2
Achilles Pl. GU21 51 A2
Addison Rd. GU21 51 D2
Albert Dri. GU21 51 F1
Alpha Rd. GU22 51 F1
Arnold Rd. GU21 51 F1
Arthurs Bri Rd. GU21 51 A3
Ashwood Park. GU22 51 D4
Ashwood Rd. GU22 51 D4
Avon Mead. GU21 51 A3
Azalea Ct. GU22 51 B4
Barrens Brae. GU22 51 E4
Barrens Clo. GU22 51 E4
Barrens Pk. GU22 51 E4
Beaufort Rd. GU22 51 F2
Beaumont Mws. GU22 51 B3
Bedford Clo. GU21 51 A1
Bedser Clo. GU21 51 D2
Beech Gdns. GU21 51 B1
Belgrave Manor. GU22 51 C4
Beta Rd. GU22 51 F1
Birch Clo. GU21 51 A4
Birch Hill. GU21 51 A4
Blackness La. GU22 51 C4
Blandford Clo. GU22 51 F3
Bluebell Ct. GU22 51 B4
Board School Rd. GU21 51 D2
Boundary Rd. GU21 51 D2
Boundary Way. GU21 51 E1
Bracken Clo. GU22 51 D3
Bradfield Clo. GU22 51 C3
Brambledene Clo. GU21 51 A3
Brewery Rd. GU21 51 B2
Bridge Barn La. GU21 51 A3
Bridge Clo. GU21 51 A3
Bridge Mews. GU21 51 A3
Brooklyn Clo. GU22 51 C4
Brooklyn Rd. GU22 51 C4
Broomhall End. GU21 51 C2
Broomhall La. GU21 51 C2
Broomhall Rd. GU21 51 C2
Brynford Clo. GU21 51 C1
Bullbeggars La. GU21 51 A2
Bury Clo. GU21 51 A2
Bury La. GU21 51 A2
Butts Rd. GU21 51 C3
Bylands. GU22 51 D4
Calluna Ct. GU22 51 D3
Candlerush Clo. GU22 51 F2
Canewden Clo. GU22 51 C4
Cavendish Rd. GU22 51 B4
Cavenham Clo. GU22 51 C4
Cawsey Way. GU21 51 C3
Century Ct. GU21 51 D2
Chapel St. GU21 51 C3
Cherry St. GU21 51 B3
Chertsey Rd. GU21 51 D2
Chobham Rd. GU21 51 C1
Chobham Rd Sth. GU21 51 D2
*Christchurch Way, West St. GU21 51 C2
Church Clo. GU21 51 B1
Church Hill. GU21 51 B2
Church Path. GU21 51 D3
Church Rd. GU21 51 B1
Church St E. GU21 51 D2
Church St W. GU21 51 C3
Cleardown. GU22 51 F4
Clover Ct. GU22 51 B4
Coley Av. GU22 51 D3
College La. GU22 51 A4
College Rd. GU22 51 F2
Commercial Way. GU21 51 C3
Constitution Hill. GU22 51 C4
Courtenay Mws. GU21 51 E2
Courtenay Rd. GU21 51 E1
Cromar Ct. GU21 51 A1
Daneshill. GU22 51 E4
De Lara Way. GU21 51 B3
Delta Rd. GU21 51 E1
Dianthus Ct. GU22 51 B4
Dinsdale Clo. GU22 51 D3
Dorchester Ct. GU22 51 E2

| Place | Ref | | Place | Ref | | Place | Ref | | Place | Ref | | Place | Ref |
|---|---|---|---|---|---|---|---|---|---|---|---|---|---|
| Dorset Dri. GU22 | 51 F3 | | Hopfield. GU21 | 51 C2 | | North Rd. GU21 | 51 E2 | | Tamerton Sq. GU22 | 51 C4 | | Birtley Rise. GU5 | 52 B3 |
| Downside Orch. GU22 | 51 E3 | | Horsell Moor. GU21 | 51 B3 | | Oak La. GU22 | 51 F2 | | The Birches. GU22 | 51 D3 | | Birtley Rd. GU5 | 52 C4 |
| Duke St. GU21 | 51 D2 | | Horsell Park. GU21 | 51 B2 | | Oakbank. GU22 | 51 C4 | | The Broadway. GU21 | 51 D3 | | Blackheath La. GU5 | 52 D1 |
| East Hill. GU22 | 51 F2 | | Horsell Park Clo. GU21 | 51 B2 | | Oaks Rd. GU21 | 51 C3 | | The Dell. GU21 | 51 A4 | | Blunden Ct. GU5 | 52 B2 |
| Eastbrook Clo. GU21 | 51 E2 | | Horsell Rise. GU21 | 51 B1 | | Ockenden Clo. GU22 | 51 D4 | | The Furlough. GU22 | 51 E2 | | Bracken Clo. GU5 | 52 C3 |
| Effingham Ct. GU22 | 51 C4 | | Horsell Rise Clo. GU21 | 51 B1 | | Ockenden Rd. GU22 | 51 D4 | | The Grove. GU21 | 51 C2 | | Brambles Pk. GU5 | 52 B3 |
| Elm Clo. GU21 | 51 B1 | | Horsell Vale. GU21 | 51 B1 | | Old Malt Way. GU21 | 51 B2 | | The Hollands. GU22 | 51 C4 | | Chestnut Way. GU5 | 52 C4 |
| Elm Rd. GU21 | 51 D1 | | Horsell Way. GU21 | 51 A1 | | Old Woking Rd. GU22 | 51 F4 | | The Mount. GU21 | 51 B4 | | Chinthurst La. GU5 | 52 B |
| Elm Rd, | | | **INDUSTRIAL & RETAIL:** | | | Oldfield Wood. GU22 | 51 F2 | | The Peacocks. GU21 | 51 C3 | | Clockhouse La. GU5 | 52 A |
| Mt Hermon. GU21 | 51 B4 | | Lion Retail Pk. GU22 | 51 E2 | | Omega Rd. GU21 | 51 E1 | | The Ridge. GU22 | 51 F2 | | Drodges Clo. GU5 | 52 A |
| Emmetts Clo. GU21 | 51 A2 | | Ivy La. GU22 | 51 F3 | | Onslow Clo. GU22 | 51 E2 | | The Rowans. GU22 | 51 C4 | | Eastwood Rd. GU5 | 52 A |
| Erica Ct. GU22 | 51 B4 | | Janoway Hill La. GU21 | 51 A4 | | Onslow Cres. GU22 | 51 E3 | | Thornash Clo. GU21 | 51 A1 | | Edencroft. GU5 | 52 B |
| Eve Rd. GU21 | 51 F1 | | Japonica Clo. GU21 | 51 A3 | | Orchard Clo. GU22 | 51 F2 | | Thornash Rd. GU21 | 51 A1 | | Firs Av. GU5 | 52 B4 |
| Everlands Clo. GU21 | 51 C4 | | Julian. GU21 | 51 A4 | | Orchard Dri. GU22 | 51 C1 | | Thornash Way. GU21 | 51 A1 | | Fisher Rowe Clo. GU5 | 52 B |
| Fairmead. GU21 | 51 A3 | | Kent Rd. GU22 | 51 F1 | | Oriental Clo. GU22 | 51 D2 | | Thorsden Clo. GU22 | 51 C4 | | Garden Clo. GU5 | 52 F4 |
| Fairview Av. GU22 | 51 C4 | | Kerry Ter. GU21 | 51 E1 | | Oriental Rd. GU22 | 51 D3 | | Thorsden Ct. GU22 | 51 C4 | | Grantley Av. GU5 | 52 D2 |
| Fairview Clo. GU22 | 51 C4 | | Kettlewell Clo. GU21 | 51 C1 | | Ormonde Rd. GU21 | 51 A2 | | Thurlton Ct. GU21 | 51 C1 | | Guildford Rd. GU5 | 52 B3 |
| Fenns Way. GU21 | 51 C1 | | Kettlewell Hill. GU21 | 51 C1 | | Pares Clo. GU21 | 51 B2 | | Tintagel Way. GU22 | 51 E2 | | Hall Rd. GU5 | 52 B2 |
| Ferndale Rd. GU21 | 51 C2 | | Kilrush Ter. GU21 | 51 E1 | | Park Dri. GU22 | 51 C4 | | Tower Clo. GU21 | 51 B2 | | High St. GU5 | 52 B3 |
| Fircroft Clo. GU22 | 51 D4 | | Kings Rd. GU21 | 51 E1 | | Park Pl. GU22 | 51 D4 | | Town Sq. GU21 | 51 C2 | | Highcroft. GU5 | 52 E3 |
| Forge End. GU21 | 51 C3 | | Kingsway. GU21 | 51 A4 | | Park Rd. GU22 | 51 D3 | | Triggs Clo. GU22 | 51 A4 | | Hill Clo. GU5 | 52 C |
| Foxgrove Dri. GU21 | 51 D1 | | Kingsway Av. GU21 | 51 A4 | | Parley Dri. GU21 | 51 A3 | | Triggs La. GU22 | 51 A4 | | Home Park Clo. GU5 | 52 A |
| Foxhanger Gdns. GU22 | 51 E2 | | Kirby Rd. GU21 | 51 A2 | | Pembroke Ct. GU22 | 51 F2 | | Tudor Clo. GU22 | 51 E3 | | Horsham Rd. GU5 | 52 A |
| Foxhills. GU21 | 51 A3 | | Knowl Hill. GU22 | 51 F4 | | Pembroke Gdns. GU22 | 51 E3 | | Vale Farm Rd. GU21 | 51 B3 | | Hull Meade. GU5 | 52 F |
| Frailey Clo. GU22 | 51 F2 | | Laleham Ct. GU21 | 51 C1 | | Pembroke Rd. GU22 | 51 E3 | | Verralls. GU22 | 51 F3 | | Hullbrook La. GU5 | 52 F |
| Frailey Hill. GU22 | 51 F2 | | Lampeter Clo. GU22 | 51 C4 | | Pollard Rd. GU22 | 51 F1 | | Victoria Rd. GU22 | 51 C3 | | Linersh Dri. GU5 | 52 B |
| Friars Rise. GU22 | 51 F2 | | Lancaster Clo. GU21 | 51 E1 | | Poole Rd. GU21 | 51 B3 | | Victoria Way. GU21 | 51 C2 | | Linersh Wood. GU5 | 52 B |
| Glendale Clo. GU21 | 51 A3 | | Langdale Clo. GU21 | 51 A2 | | Poplar Gro. GU22 | 51 C4 | | Waldens Pk Rd. GU21 | 51 A2 | | Linersh Wood Clo. | |
| Gloster Ct. GU21 | 51 A3 | | Langley Walk. GU22 | 51 F2 | | Portugal Rd. GU21 | 51 D2 | | Waldens Rd. GU21 | 51 B2 | | GU5 | 52 B |
| Goldsmiths Clo. GU21 | 51 A3 | | Lavender Rd. GU22 | 51 F2 | | Princess Gdns. GU22 | 51 F1 | | Walton Ct. GU21 | 51 E1 | | Links Rd. GU5 | 52 A |
| Goldsworth Rd. GU21 | 51 C1 | | *Littleriding, | | | Princess Rd. GU22 | 51 F1 | | Walton Rd. GU21 | 51 D2 | | Lords Hill. GU5 | 52 E |
| Graylands Clo. GU21 | 51 C2 | | Oriental Rd. GU22 | 51 F2 | | Queen Mary Clo. GU22 | 51 F1 | | Walton Ter. GU21 | 51 E1 | | Mellersh Hill Rd Sth. | |
| Greenham Walk. GU21 | 51 A4 | | Locke Way. GU21 | 51 D2 | | Radstone Ct. GU21 | 51 D4 | | Waverley Ct. GU22 | 51 C3 | | GU5 | 52 D |
| Greenheys Pl. GU22 | 51 D3 | | Lockfield Dri. GU21 | 51 A3 | | Ravenswood Ct. GU22 | 51 D4 | | Well Clo. GU21 | 51 A2 | | Mill La. GU5 | 52 A3 |
| Gregory Clo. GU21 | 51 A3 | | Lych Way. GU21 | 51 B2 | | Ridgeway. GU21 | 51 B1 | | Well La. GU21 | 51 A2 | | New Rd. GU5 | 52 D1 |
| Grobars Av. GU21 | 51 A1 | | Lyndhurst Clo. GU21 | 51 B1 | | Ridgeway Gdns. GU21 | 51 B1 | | Wendela Clo. GU22 | 51 D4 | | Norley Rd. GU5 | 52 E3 |
| Grosvenor Pl. GU2 | 51 D2 | | Lytton Rd. GU22 | 51 E2 | | Rosehill Av. GU21 | 51 A2 | | West Hill Rd. GU22 | 51 B4 | | Northcote La. GU5 | 52 E3 |
| Grove Rd. GU21 | 51 D2 | | Mabel St. GU21 | 51 A3 | | Round Hill. GU22 | 51 F4 | | West St. GU21 | 51 C2 | | Nursery Hill. GU5 | 52 E4 |
| Guildford Rd. GU22 | 51 C3 | | Manor Rd. GU21 | 51 A2 | | Round Hill Dri. GU22 | 51 F4 | | Wheatsheaf Clo. GU21 | 51 C1 | | Old Rectory Clo. GU5 | 52 B2 |
| Hall Pl. GU21 | 51 E2 | | Maple Clo. GU21 | 51 A2 | | Royal Oak Rd. GU21 | 51 E4 | | White Rose La. GU22 | 51 D3 | | Park Dri. GU5 | 52 A3 |
| Hammond Clo. GU21 | 51 A1 | | Marcus Ct. GU22 | 51 D3 | | Ruscoe Rd. GU21 | 51 E2 | | Whopshott Av. GU21 | 51 A2 | | Ricardo Ct. GU5 | 52 B3 |
| Hammond Rd. GU21 | 51 A1 | | Market Sq. GU21 | 51 C3 | | Russetts Clo. GU21 | 51 C1 | | Wilbury Rd. GU21 | 51 B3 | | Riverside Dri. GU5 | 52 B1 |
| Hanover Ct. GU22 | 51 B4 | | Marlborough Rd. GU21 | 51 D2 | | St Andrews Clo. GU21 | 51 A2 | | Wilders Clo. GU21 | 51 A4 | | Snowdenham La. GU5 | 52 A3 |
| Harelands Clo. GU21 | 51 A3 | | Maybury Hill. GU22 | 51 F2 | | St Fillans. GU22 | 51 F2 | | Wilfred St. GU21 | 51 A3 | | Stantons Wharf. GU5 | 52 B2 |
| Harelands La. GU21 | 51 A3 | | Maybury Rd. GU21 | 51 D2 | | St Johns Rd. GU21 | 51 A4 | | Wilson Way. GU21 | 51 B2 | | Station Rd. GU5 | 52 B2 |
| Heath Rd. GU21 | 51 D1 | | Mayhurst Av. GU22 | 51 F2 | | St Marys Rd. GU21 | 51 A2 | | Winnington Way. | | | Stonards Brow. GU5 | 52 E4 |
| Heather Clo. GU21 | 51 A1 | | Meadway Dri. GU21 | 51 A1 | | St Pauls Rd. GU22 | 51 E2 | | GU21 | 51 A3 | | Sweetwater Clo. GU5 | 52 E4 |
| Heathfield Clo. GU21 | 51 E3 | | Merrivale Gdns. GU21 | 51 A3 | | St Thomas Clo. GU21 | 51 A2 | | Wolsey Walk. GU21 | 51 C3 | | Sweetwater La. GU5 | 52 E4 |
| Heathfield Rd. GU22 | 51 E3 | | Midcote Clo. GU22 | 51 F2 | | Sandy Clo. GU22 | 51 F3 | | Woodham Rd. GU21 | 51 C1 | | Tanyard Rd. GU5 | 52 A1 |
| Heathside Cres. GU22 | 51 D3 | | Midhope Clo. GU22 | 51 B4 | | Sandy La. GU22 | 51 F2 | | Woodlands. GU22 | 51 C4 | | The Beeches. GU5 | 52 A2 |
| Heathside Gdns. GU22 | 51 D3 | | Midhope Gdns. GU22 | 51 B4 | | Sandy Way. GU22 | 51 D3 | | Woodlands Ct. GU22 | 51 C4 | | The Close. GU5 | 52 C2 |
| Heathside Pk Rd. GU22 | 51 D3 | | Midhope Rd. GU22 | 51 B4 | | Selhurst Clo. GU21 | 51 D1 | | Woodstock Clo. GU21 | 51 C2 | | The Coombes. GU5 | 52 C3 |
| Heathside Rd. GU22 | 51 D3 | | Montgomery Rd. GU22 | 51 C4 | | Shaftesbury Rd. GU22 | 51 E3 | | Wych Hill Pk. GU22 | 51 B4 | | The Drive. GU5 | 52 C3 |
| Hedgerley Ct. GU21 | 51 A3 | | Monument Rd. GU21 | 51 E1 | | Silversmiths Way. | | | York Rd. GU21 | 51 B4 | | The Farriers. GU5 | 52 B3 |
| High St, Horsell. GU21 | 51 A1 | | Monument Way E. | | | GU21 | 51 A3 | | | | | The Range. GU5 | 52 B4 |
| High St, Woking. GU21 | 51 C3 | | GU21 | 51 F1 | | Slocock Hill. GU21 | 51 A3 | | | | | Windrush Clo. GU5 | 52 B2 |
| Hill Clo. GU21 | 51 A1 | | Monument Way W. | | | South Clo. GU21 | 51 A1 | | **WONERSH/ BRAMLEY** | | | Wonersh Common Rd. | |
| Hill View Ct. GU22 | 51 C4 | | GU21 | 51 E1 | | South Rd. GU21 | 51 A1 | | | | | GU5 | 52 C1 |
| Hill View Rd. GU22 | 51 C4 | | Moorholme. GU22 | 51 C4 | | South View Ct. GU22 | 51 C4 | | | | | Woodhill La. GU5 | 52 F4 |
| Hockering Gdns. GU22 | 51 E3 | | Morton Clo. GU21 | 51 A1 | | Southcote. GU21 | 51 B1 | | | | | Woodrough Copse. | |
| Hockering Rd. GU22 | 51 E3 | | Morton Rd. GU21 | 51 A1 | | Stanley Rd. GU21 | 51 D2 | | Barnett Clo. GU5 | 52 D1 | | GU5 | 52 B3 |
| Holbeck Pl. GU22 | 51 C3 | | Mount Hermon Clo. | | | Station App. GU21 | 51 D3 | | Barnett Hill. GU5 | 52 C2 | | Woodyers Clo. GU5 | 52 C2 |
| Holyoake Av. GU21 | 51 A2 | | GU22 | 51 B4 | | Station Rd. GU22 | 51 C3 | | Barnett La. GU5 | 52 D1 | | | |
| Holyoake Cres. GU21 | 51 A2 | | Mount Hermon Rd. | | | Sylvan Clo. GU21 | 51 F3 | | Barton Rd. GU5 | 52 B2 | | | |
| | | | GU22 | 51 B4 | | | | | | | | | |

# ESTATE PUBLICATIONS

## LOCAL RED BOOKS

ALDERSHOT, CAMBERLEY
ALFRETON, BELPER, RIPLEY
ASHFORD, TENTERDEN
BANGOR, CAERNARFON
BARNSTAPLE, ILFRACOMBE
BASILDON, BILLERICAY
BASINGSTOKE, ANDOVER
BATH, BRADFORD-ON-AVON
BEDFORD
BOURNEMOUTH, POOLE, CHRISTCHURCH
BRACKNELL
BRENTWOOD
BRIGHTON, LEWES, NEWHAVEN, SEAFORD
BRISTOL
BROMLEY (London Bromley)
BURTON-UPON-TRENT, SWADLINCOTE
BURY ST. EDMUNDS
CAMBRIDGE
CARDIFF
CARLISLE
CHELMSFORD, BRAINTREE, MALDON, WITHAM
CHESTER
CHESTERFIELD
CHICHESTER, BOGNOR REGIS
COATBRIDGE, AIRDRIE
COLCHESTER, CLACTON
CORBY, KETTERING
CRAWLEY & MID SUSSEX
CREWE
DERBY, HEANOR, CASTLE DONINGTON
EASTBOURNE, BEXHILL, SEAFORD, NEWHAVEN
EDINBURGH, MUSSELBURGH, PENICUIK
EXETER, EXMOUTH
FALKIRK, GRANGEMOUTH
FAREHAM, GOSPORT
FLINTSHIRE TOWNS
FOLKESTONE, DOVER, DEAL & ROMNEY MARSH
GLASGOW, & PAISLEY
GLOUCESTER, CHELTENHAM
GRAVESEND, DARTFORD
GRAYS, THURROCK
GREAT YARMOUTH, LOWESTOFT
GRIMSBY, CLEETHORPES
GUILDFORD, WOKING
HAMILTON, MOTHERWELL, EAST KILBRIDE
HARLOW, BISHOPS STORTFORD
HASTINGS, BEXHILL, RYE
HEREFORD
HERTFORD, HODDESDON, WARE
HIGH WYCOMBE
HUNTINGDON, ST. NEOTS
IPSWICH, FELIXSTOWE
ISLE OF WIGHT TOWNS
KENDAL
KIDDERMINSTER
KINGSTON-UPON-HULL
LANCASTER, MORECAMBE
LEICESTER, LOUGHBOROUGH
LINCOLN
LLANDUDNO, COLWYN BAY
LUTON, DUNSTABLE
MACCLESFIELD
MAIDSTONE
MANSFIELD, MANSFIELD WOODHOUSE
MEDWAY, GILLINGHAM
MILTON KEYNES
NEW FOREST TOWNS
NEWPORT, CHEPSTOW
NEWTOWN, WELSHPOOL
NORTHAMPTON
NORTHWICH, WINSFORD
NORWICH
NOTTINGHAM, EASTWOOD, HUCKNALL, ILKESTON
OXFORD, ABINGDON
PENZANCE, ST. IVES
PETERBOROUGH
PLYMOUTH, IVYBRIDGE, SALTASH, TORPOINT
PORTSMOUTH, HAVANT, WATERLOOVILLE
READING
REDDITCH, BROMSGROVE
REIGATE, BANSTEAD, LEATHERHEAD, DORKING
RHYL, PRESTATYN
RUGBY

ST. ALBANS, WELWYN, HATFIELD
SALISBURY, AMESBURY, WILTON
SCUNTHORPE
SEVENOAKS
SHREWSBURY
SITTINGBOURNE, FAVERSHAM, ISLE OF SHEPPEY
SLOUGH, MAIDENHEAD, WINDSOR
SOUTHAMPTON, EASTLEIGH
SOUTHEND-ON-SEA
STAFFORD
STEVENAGE, HITCHIN, LETCHWORTH
STIRLING
STOKE-ON-TRENT
STROUD, NAILSWORTH
SWANSEA, NEATH, PORT TALBOT
SWINDON, CHIPPENHAM, MARLBOROUGH
TAUNTON, BRIDGWATER
TELFORD
THANET, CANTERBURY, HERNE BAY, WHITSTABLE
TORBAY (Torquay, Paignton, Newton Abbot)
TRURO, FALMOUTH
TUNBRIDGE WELLS, TONBRIDGE, CROWBOROUGH
WARWICK, ROYAL LEAMINGTON SPA &
    STRATFORD UPON AVON
WATFORD, HEMEL HEMPSTEAD
WELLINGBOROUGH
WESTON-SUPER-MARE, CLEVEDON
WEYMOUTH, DORCHESTER
WINCHESTER, NEW ARLESFORD
WORCESTER, DROITWICH
WORTHING, LITTLEHAMPTON, ARUNDEL
WREXHAM
YORK

## COUNTY RED BOOKS (Town Centre Maps)

BEDFORDSHIRE
BERKSHIRE
BUCKINGHAMSHIRE
CAMBRIDGESHIRE
CHESHIRE
CORNWALL
DERBYSHIRE
DEVON
DORSET
ESSEX
GLOUCESTERSHIRE
HAMPSHIRE
HEREFORDSHIRE
HERTFORDSHIRE
KENT
LEICESTERSHIRE & RUTLAND
LINCOLNSHIRE
NORFOLK
NORTHAMPTONSHIRE
NOTTINGHAMSHIRE
OXFORDSHIRE
SHROPSHIRE
SOMERSET
STAFFORDSHIRE
SUFFOLK
SURREY
SUSSEX (EAST)
SUSSEX (WEST)
WILTSHIRE
WORCESTERSHIRE

## OTHER MAPS

KENT TO CORNWALL (1:460,000)
COUNTY MAP - DORSET
             - SOMERSET
             - WILTSHIRE
CHINA (1:6,000,000)
INDIA (1:3,750,000)
INDONESIA (1:4,000,000)
NEPAL (1:800,000)
SOUTH EAST ASIA (1:6,000,000)
THAILAND (1:1,600,000)

## STREET PLANS

EDINBURGH TOURIST PLAN
ST. ALBANS

## OFFICIAL TOURIST & LEISURE MAPS

SOUTH EAST ENGLAND (1:200,000)
KENT & EAST SUSSEX (1:150,000)
SUSSEX & SURREY (1:150,000)
SUSSEX (1:50,000)
SOUTHERN ENGLAND (1:200,000)
ISLE OF WIGHT (1:50,000)
WESSEX (1:200,000)
DORSET (1:50,000)
DEVON & CORNWALL (1:200,000)
CORNWALL (1:180,000)
DEVON (1:200,000)
DARTMOOR & SOUTH DEVON COAST (1:100,000)
EXMOOR & NORTH DEVON COAST (1:100,000)
GREATER LONDON M25 (1:80,000)
EAST ANGLIA (1:200,000)
CHILTERNS & THAMES VALLEY (1:200,000)
THE COTSWOLDS (1:110,000)
COTSWOLDS & WYEDEAN (1:200,000)
WALES (1:250,000)
CYMRU (1:250,000)
THE SHIRES OF MIDDLE ENGLAND (1:250,000)
THE MID SHIRES (Staffs, Shrops, etc.) (1:200,000)
PEAK DISTRICT (1:100,000)
SNOWDONIA (1:125,000)
YORKSHIRE (1:200,000)
YORKSHIRE DALES (1:125,000)
NORTH YORKSHIRE MOORS (1:125,000)
NORTH WEST ENGLAND (1:200,000)
ISLE OF MAN (1:60,000)
NORTH PENNINES & LAKES (1:200,000)
LAKE DISTRICT (1:75,000)
BORDERS OF ENGLAND & SCOTLAND (1:200,000)
BURNS COUNTRY (1:200,000)
HEART OF SCOTLAND (1:200,000)
GREATER GLASGOW (1:150,000)
EDINBURGH & THE LOTHIANS (1:150,000)
ISLE OF ARRAN (1:63,360)
FIFE (1:100,000)
LOCH LOMOND & TROSSACHS (1:150,000)
ARGYLL THE ISLES & LOCH LOMOND (1:275,000)
PERTHSHIRE, DUNDEE & ANGUS (1:150,000)
FORT WILLIAM, BEN NEVIS, GLEN COE (1:185,000)
IONA (1:10,000) & MULL (1:115,000)
GRAMPIAN HIGHLANDS (1:185,000)
LOCH NESS & INVERNESS (1:150,000)
AVIEMORE & SPEY VALLEY (1:150,000)
SKYE & LOCHALSH (1:130,000)
ARGYLL & THE ISLES (1:200,000)
CAITHNESS & SUTHERLAND (1:185,000)
HIGHLANDS OF SCOTLAND (1:275,000)
WESTERN ISLES (1:125,000)
ORKNEY & SHETLAND (1:128,000)
ENGLAND & WALES (1:650,000)
SCOTLAND (1:500,000)
HISTORIC SCOTLAND (1:500,000)
SCOTLAND CLAN MAP (1:625,000)
BRITISH ISLES (1:1,100,000)
GREAT BRITAIN (1:1,100,000)

## EUROPEAN LEISURE MAPS

EUROPE (1:3,100,000)
BENELUX (1:600,000)
FRANCE (1:1,000,000)
GERMANY (1:1,000,000
IRELAND (1:625,000)
ITALY (1:1,000,000)
SPAIN & PORTUGAL (1,1,000,000)
CROSS CHANNEL VISITORS' MAP (1:530,000)
WORLD (1:35,000,000)
WORLD FLAT

TOWNS IN NORTHERN FRANCE STREET ATLAS
BOULOGNE SHOPPERS MAP
CALAIS SHOPPERS MAP
DIEPPE SHOPPERS MAP

**ESTATE PUBLICATIONS** are also
Distributors in the UK for:

INTERNATIONAL TRAVEL MAPS, Canada
HALLWAG, Switzerland
ORDNANCE SURVEY

**Catalogue and prices from:**
ESTATE PUBLICATIONS
Bridewell House, Tenterden, Kent. TN30 6EP.
Tel: 01580 764225    Fax: 01580 763720
www.estate-publications.co.uk